# Miracle of Israel

f Israel

BY

obert Gamzey

HERZL PRESS     •     NEW YORK

Printed in The U.S.A.
by
HARRY GANTT Publishers Printing Representative
NEW YORK 40, N. Y.

# Contents

To my wife
Dora

beloved daughter of Zion, who guided me through the Land of Israel, translated, interpreted, counseled, and enabled me to write honestly, deeply and authoritatively about the Miracle of Israel.

# PREFACE

What Israel needs most is understanding, the kind of knowledge that breeds compassion for its problems and a constant concern for its welfare. This profound awareness of Israel's basic needs and of the hope which it has arched across our mutual destiny is lacking in our midst. What we have instead is a welter of intense emotions. Whether these be of violent hatred on the part of the Arabs or exuberant love on the part of Jews, they all serve only to blur the image of Israel. Our vision has become narrowed because the heart is in full control. In the case of American Jews, the open purse and the jingle of coins add to the confusion. And yet what Israel needs most is empathy with its host of problems, a critical evaluation of its progress, a frank and forthright analysis of its own understandably rambunctious nature, and a clear insight into the knot of issues, affecting Jews all over the world, that have yet to be unraveled.

Outstanding books of recent date accomplishing this very purpose have been written by Robert Gamzey. The impact of his clear-eyed vision, his literary flair, his almost casual and yet penetrating glances at the complex Israeli scene, the light and deft touch of his style, and, through it all, his genuine, warm affection for Israel have been felt by everyone who has wanted to know the unvarnished truth concerning this heroic land and people. It is difficult to portray the kaleidoscope that is the Israeli scene, and many writers of talent have foundered on the rocks of their own enthusiasm because they viewed the scene with an imported lens, as it were, put into a non-objective focus long before they came to the country. The distorted images of Israel thus obtained have left the Israelis themselves bewildered and confused and the American Jews as ignorant as before.

Not so Gamzey. His is a factual, objective, honest job of reporting, written with love and understanding for Israel, its people and its problems, but without any attempt to propagandize, or to gloss over Israel's weaknesses. The epic of the Restoration is recorded in the human drama of individual stories of the simple men and women who build up the land, not with the blare of trumpets and the thrill of storming new barricades each month, but by renewing the work of creation day by day, hour by hour, modestly and humbly, a little impatiently perhaps, in the struggle to attain new human dignity. Gamzey's book is a study in depth of the old-new land in which lights and shadows inevitably blend. It presents the various sides of all issues in proper perspective. On its pages the heroic sense pounds its own unique rhythm, and the drive for survival, nurtured on the shores of the lands of exile, can be seen blossoming forth into new, pure and meaningful Jewish living.

Let us talk briefly here only of three major areas of concern: the integration of Oriental Jewry, the religious impasse and the crisis of the kibbutz.

Perhaps one of the greatest challenges to Israel today is the task of removing the barriers which today divide its Ashkenazi citizens from the Oriental newcomers. When the War of Independence ended, there were in the new State some 650,000 Jews. These were mostly immigrants from European countries such as Russia, Poland and Germany, and native-born *sabras*. They all had similar cultural traditions and formed a fairly homogeneous community. Then, after 1948, over half a million of our Oriental brethren from Iraq and Yemen, from Morocco and Algeria and other countries of the Moslem world came forth from oppression and darkness to the land for which they had yearned so long.

"These lost and forlorn tribes who have re-emerged from the darkness of their dispersion into the light of new history," as the late President Itzhak Ben Zvi described them, had to be transformed into self-respecting citizens of Israel. They had to be housed and fed, clothed and educated, trained to provide for their own livelihood, taught new standards of health and social living, and in general made to feel an integral part of this pioneer land. This new wave of immigration represented a hodgepodge of populations. By their physical characteristics, temperament, and varied backgrounds and traditions, these Jewish *olim* from the Moslem world introduced a new element into Israeli life.

The physical Ingathering of the exiles from East and West represents only the first step in a long-drawn-out process of mutual adjustment and acculturation, of establishing a common ground, of overcoming built-in prejudices and of weaving new patterns of shared living. Only when this task is done will the flower of the Ingathering emerge, the new Israeli Jew, who will represent the best from Jewish communities the world over. Robert Gamzey opens a glimpse for us into the complex problems involved: the breakup of the patriarchal family structure under the pressures of Westernized living, the emancipation of the Oriental woman, the transformation of *luftmenshen* into productive workers, and the progress already made in terms of integration in the Army, in the schools and in the factories.

Gamzey is eminently fair also in his analysis of the religious problem in Israel. Too many of us rush into print with generalizations and schematic proposals, and fail to look at the facts as they really are. The religious scene in Israel confronts us with a view of ferment and uncertainty, of contradictions and paradoxes, of a people held captive by memories of rigid authoritarianism and, of course, tremendous political pressures. American standards of measuring piety or lack thereof must fall by the wayside in the land where the voice of the Prophets was first heard and where the Sages of the Talmud laid the foundations for that legal system which served as our spiritual fortress through the ages. We see Orthodox authorities enforcing religious law and a majority which refuses to be bound by the formalities of religious observance. We see theocratic anachronisms and socialist skepticism; pious fanaticism and the sprouting of dissident, liberal groups; spiritual retardation and a renewed hunger for the word of God. What a crazy patchwork of impressions for the tourist to gather! But it need not be bewildering if we do not lose sight of the uniqueness which is the hallmark of every aspect of life in Israel. Our brethren in the Holy Land must be judged not by arbitrary standards but in terms of their own background and temperament and of the social realities with which they are faced. Robert Gamzey leads us through the labyrinth of this puzzle with the beacon of appreciation for the conflicts and compromises that are part and parcel of the restoration of Zion.

Intimately acquainted with Jewish community life in the United States Gamzey, from his editorial perch, is content to delineate rather than scold, to do no more than trace the outlines of a quest for faith that is only emerging now, with all its strange twists and sudden surprises.

To me, personally, the most moving accounts in this

book are Gamzey's descriptions of his visits to the kibbutzim, the collective farms where a new Jewish man,
the halutz, the pioneer, has arisen. The crisis which the
kibbutz is undergoing today reflects the turmoil within
a good part of Israel society, with its changes, after the
attainment of Statehood in 1948, from the exhilarating
idealism and excitement of a struggle for national independence to the daily routine of making a living and to
the search for personal advancement. Without the kibbutz, the birth of Israel would have been impossible. If
ever a saga was written upon the soil by the blood and
sweat of a people, it was that of the pioneers who devised new ways of individual and communal living even
as they made the wilderness flourish. We see the *haverim*,
the partners in a joint venture, work, eat and play together as brothers. We wonder along with them why the
promise of redemption which they feel the kibbutz holds
should have lost its fascination for the rest of their country. We listen as they express their ambivalent feelings
about their brethren in America, and their desire that
we understand their vigorous idealism.

Alfred Jospe has written in *Jewish Heritage* that Israel
is a nation of creative rebels, "which refuses to acquiesce
in the *status quo* and is ready to defy the forces of man,
of nature, of history, yes, even of God, in order to reach
out for something better, more complete and greater than
oneself." This is true without a doubt, and yet, in this
statement, too, one discerns the overtones of superlatives
and lavish praise. The new Jewish State readily lends itself to heroic and extravagant treatment. After seeing the
remnants of our people as they emerged from the concentration camps, we Jews may be forgiven for being
anxious to behold supermen of our own. But all that is
a distortion of our true dimensions and false to our historic image. Let us not pursue superhuman expectations,
or else we shall be bitterly disillusioned when the Israelis

will turn out to be men and women of mortal flesh. It is to Gamzey's credit that he drew them in authentic colors and in movement, rather than in the flamboyant still-life style that only mocks their true greatness.

Robert Gamzey has opened for us a new vista of Israel. I recommend that you allow him to guide you through the land so that you may truly come to know our brethren in Zion restored.

Rabbi Harry Essrig
University Synagogue
Los Angeles, California

# FOREWORD

*Miracle of Israel,* like *Ingathering,* its precursor, is based on a collection of reports I had originally written for the *Intermountain Jewish News,* an English-language Jewish weekly in Denver, Colorado, of which I am the editor.

*Miracle of Israel* represents the harvest of impressions gathered during five visits to Israel between 1960 and 1964, following my first introduction to the Land of Zion in 1949.

It is difficult for me to express my heartfelt gratitude to the men and women whose paths crossed mine in my journeys of discovery, who graciously granted me interviews, opened new doors for me, guided me through the land and helped make the reporter's task I had set for myself in Israel the most pleasant and deeply satisfying experience of thirty years of journalism. The reader will meet many of these people in the pages that follow. Without them, this book could not have come into being.

Thanks are due to Mr. Allen Bell, of Golden Bell Press, Denver, for permission to quote passages from *Ingathering.*

13

I wish to record my great indebtedness also to Dr. Raphael Patai, the editor of the Theodor Herzl Press, to Henry W. Levy, Public Relations Director of the Jewish Agency-American Section, and particularly to my editor, Miss Gertrude Hirschler. Miss Hirschler critically examined the manuscript and brilliantly edited my newspaper reports to shape them into this completed work which I hope will contribute to the American reader's better understanding of the miracle that is Israel.

# CHAPTER I

# FROM NEW YORK TO TEL AVIV

It was late Friday evening in Tel Aviv. My wife and I were returning home from Sabbath dinner with our friends, the Neemans. It was past ten-thirty and the streets were dark. There are no lights on Rehov Frug, just off Dizengoff Square. A woman approached. She was alone, escorted only by a poodle on a leash.

"You'd never see a woman walking by herself on a dark side street in Denver this time of night," I said to Dora.

"Oh, that's nothing," Dora replied. "You can always see women walking home alone at night from work, after visiting friends or after the show."

Dora is a Tel Avivian of twenty-five years' standing. "Who's afraid in Israel?" she demanded. "We're all Jews here. This is Tel Aviv."

This is Tel Aviv, the world's only all-Jewish city. Its population is 450,000, not including another 300,000 in its independent satellite towns, Ramat Gan, Givatayim, Bene Berak, Holon and Bat Yam.

With over 26,000 industrial establishments, Tel Aviv is Israel's metropolis, the country's center of commerce and finance. It is also the home of The Israel Philhar-

15

monic Orchestra, the Israel National Opera, and the Inbal Dance Theatre. In Tel Aviv, too, are the headquarters
of no less than twenty-one daily newspapers. The only Israeli daily published outside Tel Aviv is the English-language *Jerusalem Post.*

On what was a barren expanse of desert land less than
sixty years ago, there has risen a modern, pulsating, burgeoning metropolis with a rapidly-changing skyline dom-
inated by ten and twenty-floor hotel and office buildings
and the thirty-story Herzlia Tower.

The six Jewish families who founded Tel Aviv in 1909
had not planned to build a city. All they wanted was a
garden suburb outside Arab-dominated Jaffa where they
could live in peace. Hence, instead of parallel arteries,
there are narrow, winding streets that give apoplexy to
the harassed traffic engineers of the 1960's. One set of
streets is even laid out in the form of a seven-branch can-
delabrum. The fanciful layout is still there, just behind
what is now the city's Central Bus Terminal. As for Jaffa,
one of the world's oldest cities (the Bible makes mention
of it, and history records its invasion by the Crusaders
in 1253), it has been absorbed by the municipality of Tel
Aviv-Yafo. Once the home of 65,000 Arabs, Jaffa is being
rebuilt as a residential area for new immigrants, who live
in peace side by side with their Arab neighbors.

As Tel Aviv grew far beyond the dreams of those who
planned it, 750 acres of land were set aside for parks and
gardens. In time came five large hospitals with 650 beds
to serve Tel Aviv's citizens, of whom 80 per cent receive
free hospitalization and medical care under *Kupat Holim,* the nation-wide health insurance fund. The municipality of Tel Aviv spends IL 8,000,000 ($2,666,000) a
year on the buildings of new clinics. It maintains eighteen mother-and-child welfare stations where expectant
mothers are given free instruction in prenatal and baby
care.

In 1948, Tel Aviv had to win its own war with the Arabs of neighboring Jaffa in order to survive. The streets which run along the undefined boundaries between Tel Aviv and Jaffa were the scene of front-line fighting. Arab sharpshooters fired from the minarets of Jaffa on Tel Aviv residents in the streets below. Out of Tel Aviv, the new nation's largest population center, poured tens of thousands of *Hagana* and *Irgun Zvai Leumi* fighters and other volunteers to join Israel's newly-created Army in the War of Independence. The city has since "adopted" the Israel Armored Corps as its special favorite. Tel Aviv youths flock to volunteer for the Corps and Tel Avivians go all out to entertain the boys when they come home on furlough.

Every fourth Tel Avivian attends classes at an educational institution. In 1964 Tel Aviv's total school population was 92,167, distributed over 426 schools, including 210 kindergartens, 121 elementary schools, 20 high schools, eight teachers' seminaries and three universities — Tel Aviv University, Bar Ilan University, and the Tel Aviv branch of Jerusalem's Hebrew University. Tel Aviv University, which receives financial support from the municipality, aims to outstrip the Hebrew University's enrollment of 10,000 someday.

Adult education is in keeping with the Jewish tradition of lifelong study. Books and newspapers are widely read; 2500 Tel Avivians attend "People's University" night classes, and another 300 are enrolled in Hebrew language courses. The city has ten museums, and fifteen libraries containing a total of 300,000 volumes.

Every Friday, as the Sabbath approaches, the roar of traffic and the bustle of business and work come to a standstill. Rabbi Issar Yehuda Unterman, who was Tel Aviv's Chief Rabbi for eighteen years before being elected Ashkenazi Chief Rabbi of Israel, says that Tel Aviv-Yafo "possesses a law of tradition coupled with an up-to-date

modern approach." Rabbi Unterman told me that the
city boasts of an "ever-growing network of good schools
and academies of Jewish learning, including yeshivat,
colleges of higher Talmudic studies, whose graduates un-
doubtedly will become influential factors in the community of tomorrow."

On Rosh Hashana, the seashore and the banks of the
Yarkon River are crowded with worshippers reciting the
*tashlikh* prayers. The solemn silence that pervades Tel
Aviv on Yom Kippur turns to merrymaking on the feast
of Sukkot, when green-leafed booths sprout up from bal-
conies, on roofs and in courtyards. On Simhat Tora, Tel
Avivians dance in the streets with the Scrolls of the Law.
Passover, Shevout, Hanukka and Purim are national festivals which Tel Aviv celebrates with gusto.

Here in Tel Aviv, tourists can spend the night in luxury hotels along the shore of the Mediterranean, and go
out from there each day to tour the country. The truth
is that ordinary tourists generally do not get to know the
real Tel Aviv. They seldom take time to sit in the sidewalk cafés on Dizengoff Road, where they would be able
to see the Ingathering from the four corners of the earth
pass by. They are too busy traveling around the country
to come in close contact with Tel Avivians.

For entertainment, Tel Aviv has twenty-five motion
picture theaters which feature movies from Hollywood,
England, France, Italy, Japan, Russia and Sweden, as well
as the latest in Israeli shows. Most of the legitimate
theaters of Israel are concentrated in Tel Aviv, including
HaBima, Ohel, and Kameri theaters.

Tel Avivians love soccer, basketball, and sports in general, which they can watch at the Ramat Gan Stadium
(seating 60,000), the Bloomfield Stadium (seating 22,-
000 or the Makkabia Stadium (seating 15,000).

The Carmel Market off Allenby Road is Tel Aviv's (and
Israel's) Hester Street, crammed with an infinite variety

of food, clothing, utensils and knick-knacks, sold by hawkers and pushcart peddlers yelling their wares in nearly every language of lands where Jews have lived. Here, at Carmel Market, immigrants from Europe, Africa, Asia and South America begin as peddlers, making money to open their own stores and shops someday.

The Yafo section contains twenty churches with bells that fill the air with their melodious ringing. Jaffa's Arabs, who are now citizens of Israel, number thousands of Christians belonging to the Greek Orthodox, Armenian, Coptic, Maronite and Roman Catholic churches and to a plethora of Protestant denominations. The Moslem Arabs flock to the Great Mosque in the center of Jaffa near the Watch Tower and to a smaller mosque in Ajami. Israel's Ministry of Religions has allocated IL 50,000 to redecorate these non-Jewish houses of worship.

The natives of Tel Aviv know how to enjoy exotic foods from the world over. It's only the tourists who stay in the Dan and Sheraton Hotels and complain because the steaks in Israel aren't as large as the United States T-bone variety. The national dishes of nearly every land — from Hungarian goulash to Yemenite oxtail and Greek moussaka, from Beef Stroganoff to Mama's kneidlach soup and chopped liver — can be sampled in the small cafés with which Tel Aviv and Jaffa abound. The Casba at 32 Yirmeyahu Street features a French-Italian cuisine and serves the best crepes suzette in Tel Aviv-Yafo. Favored for Viennese dishes is the Rishon Cellar on Allenby Road. Israelis like the American-style hamburger joint at the California at the corner of Frishman and Dizengoff. *Haimishe* Jewish-style delicacies can be ordered at the Yaaqov Alster, 37 Geula Street, or at Herlinger's, 69 Ben Yehuda Street. For fish food, take a cab to Chez Jeanette on the Jaffa seafront. Also in Jaffa, on Clock Square, is the Tripolitanian Café, noted for its tasty *couscous* with sharp tomato sauce. For Greek dishes, try the Acropolis on HaMesager Street, a place popular with Army officers. Turkish fare is featured at the Istanbul at 11 Merkaz Mishari. The best steaks may be found at Herman's, on the Petah Tikva-Tel Aviv highway. The most exciting culinary treat of all is right off Allenby in the Yemenite quarter, behind the Carmel Market, where the *hummus, tehina, marak* and *shish kabab* are beyond compare. And there are always the *felafel* peddlers on the street.

Tel Aviv is the city of finance and business, where the stock exchange turnover has soared and new shares are issued almost daily. During the first three months of 1963, PIA and Yigdal, the two largest mutual funds, both sponsored by banks, increased their asset value from IL 15,-000,000 to IL 23,400,000. It is the city of industry and labor, where 147,000 workers are organized in 3,500 locals of 28 unions.

The clash of the pioneering tradition of work in the factory and on the farm with the get-rich-quick mentality of the land boom and the stock market is typified by Dizengoff sidewalk café society. Dizengoff Road is the home of the cafés like Café Kassit, where cabinet ministers may rub shoulders with "beat" poets and show people, and the Rowal, where the smart set enjoys delicious pastries and keeps an eye out for companions to invite to their weekend parties.

But although they love cafés, Tel Avivians are at their best entertaining friends at home in never-ending exchanges of social evenings. Since few have telephones, you just drop in on friends unannounced. There's always a bowl of fruit, and some tea and cakes, to welcome the guests, and much good talk about the day's events, great and small — but somehow hardly ever about the Arab threat.

This is Tel Aviv where the buses, always jammed, are followed by *sherut* taxis which trail them like vultures to pick up leftover passengers, where buses have signs in

Hebrew, Arabic and English, reading "Beware of Pick-pockets," but where it's perfectly safe for ladies to walk alone at night with just their poodles.

The tourists say they don't like Tel Aviv; they prefer the scenic beauty of Haifa's Mount Carmel, and the air of sanctity that pervades Jerusalem, and the lovely hills of Galilee. They don't like Tel Aviv because they simply don't know it. For its sons and daughters, who know and love this city, there's no place like Tel Aviv.

\* \* \*

These days you can speed from New York to Tel Aviv in ten hours aboard one of the new jet planes of El Al, Israel's national airline. In 1961 El Al established a speed record when one of its planes made the first non-stop New York-Tel Aviv flight — the longest continuous airborne route in the history of commercial aviation — in nine hours and thirty-three minutes.

Seated at the plane's controls was Captain Tom Jones, the British RAF Spitfire pilot who has been El Al's chief of flight operations since 1951. Captain Jones is proud to be working with El Al. "El Al is regarded highly among airline people," he told me. "When I say I'm with El Al, they talk with great respect for what we have accomplished in a short time with meager resources. Our introduction of English Britannia turbo-jets into transatlantic schedules in 1956 made aviation history and created a name for us in world aviation."

The fact that El Al, a fledgling as airlines go, enjoys top rating, Captain Jones explains, is due precisely to its smallness, which enables its management to remain flexible, imaginative and attentive to every detail, including the minute factors on which El Al's safety record depends.

From Captain Jones and top management down to the ground crews, the members of the El Al family beam with pride when they talk about their work and especially

about their Boeing 707 Intercontinental jet planes with
140-passenger capacity, 150-ton load, average speed of
600 miles per hour, 42,000-foot cruising altitude, 2,000-
foot-per-minute climbing speed. These giants of the air,
152 feet long, with a wingspan of 142 feet, proudly bear
the blue and white El Al emblem with the Star of David.

"There's a plane with perfect performance," proudly
declared co-pilot Arye Peer. A veteran Israel Air Force
flyer, Peer, now in his late thirties, came to Israel from
his native Rumania with Youth Aliya.

There's an infectious spirit not only of pride but also
of fellowship and camaraderie among the El Al personnel. As we whooshed through the skies over Europe and
the Mediterranean, "coming home" to Lydda Airport,
Captain Jones invited me into the cockpit and demonstrated the bewildering array of controls and gauges to
me. Then, while Captain Gad Katz, formerly of South Africa, took over the controls, an international, interfaith
crew — including Captain Tom Jones, co-pilot Peer, purser Werner Wolff (who fled Hitler's Berlin in 1933), stew-
ardess Nitza Gordon (*sabra*) and myself — kibbitzed over
a hearty breakfast.

At El Al headquarters in Tel Aviv and Lod they jok-
ingly refer to Captain Tom Jones as "the Galitzianer." He
kibbitzes with the staff, tells them he doesn't understand
a word of Hebrew but warns them he knows what they're
saying about him. But he is a tough boss, demanding
100% perfect performance from the airline's 1800 employees.

Jones, a veteran of the Battle of Britain and the Burma
campaign, who served five years with the Scandinavian Airlines before coming to El Al, divides his time between
piloting and supervising flight operations from headquarters at Lydda Airport. He was personal pilot to David
Ben-Gurion during the latter's administration as Prime
Minister of Israel, and delights in recalling how the

doughty old Premier would bounce all around the plane, talking to other passengers, quizzing the crew about their home towns, taking special pride in the ability of Israelis to operate jets, and arguing with Jones on everything from Zen philosophy to why the captain still had not applied for Israeli citizenship.

"Actually, as a foreigner, I'm entitled to certain tax exemptions, and have the right to bring in some things duty-free," Captain Jones said. "But I don't believe in taking advantage of these privileges. If I live in Israel, I believe in being like everyone else here. I'm very proud that they've accepted me as one of them, and I live in Tel Aviv just as if I were a Jew and an Israeli citizen. My children attend Christian Sunday School in addition to Israeli public schools, but we observe the Jewish holidays."

When I remarked that this was the reverse twist of the American Jew's eagerness to be accepted by his Gentile neighbors, Captain Jones smiled.

"I grew up in a small town in England where I knew only two Jews," he recalled. "From them, I acquired the impression that the Jews were very keen and sentimental people with a strict moral code. Then, in the RAF, I had a Jewish navigator who was a fine fellow and a good friend. When I joined El Al and moved to Israel, my original impression of the Jewish people was confirmed. They're keenly intelligent, quick, sentimental and good. I like living as one of them."

Also aboard the plane was Ambassador Michael Comay, Israel's chief representative to the United Nations. He and purser Wolff were conversing like two old friends. When I commented on the fact that Werner Wolff, who served us our seven-course banquet aloft, was displaying no particular deference to Comay's rank, the diplomat smiled and recalled the constant concern of his chauffeur in New York about protocol. It seems that the chauffeur, a Polish-born Israeli, was distressed that Comay's son had taken a summer job at Grossinger's as a bus boy and was receiving tips from the hotel's patrons. " 's *passt nisht*, it's just not right," the chauffeur would remonstrate with the ambassador.

"El Al wouldn't be where it is today without the wonderful patronage from American Jewish tourists and businessmen," Peter Brunswick, El Al's director of public relations in New York, declared. "Support from the United States has enabled us to rise to a respectable position among the international air lines. This is an achievement in which Jews can take pride. When Jewish travelers fly El Al, they help assure the continued existence of Israel's lifeline to the outside world. This isn't charity. Passengers get full value for their fares. And we have a service second to none in quality, with the added advantage of nonstop service to Israel that no other line offers."

The Israel airline purchased six Boeing jets at a total cost of $36,000,000, to be amortized by the Israeli Government with long term-loans.

Among its other record-breaking accomplishments, El Al boasts the highest "load factor" or the sale of the highest percentage of seats available on any transatlantic line.

The New York-Tel Aviv nonstop service flights are a decided advantage to veteran commuters to Israel. When the regular one-stop flight takes off from New York at 9:30 P.M. it lands in Paris at 10 A.M. European time, which is actually 3 A.M. Eastern Standard Time. This means that when the traveler has eaten his dinner and is ready to sleep, it is already time for the tiresome descent and a dreary hour's wait at Orly Airport for the next connection. The nonstopper taking off at 9:30 P.M. Thursdays arrives at Lod Airport around 2 P.M. Friday (Israel time) just in time for the Sabbath. Depending on tail winds, flying conditions and airport delays, the nonstop flight takes between the record nine hours and a half and ten hours and fifteen minutes.

El Al's history is replete with mandatory and costly changes in equipment, due to the rapid obsolescence of planes. Beginning operations with Constellations, El Al made the switch to Britannia turbo-jets in 1956, thus becoming the first airline with transatlantic turbo-jet service to slash the ocean hop by 20 per cent flying time. This saving in time brought El Al a substantial increase in trade and enabled it to get into the black with a 1 per cent operating profit. The acquisition of Boeing jets in 1961 further enhanced El Al's attractiveness to travelers.

This success, the *Jerusalem Post* wrily noted, has been achieved despite a handicap that no other airline suffers. Since no El Al plane can land or take off at Lod Airport on the Sabbath, El Al planes that happen to be there late Friday must stand idle for a day, while operating costs continue, schedules are knocked out of kilter and other airlines avoid Israel on weekends.

And yet El Al flies to Amsterdam, Athens, Brussels, Istanbul, Sofia, Johannesburg, London, Munich, New York, Paris, Rome and Teheran. In its first decade alone, El Al carried more than a half-million passengers. Except for the Sabbath, not an hour goes by that an El Al airliner is not aloft somewhere in the skies.

# CHAPTER II

# THE INGATHERING

Proudly flying the blue-and-white colors of Israel, the sleek white *Zim* passenger liner S.S. *Theodor Herzl* majestically slid into her home port of Haifa to the cheers, shouts, cries and tears of the immigrants and tourists on the decks and the welcoming crowd of relatives and friends on the wharf.

It is an oft-repeated scene, familiar to those who have gone to Haifa to watch the immigration ships come in, and even to those who have seen it only in pictures. It takes place nearly every day, week after week, month after month, year after year. Since 1948, when the State of Israel was established, more than one million Jewish immigrants have "come home" in an Ingathering from eighty countries that is unparalleled in the history of the world.

On that Sunday when Yitzhaq Huberman of the Jewish Agency took me to see the Ingathering in operation, the good ship *Herzl* had just docked with sixty-seven immigrant families from South America, and two hundred South American young people who came to visit Israel in a one-month *ulpan* program of intensive He-

26

brew study arranged by the Agency. Two other ships arrived that same day, both from Turkey, the *Adina,* with eight immigrant families, and the *Ordo,* with fifteen newcomer families aboard.

As soon as the *Herzl* had been tied up and the gangplank lowered, I boarded the ship together with the officials from the Jewish Agency who had come to receive the immigrants. There, in the luxurious main drawing room, were the 189 immigrant passengers — 122 from Argentina, 33 from Uruguay, 26 from Brazil, six from Chile, and two from Venezuela. They sat around the tables with their families, quietly and contentedly waiting their turn to join the orderly line which filed past tables where they went through their final processing by government and Jewish Agency officials. There was no anxiety in their smiling faces, no pushing in line. I heard no excited arguments with those who had assigned them their immediate destination. Sixty-four persons were going to kibbutzim of their own choice; seven were going to Dimona, seven to Beersheba, twenty to Jerusalem, thirteen to Ezra Bitzaron, sixteen to Holon, five to Pardes Hanna, and seven to Acre. Thirteen others remained in Haifa. Eleven went to Youth Aliya centers, twenty to ulpan institutes at various kibbutzim to get a working knowledge of Hebrew, and seven to relatives who had come before them.

The entire shipboard operation was completed three hours after the *Herzl* had steamed into Haifa harbor. Impressed, I complimented Huberman about the efficiency of the combined Government-Jewish Agency staff.

"We should have learned something by now," Huberman shrugged. "After all, we've brought in a million immigrants, haven't we?"

Who were those Jewish immigrants from South America? Why had they given up comfortable lives in their countries where Jews enjoy political and economic freedom, and the right to education and self-improvement? Why had they come to crowd their families, furniture and household possessions into small two-room apartments, mostly in the new development towns of the Negev and the Galilee, where they would have to live under frontier conditions?

A doctor from Argentina, who had been assigned to Beersheba, told me that he had been head of a staff department at a hospital in Buenos Aires. One day, the administrator asked him to come to his office. "We have twenty-five Jewish doctors here," the administrator began. The hint sufficed. "For seventeen years I was a doctor," said the immigrant physician. "But on that day I became a statistic. So I organized forty Jewish doctors in Buenos Aires and we have all come here to Israel." These doctors from Argentina willingly accepted assignments to the development towns which are desperately short of physicians.

Said another man from Buenos Aires: "I want my son to become President of Israel someday. A Jewish boy could never be President of Argentina. But here in Israel, my son has a chance to go all the way to the top."

Zalman Hirschfeld, who is in his sixties, and his wife, Esther Rappal, were stars of the Yiddish stage in Argentina. Why did they come? Their only son, Yehuda, is a second-year student at the Hebrew University in Jerusalem, and they have followed him to Israel. They have already been assigned a new apartment in Holon, a suburb of Tel Aviv, and have arranged to join a theater group. In South America, the Hirschfelds had performed with such luminaries of the Jewish stage as Maurice Schwartz, Jacob Ben-Ami, Joseph Buloff and Menashe Skulnik. During the three-week voyage to Haifa, the Hirschfelds had given nightly shows, and during the day Zalman, who had taught in a Hebrew Teachers' seminary in Buenos Aires, conducted a "seaborne ulpan" for the passengers.

The story of the Hirschfelds is much the same as that of nearly all the Jews who have come to Israel from the Latin-American countries. Most of them had fled from Poland when Hitler and his troops marched in in 1939. Now, a quarter-century later, they had pulled up roots once again.

Aside from the wish to be with their only child, what really made the Hirschfelds come? To begin with, they explained, they loved Israel. But what was more, the political and economic turmoil in Latin America is a threat to the Jews of those countries, most of whom are in business. The future in South America seems uncertain, and prospects in Israel all the brighter by comparison. Letters from friends who have preceeded them to Israel tell stories of successful integration into the new country, despite the drop in the standard of living which most of the newcomers from Latin America have had to take. Overt and violent demonstrations of anti-Semitism, the Hirschfelds hastened to add, were sporadic only and therefore not a factor in their decision to leave Argentina and make a new start in Israel.

Harry Blitzer, a furrier and photographer from Montevideo, Uruguay, his wife, their two sons, aged nine and fourteen, and Mrs. Blitzer's parents were sent to Holon. Blitzer, a handsome man in his early forties, told me that due to a cash shortage, falling prices and the buyer's advantage in dealing with emigrants who are forced to sell their holdings, the emigrants from South America lose from fifty to seventy-five per cent of the value of their business and other property when they sell out before leaving.

"It's hard to liquidate, and we've all taken a heavy loss," said Blitzer, who was born in Berlin and lived in

Montevideo for twenty-five years. "But I don't care. I'm happy to be in Israel, at any cost. I have no worries about the future here. I'm willing and able to work at anything. We've even shipped my station wagon over. We'll make out all right."

Teen-aged Mario (Mayer) Cacica, whose father is a shoemaker in Montevideo, came with two other boys, without their parents. They were sent to kibbutzim to study Hebrew at ulpan institutes there and to work the soil. But the "all for one and one for all" life on the collective is not for Mario. He wants to go to the University and study journalism. Why had Mario and his friends come to Israel? They are part of the Zionist pioneer youth movement which has a thousand members in Uruguay. This journey is the fulfillment of their dreams and hopes. This is what they trained for. Recent outbursts of anti-Semitism in Uruguay, Mario explained in Yiddish, had added impetus to the Zionist movement there and stimulated emigration to Israel.

Huberman commented that the one thousand youths in the pioneer movement represent a considerable proportion of Uruguay's Jewish population of 40,000. He pointed out that the Jews of Uruguay are strongly Zionist-oriented, and stubbornly resist assimilationist trends which are making inroads into Judaism in many other countries.

Solomon Harp, a mattress maker, also from Montevideo, has come here alone. A bachelor in his forties, he has a sister in Natanya, and for him this is a real homecoming. "Conditions are bad in Montevideo, and small shopkeepers are going under," he said.

Mayer Grupstein, his wife Ruth, and their daughters, aged nine and ten, were on their way to the new Rassco housing development at Katamon, Jerusalem, which was set up for immigrants in the academic professions. Grupstein, a journalist, had been press secretary at the Israel

Embassy in Buenos Aires, where there are two daily Spanish and Yiddish-language newspapers to serve Argentina's 450,000 Jews. Jerusalem has plenty of opportunities for journalists. Why did the Grupsteins choose Israel? "We are Zionists," Grupstein replied. "Primarily, we came for the sake of the children. It's hard to give children a proper Jewish education in Argentina." Mrs. Grupstein's brother is doing cancer research at the Weizmann Institute in Rehovot. Her parents and a sister are living in Jerusalem.

"How are the Jews from South America doing in Israel?" I asked Moshe Kitron, President of the Association of Latin American Immigrants in Israel. Kitron replied that they are making a good adjustment, for the most part. Six thousand came from Argentina in 1963. Five thousand South Americans, mostly youth, are in the kibbutzim and moshavim. Eight hundred are in the so-called liberal professions — medicine, law, engineering and education. They are doing well in the development areas of the north and the south. Small businessmen must either change their line or accept employment, unless they have brought enough money with them to open a shop or store. Kitron said that the more affluent Jews in Argentina are making large investments in Israel as a hedge against the future, but are not yet emigrating. Ninety-five per cent of the immigrants from Latin America have been successfully absorbed. Only five per cent go back across the Atlantic disappointed. This overwhelmingly successful adjustment encourages more immigration, and Jewish Agency officials expected an additional six thousand Jews to migrate to Israel from South America each year.

Ephraim Avigur, who had been a lawyer in Buenos Aires before he came to Israel fourteen years ago and is now the Jewish Agency's absorption expert for the South American immigrants, said that the Jews from the Latin

American countries adapt so well to Israel "because they want to." They have prepared themselves well in advance of leaving their former countries, and many already know Hebrew. The first few weeks are difficult, he said, but their problems are gradually resolved as time goes on and they settle down to work. Avigur explained that the real processing of the immigrants took place not on arrival but throughout the three-week crossing. Each person consults at length with Jewish Agency officials aboard the ship, discussing his occupational or professional skill and preferences, and his hopes and wishes for the future. Then the Agency, using in part funds from the United Jewish Appeal, tries to fit the immigrant into the right spot.

This is the human aspect of the overall partnership of U.J.A., Israel Bonds, Rassco, private investors and Israeli taxpayers to bring in immigrants on a large scale, to build homes for them, and to set up the factories and the business enterprises which will provide employment for the newcomers. This complex partnership continues to furnish the housing and the employment opportunities to keep pace with mass immigration. According to Louis Pincus, Treasurer of the Jewish Agency, the cost of immigration and immigrant absorption has risen in recent years from $10,000 to $12,000 per family. In 1962, 1963 and 1964, a total of $450 million was spent on immigrant transportation and absorption, construction of immigrant housing, and the establishment and consolidation of immigrant farm settlements.

When Huberman and I headed for Tel Aviv in a taxi chartered by the Jewish Agency, our companions were three other passengers, with a dozen suitcases, boxes and bags. They were Shmuel Milberg, his wife Bertha, and their pretty seventeen-year-old daughter Rosalinda, who wants to become a nurse in Israel. It was Rosalinda who insisted that her family leave Buenos Aires. She had felt the sting of anti-Semitic remarks at her high school. In Buenos Aires, Mr. Milberg manufactured and sold leather handbags. He was ready to do any kind of work in Israel. Perhaps, he said, he might be able to get a loan from the Jewish Agency to buy a machine and begin manufacturing handbags on a small scale, at home.

We delivered the Milbergs to Ezra Bitzaron, a new suburb of Tel Aviv which is known also as "Little Argentina" and whose four hundred new apartment units were already occupied by one hundred forty families from Latin America. Huberman, who discovered on the trip that he had come from the same Polish province as the Milbergs — via Auschwitz — explained that the Jewish Agency had learned from experience that each immigrant housing development should have at least fifty families from one nationality group. Otherwise, immigrants may feel lost. The South Americans are being placed with other Spanish-speaking immigrants, and we saw the dramatic result at Ezra Bitzaron.

Local Jewish Agency officials took charge of the Milbergs and brought them to their new apartment in Ezra Bitzaron. The apartment was as bare as it had been on the day the builders had completed plastering. Then, all at once, the people from the Jewish Agency filled it with chairs, a table, a one-burner kerosene stove, kitchenware and other basic household utensils, and supplied even mattresses and bedding for the newcomers. At Haifa, the Milbergs had already received from the Agency a parcel containing a ten days' food supply and ten Israeli Pounds in cash per person.

The arrival of the Milbergs at Ezra Bitzaron brought out a swarm of neighbors who helped unload the luggage and the furniture and set up the new home within minutes. They greeted the Milbergs in Spanish and Yiddish and overwhelmed them with neighborliness, friendship and sympathy. For only last week, or last month, or last year, they, too, had experienced that same unforgettable day of mixed emotions, the landing in Haifa, the first sight of the Land of Israel with its lush gardens and orchards, its new skyscrapers, burgeoning apartment projects and factories, and the move into a new home which was done with such dispatch that they were ready to go out to work the very next day.

This is Israel. This is the Ingathering. This is the unpublicized story of Israel's immigration, so prosaic that the established population of Israel is hardly aware of the statistical fact that, in sixteen years of Statehood, Israel's population which had been 660,000 in 1948, had quadrupled to 2,500,000.

The exact number of immigrants arriving in a day, a week, a month or a year is kept off the record. All the newspapers of Israel and the friendly press abroad cooperate in withholding detailed statistical information on immigration figures, sources and even points of departure in order to prevent hostile forces from exerting political pressure to block the continuing exodus.

It is no secret that much money has poured into Israel in the form of investments now totalling half a billion dollars a year from all sources — including bonds and stocks, public and private, foreign and domestic, reparations and restitution payments from Germany, and loans from the World Bank, the U.S. Import-Export Bank, and other lending agencies.

As a result, the immigrants who come in a never-ending stream from fourscore countries can be provided with jobs and homes and soon can begin to pay taxes themselves, thus helping in their turn to form new enterprises to prepare the way for still more newcomers.

Many of the immigrants from Latin America and other free countries bring capital of their own and start businesses and industries which provide jobs for those who come after them. But large numbers of Jews from

Africa and Europe come without a penny to their names and with little more than the clothes on their backs. They lack even the elementary supplies that are essential to each household — knives, forks, spoons, plates, pots and pans, winter clothes, medicines, bedding and furniture, all of which the Jewish Agency provides.

Newcomers from backward countries need to be trained in the ways of Western civilization to enable them to cope with the fast tempo of modern life in Israel. Women must be taught how to care for their children properly in keeping with the unsurpassed sanitary standards of their health-conscious nation where there are four thousand doctors and every working individual is a member of a health insurance plan, primarily the *Kupat Holim* (Sick Fund) of the Histadrut, Israel's General Federation of Labor.

"We have housing and jobs for all who want to work," said Ezra Haddad, director of Histadrut's Department of Immigrant Absorption. He denied reports that ugly *ma'abarot,* the transit camps of the early post-1948 era, have been set up again as shelters for immigrants. It is true, Haddad said, that some newcomers are being placed in temporary asbestos housing units until certain apartment projects in the development towns are completed, but no one ever remains in these makeshift quarters for longer than a year.

According to an estimate by Baruch Duvdevani, Director of the Jewish Agency's Department of Immigration, the number of immigrants is expected to average over sixty thousand a year for the next six years, forming a nucleus of Israel's third million. Duvdevani expressed the hope that eventually all the Jewish communities of the Arab countries as well as the smaller communities of Latin America will move to Israel.

As Prime Minister Levi Eshkol points out, "The multitude of difficulties in making Israel a home for newcomers is yet to be overcome. This calls for all our efforts to build housing, provide employment and speed up the cultural and educational integration of the newcomers. And all this must be done in the face of complex and almost overwhelming commitments to security for survival."

"There is a dynamism to mass immigration. It snowballs," said Yehuda Dominitz, general secretary of the Jewish Agency's Immigration Department.

From his plain, unadorned office in the Jewish Agency buildings in Jerusalem, Dominitz, who was born in Czechoslovakia and was graduated from the Hebrew University and from a yeshiva in Jerusalem, directs a worldwide network of immigration machinery. A teletype clicks out cryptic messages, signaling departures of groups of immigrants from the Americas, Africa, Europe, Asia and Australia and their arrival in Israel. Reception centers and Jewish Agency staff members welcome the immigrants at key points and speed them on to the Promised Land.

In Algeria, where 130,000 Jews were caught in the fighting between the FLN Independence Movement, the French colonials, the Moslems and the French Army, entire towns and villages were emptied of their Jewish populations by emigration. The Jewish community of Batna shrank from 1500 to 800, that of Setif from 2,400 to 700. Jews have departed *en masse* from Philippeville, Guelma, Bone, Tebessa, Biskra and Bougie. Murderous attacks by Moslem terrorists have made it plain to the Jews that there is no more room for them in Algeria.

Dominitz cited the example of the city of Constantine, where Jews have been living for the past 2,000 years.

"As the Jewish population declined rapidly, and the remaining Jews found themselves isolated in the midst of a higher proportion of Moslem neighbors, they also wanted to leave for Algiers, or to emigrate to France or Israel.

"With the Jewish population of Constantine rapidly shrinking, the Jews in the small towns of Constantine's *hinterland* felt increasingly insecure and therefore also decided to leave. The picture is much the same in every country where large masses of Jews are on the march to Israel. No government can stop it. Even a government that would like to keep its Jews realizes that it is better to let the Jews go than to force them to stay against their will."

Another incentive for immigration, Dominitz explained, is the pull of family ties, the longing to join loved ones already in Israel. New immigrants make every effort to send for their kin as soon as possible and help them settle in the Holy Land.

Despite the hardships they have suffered in the process of resettlement and adjustment, Dominitz said that 98 per cent of the immigrants are settled and self-supporting, paying taxes in their turn to help resettle and house the latest newcomers. Only two per cent of the immigrants are social cases, individuals incapable of working because of physical disability or mental illness.

"Israel expects and wants the newcomers," Dominitz declared. "It needs them to supply the manpower for its industrial expansion. True, it takes a year or two for an immigrant to become fully integrated, and the process is difficult for Israel as well as for the newcomers, but we are sure they will be absorbed."

Perhaps the classic place in which to study the modern miracle that is taking place in Israel, the creation of a home for the million newcomers who have come to the land since 1948 is Beersheba, the Biblical city in the Negev.

Tourist guides will point out the place where, according to the Book of Genesis, Abraham went to the well.

But around this ancient Biblical landmark there has risen a new city of 80,000 Israelis gathered from all the continents of the earth, who live in modern apartment houses and earn their livelihood from local industries and businesses that came into being since 1948.

In 1949, Beersheba was a lonely Bedouin desert trading outpost where some two hundred Jews and Arabs lived in ancient stone huts. What has happened in Beersheba since then has come to pass — though in a lesser degree — also in 26 smaller new "development towns" Kiryat Shmoneh, Shelomi, Maalot, Hatzor, Safed, Tiberias, Carmiel, Migdal HaEmek, Upper Nazareth, Afula, Bet Shean, Or Akiva, Yavne, Bet Shemesh, Ashdod, Ashkelon, Kiryat Gat, Kiryat Malachi, Netivot, Sederot, Ofakim, Arad, Dimona, Kefar Yeruham, Mitzpe Ramon, Elat.

The unprecedented policy of providing a new apartment for every immigrant family settling in a new town is the basis of Israel's program of colonization and social absorption, David Tanne, a housing ministry expert with the Israeli Government told me. "Housing," he declared, "is the fundamental instrument of absorption. It is basically instrumental in implementing any program for the distribution of the population away from the big cities, into the arid regions of the Negev and the hills of Galilee."

The main purpose of Israel's housing program is to provide living quarters adequate for normal family life — a determining factor in the education of the younger generation. Only when these satisfactory conditions exist can productivity and initiative in labor be assured and the vocational training of immigrants be begun.

Housing expansion is not confined to the new development towns which have sprung up since 1948, but has taken place also in Tel Aviv, Jerusalem, Haifa, Jaffa, Safed, Tiberias, Acre, Hadera, Petah Tikva, Ramle, Reh-

ovot, Afula, Nahariya, Zikhron Yaakov, Athlit, Nathan-
ya, Ra'anana, K'far Saba, Lod, Rishon LeZion, Gedera,
Ramat Gan, Bat Yam, Holon and Herzliya.

Golda Meir, Israel's Foreign Minister, who at one time
headed the housing program, has said that the housing
of a million immigrants "means that a new geography
has been created in place of the old, in which the Jewish population of Israel had been confined to the coastal
plain and the valleys. A quantitative revolution has got
under way which will, in the nature of things, bring a
new quality into every sphere of our lives. The story of
how homes were provided for hundreds of thousands,
this part of the collective endeavor of our lives, will also
eventually crystallize into one more proud chapter in
our nation's history of glory, suffering and struggling for
a life of truth and justice."

In practical terms, the Battle of Housing, which is being won in the face of a ceaseless torrent of mass immigration, is only one of the two decisive peacetime strug-
gles being fought out on Israel's home front. The other
is the creation of jobs for the newcomers.

The mass housing program has given rise to a substantial construction and building material industry
which now employs 70,000 persons. Thus, even as it
provides apartments for immigrants, Israel's housing expansion program also has created 70,000 new jobs.

Israel now produces and processes its own building
stone, cement blocks, lumber, plywood, tile, brick, aluminum, paper, and electrical equipment. As a matter of
fact, one-third of Israel's output of building materials,
such as cement and glass, is tagged for export. Iron and
steel are used only sparingly in construction. Iron ingots
are imported from abroad, but are finished in Israel.

Who pays for immigrant housing?

The money comes from many sources including the
United Jewish Appeal, Israel Bonds, reparations from

Germany, grants-in-aid from the United States, taxes, compulsory loans, land sales and customs duties including indirect levies on building materials.

Israeli taxpayers, already groaning under a tax burden amounting to one-fourth to one-third of weekly wages that range between $40 and $50, must also contribute to a compulsory loan of $12,500,000 for immigrant housing. Funds provided by the United Jewish Appeal go primarily for the transportation and initial resettlement of the newcomers. Two out of every three dollars of the costs of immigrant absorption are provided by the taxpayers of the State of Israel.

The story of the first three years of Israel's Statehood, when the new-born State doubled its population, seems almost inconceivable today.

"Housing hundreds of thousands of people was a problem that could have blown immigration sky high and wrecked the whole enterprise of rescue," Golda Meir recalled. "This was an appalling risk to take, one of those risks that put the fate of a nation in the balance, and it was perhaps one of the miracles of our restoration that we stood up to the risk and overcame its dangers."

Mrs. Meir says that those early years of large-scale immigration and housing construction provided a wealth of experience that makes today's mass influx easier to handle.

H. Darin-Drabkin, economic advisor to the Housing Division and planner of immigrant absorption and employment in Israel's Ministry of Labor, describes the drama of the immense task in his book entitled *Housing in Israel*. Mr. Darin-Drabkin who studied economics at the University of Warsaw, likens the mass immigration that followed the establishment of the State in 1948 to the Exodus of an entire people, including whole communities which abandoned the places in which they had lived for centuries, in order to return to the land of their fathers. They came as they were, the old and the young, the healthy and the sick. Israel is the only country in the world that is ready to accept the sick and the ailing, for it is inconceivable that communities and families should leave their sick behind."

Darin-Drabkin, who is also a sociologist of note, clearly explains the reason for this open-door immigration policy. "The basis of the young State, indeed, the whole purpose of its existence," he writes, "was the opportunity it afforded for the ingathering of the exiles and the consolidation of the Jewish people. The pressure of the refugees, the requirements of security, the vital necessity for immediate settlement measures in order to populate development and border areas, left no time for selection and experimentation. What had to be done was to bring in Jews, whatever might befall, and it had to be done in accordance with the high historic principle that the gates of the country remain open to all Jews who wish to immigrate."

Why did Israel not spread out its immigration over a longer period of time? Why did the State of Israel endanger its very existence by letting in 684,201 immigrants during the first three years of its existence?

According to Darin-Drabkin, the answer is that Israel does not hold the keys to immigration, nor can it control the size or the tempo of the Exodus. The keys, he asserts, are in the hands of other countries, which can open their gates or close them at will.

"In many lands," he observed, "the problem for the would-be immigrants was the acute and brutal one of making a choice between immediate emigration and the chance that all possibilities of departure might be cut off in the not-too distant future."

What took place between 1948 and 1951 was one of the greatest stories of mass rescue in the history of mankind. Even as the Jewish State was proclaimed on May 14,

1948, and was immediately attacked by six invading Arab countries, the surviving Jews in the displaced-persons camps of Europe were being assembled for hazardous treks across Europe to ports in France and Italy, from which ancient hulks moved them to Haifa.

The camp set up by the British in Cyprus for the internment of illegal would-be immigrants to what once had been Palestine was emptied. Veterans of anti-Nazi underground bands in Europe made their way to Israel to join the Hagana, the new Defense Army of the new State, in the fight against the Arab invaders. Nearly fifty thousand Jews left Turkey. Czechoslovakia, which sold armaments and planes to the hard-pressed Israeli army, allowed its surviving Jews to depart in contingents of twenty thousand each year. Bulgaria's Jewish community of thirty-six thousand moved to Israel *en masse* within two years, beginning with October 1948. Seven thousand Jews emigrated from Yugoslavia.

Then came the Exodus from the Kingdom of Yemen. In 1949, the Imam of Yemen gave his Jews permission to leave the country. Within eighteen months, El Al's "Operation Magic Carpet" had airlifted forty-five thousand dark-complexioned, wizened, skinny, peppery and pious Jews from Yemen to Israel. For these throwbacks to the Biblical era, the flight to Israel was a leap of a thousand years from medieval ghetto life to modern civilization, made within a few hours of flight time.

Civil war drove out five thousand Jews from China, and they took off for Israel.

The birth of the Jewish State touched off a mass Exodus from North Africa. Within a period of three years, thirty-five thousand Jews had left Morocco, Tunisia and Algeria for the Promised Land.

The Iron Curtain was temporarily lifted in 1949. Between December 1949 and February 1951, Poland let out twenty-eight thousand survivors of Naziism. Rumania permitted the ship *Transylvania* to make weekly voyages to Haifa, bringing to Israel a total of eighty-eight thousand Jews, and when Hungary opened its gates, three thousand Jews left there each month.

During the first eighteen months following the signing of Israel's Proclamation of Independence, a total of 341,000 Jews poured into the land despite the war which it was fighting against the Arabs for its very survival. Young men went directly from ship or plane to the army and into battle. Able-bodied immigrants of middle age found jobs in war industries. Forty former British army camps were hastily converted into immigrant reception centers.

Israel had no time to take a breathing spell from this human deluge. Suddenly, a stream of Jews gushed forth from hostile Arab countries. Iran permitted its Jews to leave. In 1950, Iraq enacted an emigration law, permitting Jews to emigrate during a specified period of twelve months. Before the deadline had passed, a hundred thousand Iraqi Jews had been swept into Israel by a phenomenal airlift operation.

Where did Israel put all these new arrivals in the beginning?

The houses abandoned by the Arabs were quickly filled. The former British army camps were overcrowded with immigrants. Tent camps were put together; prefabricated wood and tin huts were set up, too hot in the summer, too cold in the winter, but providing a roof over the newcomers' heads. The boast of the Israeli housing authorities to this day is that there was never even so much as one immigrant without shelter, even if it was only a canvas covering. Nobody had to sleep in the open, and no one starved. Food was rationed.

The year 1950 saw the rise of the ma'abarot, transit camps of barrack-like temporary housing units mushrooming on the outskirts of Israel's cities. Occupants of the ma'abarot would go to the cities and towns each day to work. Medical, educational, social and vocational services were provided by the government and the Jewish Agency. By the end of 1951, Israel had 123 ma'abarot which sheltered a total of 227,000 immigrants.

Many newcomers found life in the ma'abarot unbearable. In 1952, immigration dropped to 24,369 from its peak figures of 239,000 in 1949, 170,249 in 1950 and 175,095 in 1951. During the ten years that followed, immigration fluctuated from a low of 11,326 in 1953 to a high of 71,224 in 1957.

With the tapering-off of immigration in 1952, the government began its program of directing immigration away from the cities to development towns and border villages. The ma'abarot which had degenerated into sores upon the face of Israel were slowly dismantled, and by 1955, the "ship-to-settlement" plan of immigrant distribution had become an actuality.

It was this "ship-to-settlement" process that brought order out of chaos and accomplished the parallel miracles of providing decent housing and building up new towns in the Negev and undeveloped parts of the Galilee on the one hand, and furnishing manpower to the new factories arising in the development towns on the other.

Despite the burden placed upon it by mass immigration, Israel's economy is booming. Its industries, business enterprises and farms are short of labor, its agriculture is exporting a food surplus, and the settled citizens of Israel who have money to spare are speculating in stocks and real estate. The new immigrants, going to work immediately after arrival, became consumers and productive citizens, thus adding to the buying power which creates new demands for food, clothing, furniture and other products. Thus, immigration accelerates the momentum of a prospering economy.

In the face of such optimistic reports, people in the

United States and elsewhere are naturally inclined to ask: "Does Israel need our money?"

The answer is a complex "Yes and no."

Yes, Israel is in need of more investment funds than ever to build up its industry to provide housing and full employment for its immigrants. This means that Israel Bonds, Rassco, Israel Investors Corporation, Palestine Economic Corporation, Ampal and the other legitimate Israeli investment opportunities are still needed to keep the economy growing. Those who make such investments are assured of good dividends, and prospective long-term added values, based on the promise which the future of Israel holds. And while they are earning dividends, the men and women the world over who are investing in the State of Israel are also carrying out the great *mitzva* of helping our brethren in Israel help themselves become self supporting.

Israel does not get "charity money" from the United Jewish Appeal. Such a direct transfer of funds is, in fact, prohibited by the tax laws of the United States to which the United Jewish Appeal, as an American organization, is subject. The contributions given to the United Jewish Appeal go to the Jewish Agency which uses these funds to organize mass immigration operations from Africa, Europe, Asia and the countries of the Western Hemisphere. With these funds, too, the Agency subsidizes the immigration of those who cannot afford to pay their own ship or plane fares. The Jewish Agency processes the immigrants before they arrive in Haifa or at Lod and sends them where they are needed and where jobs and housing await them.

The Jewish Agency is the helpful "Uncle *Sochnut*" (*Sochnut* being the Hebrew for "Agency") to the immigrants during the time of their adjustment to Israel, supplying them with cash, food and housekeeping essentials until they are in a position to provide for their

needs by themselves. The Agency makes loans to craftsmen so that they may start in business and provide employment for others, and to struggling agricultural settlements to put them on their feet. The Jewish Agency
supports ulpanim (intensive Hebrew language courses)
and vocational training centers for immigrants, and looks
after those newcomers who have trouble in adjusting or
in finding the right employment.

With mass immigration continuing, the grand total of
all funds raised by the United Jewish Appeal is far below the overall cost of the Jewish Agency's immigration
program. To make up for this deficit, the Agency bor-
rows money, and draws on support from the hard pressed
Israeli government.

It is simply not true that contributors to the United
Jewish Appeal in America are "giving money" to Israel
or to Israelis. The Israeli taxpayer is giving much more,
proportionately, through regular taxes and a "voluntary"
immigration housing tax, than his American cousins.

Israel is not, by any means, a "charity," and should
not be regarded as such.

Does poverty still exist in booming Israel? To get the
facts on poverty in the Jewish State, Rabbi Herbert A.
Friedman, who is Executive Vice-Chairman of the United Jewish Appeal, sent the noted author Ruth Gruber to
the Holy Land to hunt out pockets of suffering. She found
them, in the small immigrant towns of the Negev and
the Galilee that you rarely, if ever, hear about — Shlomi,
Ma'alot, Hatzor, Bet Shean, Shderot, Yavne, Kfar Yer-
uhim, Netivot, Afikim and Mitzpe Ramon. Unlike the
successful development towns of the Negev — Beersheba, Dimona, Ashdod, Ashkelon, Kiryat Gat — whose primary problem is the shortage of labor — these smaller
towns suffer from unemployment and their large immigrant families have insufficient incomes. The Shderots
and Bet She'ans have no large factories as yet, because

they are still in the early stages of development. Ruth Gruber reports that in the villages she visited, the idle are not registered with the labor exchanges because of the scarcity of local industries and business enterprises which would give them employment.

Israel's social welfare policy is based on the premise that no one must be allowed to starve. At the same time, the rule in Israel is that everyone must do some kind of work for his money. Unless he is so seriously ill or handicapped that he can do nothing at all, no unemployed person in Israel receives handouts. Where no jobs are available, Israel creates *dahak* or "planned labor," to give a measure of dignity and self-respect to those "on relief," who are preferably spoken of as "social" cases. There are 20,000 Israelis on "work relief," employed on public projects such as building highways, planting trees, weeding parks and cleaning streets. It has been estimated that of these 20,000, 16,000 are old, illiterate, or partially disabled. Most of them work five hours a day, earning daily wages of IL 5.10 or $1.70. Married men are given up to twenty-four days of *dahak* work per month according to number of dependents, so that they can earn a maximum of $40.80 per month toward the support of their families. If they are recent immigrants, they also receive the customary allocations from the Jewish Agency. Wives and older children, too, work to supplement the family income. In addition, a cut-rate food surplus allotment program helps fill the breadbaskets of *dahak* families.

According to Miss Gruber, there is no unemployment for the skilled in Israel. Actually, she reports, 97 per cent of the labor force is at work — a spectacular figure of full employment. But in the development towns employment is still a very real problem for those who have no special skills.

Rabbi Friedman, emphasizing the need for increased

giving to the United Jewish Appeal to meet mounting costs of mass immigration, informed me that, "until an immigrant becomes firmly integrated in an area where employment opportunities abound, schools are available for his children, etc., he and his family remain a charge, in one way or another, of the Jewish Agency. This is what we mean when we say that one out of four of Israel's immigrants are still unabsorbed."

The UJA chief stressed the need to help struggling agricultural settlements become self-sufficient. Despite the increasingly successful economy, Rabbi Friedman stated, there are still tremendous pockets of human suffering and deprivation which the United Jewish Appeal and the Jewish Agency strive to alleviate.

"While normal indices show a glowing picture of booming industry, skilled labor shortages, rising exports, etc.," the UJA leader declared, "Israel's abnormal situation can be righted only by continued and considerably greater assistance from UJA and other philanthropic sources."

Rabbi Friedman warned against ignoring the "Extraordinary security burden which seriously distorts Israel's economic development." He stressed that, "To an Israel surrounded by 40 million hostile Arabs, military preparedness is a life or death matter. Israel must maintain this costly military establishment at a time when it is receiving and absorbing scores of thousands of immigrants each year, each of whom constitutes an enormous charge upon the country's resources until he gets on his feet. The only way a small, hard pressed, resource-poor country like Israel can assure a secure and viable future for itself is by budgeting an unusually high amount of its national income for education. Only by the highest degree of scientific and allied accomplishments both from the present generation and the children of these immigrants will Israel be in a position to hold its own — not only against the sheer weight of numbers represented by the Arabs, but also in competition for world markets with the technical skills of friendly nations.

* * *

Seated in his office in the Jewish Agency building is a newcomer representing an entirely different type of immigrant. He is Rabbi Israel Goldstein, former President of the Zionist Organization of America, the World Confederation of Zionists, and the Jewish National Fund in the United States. Before coming to Israel to assume the presidency of *Keren HaYesod*-United Israel Appeal, Dr. Goldstein had a distinguished career of over four decades in the American Conservative rabbinate, until he became rabbi emeritus of his congregation. In 1961 he and his wife came from New York to settle in a villa they built in Jerusalem. Rabbi Goldstein regards his move to the Land as an act of self-fulfillment.

"I have not had a single moment of regret," he told me, as he leaned back in his swivel chair in the Jewish Agency building. "Israel is in a class by itself for complete personal self-fulfillment as a Jew. I can live a full, uninhibited Jewish life only in Israel. Here I feel a national sense of purpose unlike anywhere else. I am part of it."

Notwithstanding some pointed criticisms he has to make of life in the Jewish State, particularly the stranglehold of Orthodoxy on religion in the country, Rabbi Goldstein, who is in his late sixties, appeared to be the perfectly "adjusted" American Jewish immigrant to Israel.

For less illustrious Jews from the United States who have answered Ben Gurion's call for *aliya* from the English-speaking countries, the adjustment is not quite so easy.

I met Murray Greenfield, formerly of Brooklyn and

a veteran of Israel's War of Independence, who is the founder and president of the Association of Americans and Canadians in Israel, a group with a membership of over 10,000. He estimated that there are in Israel some 13,000 immigrants from the United States and Canada. Of these approximately 1,500 live in Kibbutzim, and about 800 are elderly people who came to Israel to retire.

Why the sudden influx from the United States?

Some say that Leon Uris' best-seller, *Exodus,* presented to millions of Americans between hard covers, in paperbacks and on the motion picture screen, stimulated the desire to settle in Israel. Then there is the Peace Corps, inaugurated in the administration of the late President Kennedy, which made pioneering for the purpose of helping new nations in many continents a highly respectable thing to do. Still others look on Israel as a challenge, a new frontier, an opportunity to live an exciting, meaningful life as a full Jew, in the most dynamic, fastest-growing country in the world.

The young man or woman who emigrates to Israel for idealistic reasons has a chance to do well here, provided he has been prepared for the difficulties he may encounter and he is blessed with a sense of humor, tolerance, and love for his fellow-Jews. It is not a bad idea, I am told, to have a reserve of $5,000 to tide one over the transition period.

Only half of the American aliya sticks it out, Greenfield said. The other half return disillusioned. They complain about lack of amenities taken for granted in the States, lower standards of living, the struggle to make ends meet, and the exorbitant price of housing in Tel Aviv. Many American olim feel that the Israelis show a callous lack of concern for their welfare and happiness.

Meyer Levin, the novelist, who is living near Tel Aviv, said the discrimination and disdain to which Americans settling in Israel are subjected represent "the strongest cause of maladjustment of Americans in Israel."

Greenfield criticized Ben-Gurion for his attitude toward American immigrants while he was Premier. While the veteran statesman repeatedly called for aliya from America, he did little to make the Jews from America welcome when they did arrive to settle. As president of the organization of American and Canadian immigrants to Israel, Greenfield met with Ben-Gurion three times in an effort to get him to appoint one central government authority to work with Western immigrants instead of letting the newcomers from the Anglo-Saxon countries race around to as many as fifteen different offices and agencies dealing with English-speaking arrivals.

Greenfield recalls the main points of his fruitless talks with the then Prime Minister.

"The important thing is not how many immigrants you get from America, but how well Israel can absorb them," Greenfield told Ben-Gurion. "The Americans want some courtesy extended to them when they arrive. They object to getting the run-around wherever they go. Customs procedures alone take days and weeks. And then they need long-term mortgages. It takes $15,000 just to buy a small apartment in Tel Aviv, with a down payment of $13,000."

"That's all unimportant," Ben-Gurion insisted. "Immigrants have to pioneer. When I came here, nobody did anything for me."

"But you have to remember that this is the first aliya which comes here out of love for Israel and not out of fear. They have come and they stay because they find life here stimulating and are convinced that there's no other place in the world where Jewish children can grow up as freely and normally as in Israel. These people aren't refugees from oppression," the American replied.

"There's no real aliya from the United States," retorted Ben-Gurion.

"I have the figures here," Greenfield countered. "One thousand came in 1960, 1,300 in 1961 and 1,700 in 1963."

"I don't believe it," was Ben-Gurion's answer. "And besides, if anything's wrong with the adjustment of Americans here, it's your American Zionist organizations who're to blame."

Today, Greenfield says: "I opposed Ben-Gurion's call for a wholesale American aliya. I felt that Israel really did not need it. If the Israelis had really wanted immigrants from America, they would have done something to make aliya attractive to Americans. After all, when Israel was in need of money from abroad, the government actually changed its policies in order to encourage foreign investors to put their capital into Israeli industries."

Greenfield pointed out that there is one type of American immigrant who is really more of a burden than an asset to Israel. "There are plenty of people in the States who regard Israel as some sort of an asylum for nuts," he said. "Too many families with a young mental case on their hands think Israel will solve his emotional problems. One such character even wrote to our office that his psychiatrist had told him to settle in Israel. We send the nuts back as fast as they come. It's become so that we're able to tell them by the letters they write. And we weed them out pronto."

*      *      *

Menahem Beigin, leader of Israel's Herut Party and chief of the extremist Irgun Zvai Leumi under the British Mandate, feels that South America and South Africa are substantial sources of immigration to Israel — with wealth to invest in the rapid industrialization of the Negev and Galilee.

He told me that South American Jewish businessmen

and industrialists are concerned about the spreading influence of Castro Communism, and pointed out that South Africa is on the verge of a racial explosion over the *apartheid* issue.

Beigin, who has many supporters in South Africa, said that the Jews there might become the victims of a great struggle between Negroes and Whites.

"I say to every guest: Why not come here to Israel to live?" he said. "South African and South American Jewries should come here *en masse*. Why wait until things get worse and you lose your property? Come here with your wealth while you still have it. Invest in our country. Build it up. It's a good country and it will be good for your children."

Unfortunately, Beigin observed, the tragedy of Jewish history has always been that Jewish communities never expect anti-Semitism to overrun them and therefore they wait until it is too late. By the time the situation becomes acutely uncomfortable, the emigrants have difficulties in selling their property at the "right price," and many arrive in Israel practically penniless.

"We have no fear of war with the Arabs," Beigin told me. He did not expect peace in the near future, but predicted that it would be made first with Egypt after Nasser falls. "We believe there will be no general war. I have absolute faith in our army's ability to repel any attack. Our people are not nervous about the Arab enemies. We get stronger. The Arabs know they cannot defeat Israel. And so we go forward to our two-fold goal—to develop the country and to complete the Ingathering of the Exiles."

# CHAPTER III

# "THE SECOND ISRAEL"

I was the "tenth man" on a Sabbath in Tel Aviv, in a little Yemenite synagogue just off Carmel Market. Then Moshe, a boy of fifteen, entered, making the total attendance eleven. No more worshippers came that Sabbath morning to the fifteen-by-fifteen room which houses one of the eighteen synagogues in the Yemenite quarter of Israel's metropolis. But what the *minyan* lacked in numbers was more than offset by the fervor with which these Yemenites, whom a historian has called "the most Jewish of all Jews," worshipped that day.

The prayers of the Yemenites are virtually the same as those recited in the Orthodox synagogues of their Ashkenazi brethren in the Western world, but the chant to which they read them is strange and intriguing. Their synagogues as such are nothing more than tiny rooms with rather scanty decorations, but they have brought with them from Yemen their wood and silver encased Scrolls of the Law. These and their other ceremonial objects reveal that artistry and sense of beauty which has made Yemenite filigree silverwork known and enjoyed the world over.

Moshe Cohen, the young man who deprived me of the unexpected privilege of being the "tenth man," left the synagogue with me at the end of the service. As we walked through the Carmel Market — strangely quiet and deserted on the Day of Rest — he told me that he wanted to be a doctor. His friend, Shlomo Shaare, who was eighteen, said that he was attending high school at nearby Rehovot and hoped to win a scholarship to Bar Ilan University after completing his two years of compulsory service in the Army. Shlomo wants to teach Bible in the secondary schools.

Moshe and Shlomo represent the new generation of Yemenites making the transition from a culture which had stagnated in centuries of isolation to the modern civilization which the Jews from Yemen found when they arrived in the Promised Land in the "Operation Magic Carpet" airlift of 1949-50. These young men are bright, intelligent, ambitious, and willing to work hard to get a higher education, to become part and parcel of the Land for which their people have yearned so long.

To many of the pious Yemenites, who preserved their Judaism through many generations of isolation and oppression, the establishment of the State of Israel in 1948 signified a Messianic call to a wholesale "return to Zion".

Yehiel Wahab gave up his prosperous textile business at Sana, sold his home at half-price, and came to Israel in 1951 with his wife Urah and their four children. With him on the plane were twenty-four members of his clan. Now Yehiel lives with his wife and children in a tiny two-room flat in a Jaffa slum. His teaching position at Yeshiva Ateret Zeqenim brings him IL 25 per month. Occasionally he earns a few additional pounds repairing Scrolls of the Law. His wife works as an *ozeret* or housemaid, four hours each day. She brings home IL 120 a month — almost five times as much as her husband.

In his fifties, Yehiel Wahab has had to get accustomed

to a new order of things — poverty, slum living, and the fact that Urah, a mere woman, is now the real bread-winner of the family. But he has no regrets and would not think of returning to Yemen. "Israel is my home-land," he declared. His only complaint is that the home-land of the Jewish people is not sufficiently religious. "The Sabbath isn't observed properly here," he said, but he prays that Israel may yet become a religious State.

We dropped in on Yehuda Arkabi, his wife Galya, and their six children, whose home is a bare cottage in the village of Neve Hadar on the outskirts of Tel Aviv. The Arkabis came to Israel in 1949. Now they eke out a scant living with their vegetables, a cow, some goats and scrawny chickens. Their tiny house contains only a few rickety beds and chairs, with mattresses piled up along the walls during the day and laid on the floor at night. The whole family sleeps in one room.

Yehuda is sixty-five, but his eyes burn with passion as he speaks in the strong stentorian voice that is charac-teristic of many a Yemenite. In his pure Biblical Hebrew, he described the "Magic Carpet" that bore him to Israel "upon the wings of an eagle."

When he first arrived in Israel, he worked on a mo-shav. When Galya, now in her forties (she is his third wife), suffered her fifth miscarriage, they decided to leave the moshav and move to Neve Hadar to "change their luck."

Arkabi acts as Tora reader in one of the two Yemen-ite synagogues at Neve Hadar. The Yemenites may be poor, but they're individualists, and when worshippers can't agree, one synagogue is just not enough.

The Arkabi children, ranging in age from three to fourteen, attend a religious public school at nearby Kfar Nitzahon.

"We prayed for the moment to come when we would be able to go to Israel," their father told me. "It was the will of God." It is this simple outlook on life, based on an unquestioning faith in God, that guides the Yemenites of Arkabi's generation. When I inquired whether he and his family did not find it difficult to make ends meet, he replied: "Material things mean nothing to me. I forget them. It is not the profane, but only the holy that I remember."

You find Yemenites working at the most menial of tasks, as maids, street-cleaners, janitors and newspaper peddlers. You see them as day laborers on the kibbutzim, in orange groves, highways, and in factories. You see Yemenite gold and silver embroidery on the stylish Israeli blouses, and in filigree work that is in demand throughout the world. And you will come upon Yemenites in the slums in the side streets of Tel Aviv, Jaffa, Jerusalem and small towns, sitting on their doorstoops, idle, dozing, dreaming in the manner of the Moslem world, where life is leisurely and there's always time to do things tomorrow.

Dr. Shlomo Dov Goitein, an Orientalist who made a study of a Yemenite community of weavers, pointed out that the Yemenites cannot be regarded as one community but should be viewed in "sub-sections" representing widely divergent groups, coming as they do from 1030 different places in Yemen, each group differing from the others in economic, social and intellectual background.

"I have met Yemenites with an almost European mind," he said, "and other groups — fortunately a small minority only — who are inarticulate and primitive. Some communities impress one as closely-knit, well-organized units, while others tend to disintegrate over issues that seem trivial."

Goitein, who has specialized in the study of Yemenite Jews, found that they followed 66 different trades, including agriculture. "The real tragedy of the Yemenites," he declared, "is that the whole economy of Israel

is so different from that with which the Yemenites are
familiar. Not a single one of the 66 arts and crafts they
practiced in Yemen could be put to use in Israel without
some profound changes. The Yemenite Jew, who had
been a skilled master craftsman at home, found himself
an unskilled laborer in Israel."

"The greatest tragedy of all," Goitein added, "was that
the religious element among the working people of Israel was far too small to cope with the needs of this mass
immigration of religious Jews. The Yemenites are the
most Jewish of all Jews. In a country which was itself
a medieval theocracy, they had preserved in their remote
isolation much of the character of a genuinely Jewish
society. Therefore, their ingathering to the land of their
fathers was not only a redemption of the body; it was
a return of the spirit."

The predominance of the irreligious among the working people in Israel meant that the Israeli social workers and instructors who dealt with the Yemenite newcomers did not talk the same language as their charges,
religiously speaking.

Yet, Goitein feels that the integration of the Yemenite
Jews in Israeli society is progressing rapidly and well.

"We are interested in strengthening their attachment
to the positive values they have brought with them," he
said. "For the truer a Yemenite remains to the positive
aspects of his tradition, the better an Israeli is he likely
to make."

According to Yemenite Jewish tradition, their ancestors arrived in Yemen shortly after the destruction of the
First Temple in Jerusalem by Nebuchadnezzar in 568
B.C.E. At one time, they prospered greatly. In the sixth
century of the Christian era, they succeeded in converting
the ruler and the royal household of the Himyarite kingdom in Yemen, an event which resulted in the wholesale conversion of Himyarites. But after the death of

King Dhu Nuwas, who had adopted the Jewish name of Yusuf (Joseph), and the advent of the faith of Islam, the Jews of Yemen suffered increasingly from oppression and isolation. For a period of thirteen hundred years they turned inward to cultivate a strong religious life, motivated by a deep faith in the coming of the days of the Messiah. Beginning with the early 1880's, a few thousand Yemenites came to what then was Palestine, but there was no mass emigration from Yemen until 1948, when Israel was reborn and silvery birds came on giant wings to carry them to the Promised Land.

They left Yemen by the thousands, their eyes turned to the land of their Father Abraham, bearing with them their prayer books and their richly ornamented Scrolls of the Law, but little else.

Today, there are about 100,000 Yemenites in Israel.

* * *

The Negev bus was crowded and I pushed into the last vacant seat in the back row as two young men moved over to make room for me.

The one next to me unhooked his holster and placed his revolver in his lap so the gun would not poke my ribs. It made a handy conversation piece. The gun toter was Yosef Mishari, a veteran of the Israel Army at 23. Yosef represents the new type of Israel pioneer. He was going to Arad, the newest industrial development town in the Negev desert, to work as a tractor driver. In a lonely frontier post where Bedouins roam the rolling desert sands, the gun is just as much standard equipment as it was in the Dakota badlands of the American Wild West.

Yosef and his family came to Israel from Iraq in 1950, refugees from persecution by the Iraqi government which was then still smarting from its ignominious defeat by the Israeli Army in 1948.

He was just nine when he and his clan of 123 relatives, including his parents, four brothers and five sisters, were flown to Israel from Baghdad.

What has happened to the Mishari clan is a miniature version of the epic drama of the exodus of a million Jews to Israel from the Moslem countries.

Abraham, Yosef's father, who is close to sixty, was a well-to-do restaurant owner in Baghdad, where Jews had resided for over two thousand years. Yosef estimated that his family had a fortune of $75,000 before their home and their family business were confiscated.

They arrived in Israel without a penny. From Lod Airport they were taken at once to a ma'abara at Ramatayim, north of Tel Aviv, where they spent five years.

"Life was very bad," handsome Yosef sadly recalled as our Egged bus rolled southward. "Never in my life will I forget the horrible ma'abara. For three years, we lived in tents. The tents kept collapsing. Then they built huts where we lived for two years. During the rainy season it was cold, and the roofs were leaking. There was plenty of sickness. There were snakes in the mud, too. Father was working in the orange groves and the older children worked after school. Finally, we had saved up enough money to lay out IL 1,250.00 for a down payment on a little farmhouse near the ma'abara. That's where we kids grew up. We all went to school, but we kept on working after school hours to help support the family."

Yosef ran down the roster of the Mishari family. Sasson, his oldest brother, 28, is living with his wife and six children on a moshav at Kedma. Batya, 26, lives at Ramatayim with her husband and seven children. Batya's husband earns IL 11.00 a day feeding chickens in an agricultural cooperative. Ilana, 24, is the mother of three; her husband is a clerk. Yosef at the time was still unmarried. Shaul, 20, was released from the Army before the end of his term of service to help support his family.

He makes IL 250.00 a month from his own moving and transport business, a one-man, one-horse operation. Zalman, 18, is in the Army. Three children are still at home; Nigega, 16, supplements the family income with her monthly profit of IL 140.00 which she earns by raising chickens. Carmela, 13, is too young to help the family along, but she hopes to be a doctor when she grows up. The youngest is Eli, who is just eight. A little girl, Sabena, died in Baghdad at two, of typhus.

After fourteen years in Israel, the Misharis do not lead a life of ease, but they are not dependent on charity. They are self-supporting and pay heavy taxes to help absorb new waves of immigrants. While Yosef is leveling the ground at Arad with his tractor for the building of new homes for immigrants, his parents, brothers and sisters are producing food for their own sustenance and for sale to help feed the new arrivals.

Social workers like Ezra Haddad of Histadrut have thrown themselves into the task of aiding the newcomers from Iraq. Haddad, who himself came to Israel from Baghdad in 1951 and has risen to his present post through the Histadrut ranks, spoke of the noble tradition of which the Iraqi Jews were the proud bearers for 2,500 years. It was in Iraq, the Mesopotamia of the Bible and later part of the Babylonian Empire, that the Jewish exiles sat "by the waters of Babylon" and mourned the destruction of the First Temple. Eventually, Babylonia became the seat of the famed Talmudic academies of Sura and Pumbedita where the great Gaonim expounded the Law. It was only natural that Talmudic training should have sharpened the minds of their disciples and thus indirectly helped produce brilliant legal and medical minds, writers and poets. Jewish traders went forth from Babylonia to do business in Central Asia and as far away as India and China. Many of the sons of these cosmopolitan merchants rose to posts of distinction at the courts of Oriental potentates.

There were also times of oppression and persecution, depending on the mood of the rulers who happened to be in power, but never had conditions been such as to compel the Jews to leave the country in a mass exodus.

In the main, the Jews of Iraq had been prosperous. In the early days of modern Palestine, Iraqi Jews sent generous financial support to yeshivot, schools and agricultural settlements in the Holy Land. They had never forgotten Jerusalem.

In 1948, there were 125,000 Jews in the Kingdom of Iraq.

"In fact, it was the Jews who introduced many of the ways of Western civilization into Iraq," Haddad said. "And then, suddenly, Iraq turned against the Jews who'd lived there 1300 years longer than the Arabs. We all thought we had lasting roots in Iraq. But then came destruction, pogroms in the streets of Baghdad, with 235 Jewish men, women and children killed in one day. Young Jews were cast into dungeons and tortured. Some had the nails torn from their fingers. Thousands of Jewish homes, shops and institutions were sacked. Hebrew books were confiscated, synagogues were closed, and Jews were forbidden to teach Hebrew to their children. There had been a time when I could hardly draw a line between my Jewishness and my identification with the Iraqi people. But when this blow came, I resolved to dedicate myself to the Jewish people and prepare the youngsters I was teaching for emigration to Israel."

However, emigration was not immediately possible. The Iraqi government refused to let the Jews leave. Iraqi Jewry appealed to Israel for help, and requested the United States to exert pressure on Baghdad to let the Jews go. In the end, the Iraqi Parliament passed a decree that any Jew desiring to do so would be permitted to emigrate to Israel but that such emigrants had to forfeit their Iraqi citizenship and give up all their property and assets.

"We had to leave everything behind," Haddad told me.

In a period of nine months in 1950 and 1951, a rescue airlift flew 100,000 Iraqi Jews to Israel.

"I landed in Lod," Haddad recalled, "and found myself a free man in a free country. I was dazzled by the bright light of liberty. But for us Iraqi Jews, a long and difficult process of adjustment was only beginning. It was not easy. Among the Jews of Iraq there was not one farmer, not one carpenter, bricklayer or factory worker. We were traders, shopkeepers, bankers, clerks, teachers, rabbis, doctors, lawyers — but not workers. And Israel needed workers to reclaim the Negev and the Galilee, to build factories and farms, to till the soil and make the desert bloom."

"I am amazed to see my fellow-Iraqis work in factories, on the scaffolding of new buildings, on the highways, on the farms, at all kinds of hard physical labor. They came from a country where the better-class citizen was taught that it was a disgrace to do manual work. But Israel has changed their lives," Haddad told me. "I really should say that Israel has *saved* our lives, and for this we will always be grateful."

Zalman Mizhari (no relation to Yosef of Arad), Haddad's deputy at the Department of Immigrant Absorption, recalled how the Iraqi newcomers were sped from the airport to ma'abarot, and eventually transferred to the former Arab quarters in Lod, Ramle, Jaffa and Haifa which the Arabs had hurriedly abandoned in the War of Independence. Then, along with other immigrants, the Iraqis were trained in the work that Israel needed and brought to new housing in 26 new towns in the Negev and the Galilee.

"You throw these immigrants out into the wilderness,

without water, without jobs. How will they live?" opponents of the development town scheme demanded.

"Well, just come with me to a place like Ashdod," said Mizhari, who had come to Israel from Poland in 1926, worked in orange groves near Petah Tikva and had personally supervised the erection of seventy immigrant settlements throughout the country. "You'll see a town full of life and industry and with good living conditions. Five years ago, they asked how they would make a living. Today they ask, when will more people come to fill the vacancies in factories and building trades? It's the same story in the other 25 towns. Some grow faster, some slower."

\* \* \*

Eliahu Cohen, formerly a tailor in Marrakesh, is a farmer at a cooperative settlement in the Lakhish region. He and his family had not suffered want or oppression in Morocco, but they did not know what the next day might bring. "Therefore," he recalled, "when we had a chance to emigrate to Israel, we didn't think too long."

Rabbi Isaac Benizi, spiritual leader of the Jewish community of Sifrou, personally led his flock of 800 men, women and children to Israel in 1957 and founded Yad Rambam. Yad Rambam is a moshav, a settlement where each member has his own home and property, but the farming is done on a cooperative basis. He saw that there would be no future for his brethren in Morocco. Despite difficulties and insufficient income, Rabbi Benizi and his disciples are happy to be in Israel.

Yosef Levi, a man in his fifties, came to Israel in 1959 from Casablanca where he had owned a large clothing store. Now he lives in a three-room house at Neve Hadar, near Tel Aviv, and barely makes ends meet as a part-time house painter. He manages to get 15 to 20 days of work a month, earning the equivalent of $4.25 a day. He does a little farming on the side. With chicken prices down, he asserted, it did not pay to buy feed for poultry-raising on the small plot of ground that surrounds his home. And with irrigation as costly as it is, he did not consider it economical to go into large-scale vegetable growing.

"How do you manage to make a living?" I asked him.

"If you work and earn well, you eat well," Levi replied. "If you don't work, you don't eat well. But we have enough."

While we talked, his wife Hanna, granddaughter of the Grand Rabbi of the Moroccan town of Mogador, was setting the table with an array of thick, sweet preserves, dates and figs.

I asked Mr. Levi why he had chosen to exchange his prosperous store in Casablanca for near-poverty in Israel.

"I was no fool," he replied. "I followed political developments. I saw what was coming. All my friends told me I was insane. But I got out while I still could sell my store. France was still in control of Morocco then, but I knew what would happen to the Jews once the French left. My friends, like fools, kept on expanding their businesses and investing money. I told them, 'You're only building for the Arabs. They will take it all from you.' "

Yosef Levi brought his entire family to Israel with him. His brother is working in Rishon LeZion, the center of Israel's wine, beer and whiskey industry. His mother lives in Afikim with another brother. Hanna is not so fortunate. Part of her family is still in Tangiers, and since postal communications between Morocco and Israel have been cut off, she has no news from these relatives.

Since Levi came to Israel at his own expense and had brought some money with him, he paid for his home, and added two extra rooms, doing part of the work himself. Less fortunate newcomers who left Morocco when it was no longer possible to take out money from the country were placed in ma'abarot. If they agreed to settle in one of the newly-created development towns they were supplied with both work and shelter. Others, like Eliahu Cohen and Rabbi Benizi, were settled in moshavot.

I asked Mr. Levi whether he felt that the Ashkenazim were discriminating against the newcomers from the Oriental countries.

He had no complaints about the Ashkenazim. "If not for them, there would be no Israel today," he said. "Hitler pushed them out of Europe, and so they settled here and built up the land."

The history of North African Jewry, like that of their brethren in Iraq and Yemen, goes back 2000 years, and is well-documented by archaeological excavations, and by records of Jewish, Roman and Christian chroniclers.

"From Tyre to Carthage, all know the people of Israel and their Father in Heaven," Rav Hisda states in the Talmud.

Some of North Africa's Berber tribes converted to Judaism. In 707 C. E, Dahia Al-Kahina, a Berber queen who had embraced the Jewish faith, was killed fighting against the Moslems.

As Christianity and Mohammedanism were locked in a struggle for supremacy in North Africa, the Jews were caught in the middle. In 1,032, six thousand Jews were massacred in Fez, Morocco, by the Emir of Afran.

However, in that same century, the Jews in Wadi Dera established an independent government which lasted for over one hundred years and was headed by a succession of Jewish kings — Yusef, Jacob and Samuel.

In the thirteenth century, the Jews suffered persecution at the hands of the fanatical Almohades, who instilled into the Moslems of North Africa a deep-seated hatred of Jews which has persisted to this day.

Periods of relative peace were marked by revivals of Jewish scholarship and culture. The Talmudic academies of Fez and Kairuwan were centers of higher Jewish learning. The influx of cultured and erudite refugees from Spain after 1492 was a valuable addition to the Jewish communities of North Africa. This merger of Spanish and African Jewries was followed by a brief but important era of illustrious scholars and scientists, culminating with Maimonides.

As early as the twelfth century, a Moroccan Jewish community settled in Jerusalem. These Jews and their descendants established yeshivot in Jerusalem, Safed, Tiberias, Jaffa and Haifa.

In the years immediately preceding the establishment of Morocco as an independent state, 70 per cent of the Jews of Casablanca were wealthy or middle-class businessmen. The others were poor peddlers or workers. But in those days, Yosef Levi recalled, even the poor man in Morocco ate better than the rich man in the new State of Israel.

When the French left Morocco, the position of the Jews became increasingly insecure.

In 1963, 80,000 Jews were still living in Casablanca, at least half of them crowded into the filthy *mellah* (ghetto). Marrakeesh and Rabat had 11,000 Jews each. Their activities have been greatly restricted. Many are dependent on the welfare programs sponsored by the American Jewish Joint Distribution Committee.

Eliahu Cohen, Rabbi Isaac Benizi, Yosef Levi, and the many who followed their lead and came to Israel, had nothing to lose in Morocco.

* * *

Three-fourths of the immigrants who have come to Israel from the Moslem countries have chosen to settle in moshavim and development towns where jobs and apartments — or cottages were waiting for them.

But what of those who preferred to live in the cities, in Tel Aviv, Haifa or Jerusalem? For them, it was a hard struggle to make ends meet.

Some succeeded in climbing up, on and over the backs of others, to set up a shop or a small factory. At the bottom of the economic heap are the street hawkers. A new immigrant, or a not-so-new arrival, starts out by opening a suitcase filled with neckties, shirts, jewelry, odds and ends, and cries out his wares. If a policeman or tax official gets tough and invokes the municipal ordinance which prohibits street hawkers on the main thoroughfares, the peddler may be hauled into court and fined IL 3.00 ($1.00) for selling without a license. Then he goes back to his old corner or finds a new place to peddle his wares. During one recent year, the city of Tel Aviv collected a total of $25,000.00 from 2,500 street hawkers. Many of these out-of-suitcase merchants who interfere with traffic and, with their minimal overhead, create unfair competition for storekeepers, seem able-bodied and well suited, at least physically for factory or farm work.

One rung higher than the sidewalk hawkers are the pushcart peddlers of Carmel Market, just off Allenby Road, Tel Aviv's main artery. Here you see faces from the world over, from Europe as well as from Asia, and Africa. You can hear the street cries that reveal national origins in accented Hebrew.

There are many surprises. The Moroccans, for instance. Young army veterans stand atop a table laden with sweaters. "Shmone!" yells a youthful Moroccan as he scoops up an armful of sweaters and throws them high into the air. "Shmone!" His one-word sales pitch means "eight." One sweater sells for eight pounds, or $2.66.

"Hey, Shmone!" I yelled, brandishing my camera. "Shmone" posed for me with a broad smile and a gruff greeting in Hebrew, and across the lands and seas that separate Fez, Morocco, from Denver, Colorado, a bond of brotherhood was forged which transcended the barriers of nationality, language and culture. We are both Jews, "Shmone" from Fez and I. He is no darker than I am. Most Moroccans have dark complexions, but not more than any golfer at summer's end. To a man, the young immigrants from Morocco are strong, muscular, broad-shouldered, and toughened by Army service.

"Shmone" is tough enough to do the heaviest type of work on the farm, on the docks or in a factory. But he prefers the excitement of Carmel Market, that lively competition, the city's night life, the shady deals and the girls of the street.

"Shmone" may be a typical example of the tragedy that has befallen so many Moroccan Jewish families. Soon after the signing of the Proclamation of Independence, 100,000 Jews from Morocco entered Israel. The children were the first to be brought in by the Jewish Agency. When the first wave of immigration from Morocco was suddenly cut off a decade ago, thousands of parents found that they could not follow their children to Israel. When Morocco, pressured by its allies in the Arab League, stopped postal communications with Israel, the separation of parents and children was tragically complete.

Cast adrift in Israel without family ties, "Shmone" grew up in a Youth Aliya village, then graduated into the Army. He came out of the service as a rebel against authority, preferring the streets and the Carmel Market to the trades and skills the Army teaches immigrants to prepare them for productive jobs in industry, agriculture or communications.

On the side, to bolster his income from the sweater business, "Shmone" and others like him might be procurers. Tel Aviv police authorities estimate that their city has some 300 prostitutes working in cafés or receiving clients at private addresses, with 150 procurers drumming up business for them.

Mrs. Victoria Nissan, director of psychological and social services for Israel's prisons, explained the factors that
might lead an immigrant girl, particularly one from the
Oriental countries, into prostitution. Mrs. Nissan — herself an immigrant from Iraq — has had considerable experience with these young women.

"Simha, or Benita, or whatever her name may be," she
said, "arrives with her family from Morocco or another
one of the countries of the Moslem world. Or perhaps she
has come alone. In either case, she grew up the hard way.
Maybe she has been rejected by her parents because they
do not understand the ways of Israel or modern youth.
Uncultured, uneducated, with no family background, she
doesn't know how to sit with a boy for two hours and just
talk. Before long, she meets a procurer who takes advantage of her ignorance. She learns that she can sell her body
and make IL 200.00 a day, before splitting her profit.
Compare this with the IL 300.00 which a government
official takes home for a month's work. It is our task to
re-educate these wayward girls and train them for jobs,
professions and careers. We must prepare them to become
homemakers and mothers. We don't send streetwalkers to
prison for prostitution, though we may take them in on
charges of solicitation or theft. Many of them also steal."

Mrs. Nissan gave me one specific case history. The girl
was from Morocco. Her mother had died in childbirth and
she was raised by a harsh stepmother who limited her
love to her own children and rejected the stepdaughter.
By the time the girl was twenty she was ready to use her
body to break away from the family that did not care for
her.

"She assumed an aggressive personality in order to defend herself against the hurt of rejection," Mrs. Nissan
explained. "A man in the same situation might vent his
hostile feelings by getting into fights, or by entering a
career of burglary or crime. But the girl who has suffered

rejection can use as her weapon only the one thing about herself that she knows is desirable. By selling herself in order to make money, she gets a feeling of being wanted, of being worth something, after all. The fact that she is defying the mores and laws of society means nothing to her."

In the case of the Simhas and the Benitas, the religious foundations which guide the lives of the Oriental Jews were of no avail because their parents failed to give them love and understanding. The commandment to "honor thy father and mother" went unheeded because the parents had neglected to respect their children as human beings.

* * *

The Oriental Jewish family at its best is founded on the Biblical commandment concerning honor due one's parents. No matter how overcrowded his hut or tenement, or how scanty his meals, the Oriental Jew does not forsake his parents or grandparents in their old age and cast the responsibility for their care on public welfare agencies.

The grandfather is honored as the patriarch, the supreme authority in his family. It is when the patriarch's authoritarian rule clashes head-on with the democratic ways his children or grandchildren have acquired in Israel's schools, that trouble comes.

In this clash between the cultures, there is no question about which will come out the winner — Oriental or Ashkenazi. It's not a matter of quantity because with their higher birth and immigration rate, the Orientals outnumber the Western-descended Jews. The deciding factor is that modern Israel has already committed itself to a certain way of life — vigorous, productive, ambitious, restless and materialistic — the Western way, as opposed to the leisurely pace of the Oriental society, where ambition is at a low ebb and time of little importance.

Most of the Oriental immigrants soon catch on to the swing of Israeli life, and adopt the clock, the machine, the bus, the supermarket and the apartment as part and parcel of the new way of living.

This switch to the west throws the Oriental patriarchal society out of kilter. The father's status in the family is lowered. In the old country he might have managed to get by on the outer fringes of the economy as a tradesman, a peddler, a small shopkeeper or perhaps as a teacher. In Israel he may be forced to accept a job where he has to report every day at a set time and put in a full day's work. And if he is over forty, he finds little use for his services, especially when prospective employers realize that they must invest many unproductive weeks into training him for the work they need done. If he takes on a government-sponsored "work relief" job, he loses status in the eyes of his children and grandchildren.

In the meantime, his wife may go out to work in a textile mill, or do home work with a new sewing machine or loom which governmental or quasi-governmental agencies provide for her on liberal financial terms. Or she may enter domestic service and find that she is earning much more than her husband. She acquires a new sense of self-assurance and worth. Getting out into the factory and into Israeli households, she meets a new world. She begins to crave for better ways of living.

She learns from her Ashkenazi mistress that getting a baby each year is not unavoidable but can be prevented without her husband's knowledge. At home, she receives regular visits from social workers and from volunteers sent out by the Pioneer Women's Organization. She is taught new ways of cooking, nutrition and child care.

The children go to school and learn a new set of manners. In Morocco, Iraq, Iran and Yemen, families would sit cross-legged around a big bowl on the floor, using hands and fingers to scoop up the thick mixture of spiced meat, vegetables and rice. They would piously observe the Jewish rite of washing their hands before meals, but this laving, which is purely ritual, does not clean the hands as throughly as the liberal use of soap and water. Among the traditional families, the father is the first to eat, and he frequently takes for himself most of the scanty food supply available, leaving his wife and children to make do with whatever remains. Even in the more well-to-do families, the father breaks up the chicken with his hands and takes the largest portion for himself before giving out the rest to the others. Social workers calling on Oriental newcomer families found that most of them did not have regular mealtimes. When a youngster was sent to the grocery for a loaf of bread, he would eat half the loaf by the time he returned. Many of the children subsisted on bread, raw carrots, or onions and olives. Quite a few were avid coffee-drinkers, and their parents had to be told that coffee tended to stunt growth in young boys and girls.

Over and beyond these amenities, the children learn attitudes to life which conflict with some of the views cherished by their elders. Most of the children from Oriental families are enrolled in the religious public schools rather than in those of the "general" or non-religious type. In these schools their religious way of life is not questioned, but they learn that they have a right to make their own decisions with regards to careers and vocational choices, and that secular education is not a luxury but the key to a better future. At this point the conflict begins. The children are anxious to continue their schooling beyond the elementary level, and the government encourages their ambition by providing complete or partial scholarships to pay high school tuition. But their parents want them to go to work as quickly as possible so that they can make their contribution to the family's support.

In the Moslem countries, daughters remained at home

until they became eligible for marriage, at which time their fathers would select their husbands. In Israel the daughters of the Oriental newcomers learn that women can be human beings, free to choose their own marriage partners, and enjoy a position of respect in a society which, in fact, shows strong matriarchal tendencies. The girls keep some of their earnings themselves, and buy the latest Israeli fashions which are among the smartest in the world of women's wear. They are avid fans of Hollywood and European films which they go to see with their dates who may be Ashkenazi youths, from an entirely different background. When fathers and mothers attempt to offer resistance, the girls may move away from home.

In some of the development villages, where the youngsters from Oriental families attend school with children of similar background only, the real conflict may not come until they enter the Army — Israel's great melting pot.

In the Army, the young Israeli from Iraq, Yemen or Morocco, in whose family not only the law of the Tora but the rules laid down by the father were strictly observed, lives, eats and sleeps together with sabras and Ashkenazim of his own age, who represent a free, democratic way of life, mostly non-religious and definitely not based on unquestioning obedience to the commands of a father or grandfather. Frequently, the result of this meeting between two cultures is that the Oriental soldier discards his tallith and tefillin together with the rest of the ways he has brought with him from the Moslem country of his birth. But sabra living has no stable, ideological replacement to offer for the religion he has dropped. The army youth is in need of patient paternal guidance or of an understanding rabbi to help him cope with the problems raised by this head-on challenge to centuries of Levantine background. But in most instances he receives no such assistance. His father is likely to be hundreds of years removed from him, and only a few of Israel's rabbis are willing and able to see his point of view and to advise him accordingly. Thus he graduates from military service a tough, trained veteran with vocational skills he may put to use in civilian life, but without a sense of direction or a philosophical basis to guide his future life.

* * *

Israel's leaders are working, within the limits of the budgets set for their agencies, to create broader educational opportunities for newcomers of all backgrounds, Ashkenazi and Oriental alike. Yitzhaq Navon, formerly secretary to David Ben-Gurion, is directing the anti-illiteracy campaign of the Ministry of Education and making plans for more secondary schools, more scholarships, and for "long-day schools" to provide children from large Oriental families with a place to study and with tutors to help them with their studies after school hours. The proportion of illiterates among the immigrants from Asia and Africa is 30 and 53 per cent respectively. Among the European-born, the percentage is nine for men and thirteen for women. Navon estimated that one adult Israeli Jew out of four is illiterate. In 120 villages, between half and three-quarters of the population is unable to read and write. Navon has drawn up a three-year plan of study to enable the majority of adult illiterates and semi-literates to read a newspaper written in elementary Hebrew, to write a short, uncomplicated letter, and to use the fundamentals of arithmetic.

According to Ezra Haddad, the formidable rate of illiteracy among Israelis of Oriental origin is due in part to the fact that the parents of these youngsters are eager to have them work to supplement family income. "Most Ashkenazi parents will go hungry if need be so that their children will have the tuition for high school and university. But what's an Oriental family to do, when a fa-

ther, mother and ten children all have to live from IL
300.00 a month, and they still keep on following the
commandment, 'be fruitful and multiply'?" Haddad
asked.

The more progressive elements among the Oriental
immigrants, on the other hand, show considerable concern about the education of their young.

"We are not interested in shops, money, work, or licenses," said Meir Ben Yair, a member of the Beersheba
Municipal Council who came to Israel from Morocco in
1949. "We want to make sure that our children receive
an adequate education. I demand that the children of
immigrants from Morocco get exactly the same educational opportunities as they would have had in Morocco.
In Morocco today, all children can enroll at a high school
without having to pay tuition. We refuse to accept this
'educational gap' as a result of which immigrant children
will suffer all their lives simply because their parents left
their homes and came to Israel."

\*    \*    \*

David Sitton, a third-generation Jerusalem sabra and
former member of the staff of *HaBoker,* a General Zionist daily, is chairman of the Council of the Sephardic
Community of Jerusalem. The primary aim of this organization of Jews of Sephardic and Oriental descent is to
organize the strength of what is actually the majority of
Israel's population in order to speed its educational, social and economic integration into Israeli society.

Sitton is proud of the progress that has been made in
this area, but knows that much remains to be done.

Replying to arguments that in view of the financial
burden imposed by defense and the resettlement of immigrants, the Israeli government cannot at this time
make a free high school education the right of every citizen, Sitton said:

"Defense and education are equally important. If we educate the new generation, we have the guarantee that it will be ready to defend our country. But if we fail to give our youth an adequate education, Israel eventually will become a Levantine state like all its neighboring nations, with the low standard of living that is the result of lack of schooling." A generation grown Levantine in spirit would not be able to defend Israel as successfully as had the fighters of the wars of 1948 and 1956.

Sitton demands for his people not only the benefit of universal free high school education, but also an opportunity for training in the liberal arts rather than in the trades only. "We don't want our youth to be common laborers and farm workers only. We want to have our share of future leaders too."

"Let me say one important thing," he interrupted himself. "Our problem is not just educational but also social and economic."

"Ten years ago," he recalled, "ears were deaf to us. Today, things have changed. The Orientals have become articulate. The Wadi Salib riots of Oriental immigrants in Haifa and disturbances in development areas have made the country sit up and take notice. Let me put it bluntly. We Sephardim and Orientals feel that we are being discriminated against here in Israel."

Sitton handed me a pamphlet that bore the title *From Ingathering to Integration*. Written by Abraham Abbas, a member of the Knesset, shortly before his death in 1958, it has 32 pages loaded with shocking facts. Abbas, who came to Israel with a Youth Aliya transport from Syria, made this survey on behalf of the World Federation of Sephardi Jews which sponsored its publication. It is a study of the problems of the Oriental immigrants in Israel, and much of what it disclosed is still a cause of concern in the country today.

Abbas declares that the full integration of the immigrants from the Oriental countries is the key problem of Israel and that the very survival of the State depends on its just and equitable solution.

To underscore the magnitude of the problem, he submits a statistical breakdown of Sephardic and Oriental immigration figures as of 1958: Algeria, Morocco, Tunisia — 150,000; Iraq — 125,000; Yemen — 50,000; Bulgaria 40,000; Turkey — 40,000; Libya — 40,000; Iran — 35,-000; Egypt — 40,000; India and Aden — 10,000; Greece and Yugoslavia — 10,000; other Arab countries — 10,000. By 1965, Israel's total population was 2,500,000, of which 55% were of Sephardi and Oriental origin.

Abbas pointed out that while many of these immigrants had already been absorbed in various branches of Israel's economy, and had been provided with housing and employment on a large scale, they had not been socially integrated.

"In the social and cultural spheres, there is an almost unbridgeable chasm between the so-called 'First Israel' (the sabra and European-descended elements) and what is called the 'second Israel' (the Sephardi and Oriental elements who have arrived in Israel more recently)," Abbas wrote.

The Abbas report stresses the role of the Oriental immigrants in the repopulation of the Negev. By settling in the wilderness, they succeeded not only in turning the desert into a flourishing region of industrial and agricultural development, but also in transforming themselves from petty traders and peddlers into builders, farmers and factory workers.

At the time of the survey, 67 per cent of the population of Israel's development areas was Oriental. Abbas paid tribute to the Oriental element for refusing to abandon these outlying areas despite such hardships as inadequate lighting, bad road communications and the danger of enemy attack.

Abbas felt that the assignment of immigrants to agricultural communities according to their lands of origin presented "a grave danger to the process of integration and, in fact, puts off integration and crystallizes present 'communal' divisions." His survey does not state the reason for this policy; namely, that an earlier attempt to mix the immigrant elements indiscriminately without regard to national and cultural background in immigrant villages had resulted in dissension and fighting among the settlers — even among newcomers from different places in the same Moslem country.

Another factor making for "the continuation of communal isolation and separation" was the high incidence of school dropouts among Oriental youngsters. Of the 3 per cent of all Israeli children quitting elementary school before graduation — and this "little" 3 per cent represents a total of 15,000 children — 90 per cent are of Oriental families. Such children can hope for no more than the most poorly paid jobs in the factory and on the farm.

A study made of dropouts in the schools of Beersheba revealed the following reasons why boys and girls fail to complete their education:

1. Poverty, which forces parents to send out their children to sell papers, shine shoes or run errands to bring in extra money, at the expense of their schooling.

2. Study made difficult by overcrowded housing, with families of ten and twelve occupying one-bedroom dwellings.

3. Undernourishment.

4. Inadequate school buildings.

5. Lack of textbooks.

6. Inability of large, low-income families to afford high school tuition.

7. Poorly trained, inexperienced teaching personnel, unable to cope with the mentality and problems of pupils from Oriental families. Competent teachers prefer posi-

tions in the large cities to posts in frontier areas.

Notwithstanding excuses and counter-arguments from government officials, the fact remains that this condition still constitutes what Abbas terms a "social explosive."

Abbas pictured these drop-outs as "doomed to a life of idleness, indeed, exposed to a life of destitution, cruel, bitter and degrading, without a single redeeming feature to brighten the darkness of their dismal existence . . . They represent the most dangerous social 'explosives'."

In 1958, Oriental youth in the 14-17 age group constituted 55 per cent of the entire youth population of Israel, Abbas reported, but only 17 per cent of the enrollment in Israel's high schools, trade schools and farm training institutions. At the college level, the proportion was even lower. Only 5 per cent of the student body of the Hebrew University was of Oriental origin. At the Haifa Technion, only 14 out of a freshman class of 436 were Orientals.

But in that same year, Orientals comprised 80 per cent of all hired farm help, 90 per cent of all building workers, and 95 per cent of all applicants to labor exchanges.

As to the social and political integration of the immigrants from the Oriental countries, Abbas presents a picture that is hardly more cheerful. To those who pointed to the role of intermarriage in erasing the barriers between the Orientals and their Ashkenazi brethren, he replied that, of 13,530 marriages, only 7.5 per cent were between Ashkenazi men and Oriental women, and a mere 4.3 per cent between Oriental men and Ashkenazi women.

Abbas asserted that the Ashkenazim of Israel were discriminating against the Sephardi and Oriental element. The worst offenders, he claimed, were the Zionist institutions and organizations, and the political parties, some of which have no Orientals at all or only one or two, for show purposes, in their executive councils.

The Knesset elections of August 1961 seemed to bear out the statement made by Abbas three years before. Mapai had only six Orientals among its first 36 Parliamentary candidates, Herut only three among its first 15, and the Liberal Party had its first Sephardi candidate as the seventeenth name on its list.

The National Religious Party, whose membership is two-thirds Sephardi and Oriental, does not have even one representative of these elements in its policy-making councils. Nor is there even one Sephardi in Israel's Supreme Court or the Executive of the Jewish Agency.

David Hakham, an articulate spokesman of the Iraqi element in Israel, voiced indignation at the practice of referring to Israelis by their former nationality.

"In Iraq," he said, "the Jews are called Jews. But when they get to Israel, all of a sudden, they're 'Iraqis.' And the same goes for all the other newcomers from the Moslem countries, even though they've all either lost their original citizenship or given it up, and became Israelis immediately on arrival here."

It cannot be denied that there is plenty of prejudice against the Orientals among the Ashkenazis and the Sabras. Many refer to the newcomers from the Moslem world by such unlovely names as the *"shvartze"* ("blacks"), "Frenks" or "Frenkeles." One Tel Aviv municipal employee wryly commented that it would take Israel as long to absorb the Orientals as it took Moses to weld the Hebrew tribes into one nation in the wilderness.

"I wouldn't want a daughter of mine to marry one of the *shvartze*," he told me. "It's not because of their color. There are other things. To begin with, their family background is so different from ours. With most of their families you couldn't even eat at the same table. For one thing, they eat with their hands. They're hot-blooded and completely uninhibited. They tell you what they think without worrying about the feelings of others, and when they get angry, they either become violent or they explode into vicious curses. And they keep on having babies. I wouldn't want my daughter to spend all her good years as a baby-breeder. And their living standards are lower. They lack the ambition of our kind, because they don't feel the need for any of the things we consider essential."

He complained that some of the less desirable traits of these newcomers are rubbing off on the Ashkenazi youth which patronizes Oriental restaurants and cafés.

"It's easier to learn bad manners than good manners," he sighed.

The "Frenks" retaliate with a pet name of their own for their sabra and Ashkenazi brethren — "Vus-Vus" ("What? What?") which is what all Yiddish sounds like to them.

Ezra Haddad told me that until a few years ago *"haf-laya"* — discrimination — was a household word among the newcomers from the Moslem lands. "If the roof of a hut leaked, or someone was out of work, or a child couldn't go on to high school, they'd blame the trouble on *haflaya*. The Orientals thought that the State and the Histadrut ought to give them everything they needed; anything else constituted deliberate discrimination. But by now they have learned that in order to get things they have to work, like everyone else here, and that physical labor is nothing to be ashamed of."

Unlike Hakham and Sitton, Ezra Haddad felt that there has been a marked improvement in the overall situation.

"People don't talk in terms of segregation and discrimination so much today," he said.

Neither the Israeli Government nor the Jewish Agency practice discrimination against immigrants. All new-comers, regardless of nationality background, receive help in resettlement and in the search for housing and employment. The Israel Education Fund in America and candid discussion of "Two Israels" in the Knesset are making U. S. Jews and Israelis conscious of the need to unify the Tribes of Israel and eliminate discrimination.

All citizens of Israel, regardless of color or background, Oriental or Ashkenazi, Jewish, Christian or Arab, have the right to vote, and are guaranteed freedom of speech, press, assembly and conscience.

Immigrants from the Oriental countries have the same right to hold public office as any other citizens of Israel. Armon Laredo, former mayor of Dimona, a development town in the Negev, is from Morocco. Mayor Eliahu Navi of Beersheba is from Iraq.

And if you sit down with some of the Ashkenazi old-timers who complain the loudest about the *shvartze* and the "Frenkeles," you will find that, in the end, they admit that the Orientals are indispensible to Israel.

"We need them," say the *Vus-Vus*. "It will take a generation or two to absorb them. Or maybe they'll absorb us. But we need them. We will educate them. We will train them to work. We need hands in our shops, on our farms and in our factories. We need young men for the Army. We're beset by enemies on all sides. We are only two million surrounded by forty million Arabs. The 'Franks' make good fighters. They'll be a good element in our country. In the end, our sons and daughters will intermarry with them. We'll be one people yet, one Israel."

Some hopefully venture that it will take no more than ten years for the "Frenkeles" to be absorbed. Others are not quite so sanguine in their prognosis. Those who know the rigidity of social structure within some of the

villages and moshavim believe that more than one generation will have to pass before acculturation will go beyond the phase of token adjustment.

But whether it will take ten years, or two generations
to raze the barriers that keep Ashkenazim and Sephard-
dim apart, most Israelis believe, and hope, that in the
not too distant future, Israel will indeed be one, even
as the God of Israel is One.

# CHAPTER IV
## EIGHT PATHS TO ONE ISRAEL

How do the Israelis expect to mold men and women of a seemingly endless variety of national, cultural and social backgrounds into one united people?

In a free country of 2,500,000 individualists, you could expect 2,500,000 different answers. But basically, all these answers could be catalogued into eight major views now current on Israel's Number One long-range problem, the creation of one Israel from an Ingathering of over a million immigrants from every part of the world. These eight views, representing eight distinct schools of thought, are as follows: (1) The Marxist View; (2) The Religious View; (3) The Nationalist View; (4) The Anthropocentric View; (5) The Sociological View; (6) The Philosophy of Categorical Values; (7) The "Primitiveness" View; and (8) The *Gestalt* Psychology View.

A brief survey of each of these schools of thought should be of help in gaining an understanding not only of the complexity of the process of Ingathering but also of the different political, religious and philosophical outlooks which contend for supremacy in this land of contrasts.

*The Marxist View.* In a country built by Labor Zionist pioneers imbued with the socialist ideals that have been incorporated into the party platforms of Mapam, Ahdut Ha'Avoda, and leftist elements in the ruling Mapai party, it should come as no surprise that the Marxist view plays an influential, though not necessarily crucial role.

Marxist thinkers, mainly from the kibbutzim, who see the world in the red and black colors of economic determinism, are inclined to minimize the significance of ethnic and cultural differences between Israelis from North Africa, Iraq, Yemen, Poland, Rumania and Germany. The cultural disparities between these nationality groups, they argue, derive solely from differences in living standards. The Marxist remedy for this is amazingly simple. Give the Oriental Jews and the Ashkenazim the same economic opportunities, the same work, the same housing, health and sanitation facilities and the same chance for a free education, and any and all differences between the two will vanish and you will indeed have one united Israel.

Despite the fact that the masses of post-State immigrants have not joined kibbutzim, the Marxists have remained firm in their belief that the collective settlement is the ideal place for Orientals and Ashkenazim alike. Rather than accept the fact that most newcomers do not go to kibbutzim as evidence that these immigrants do not believe in the collective way of life, they are convinced that the Government is to blame for not giving sufficient encouragement to immigrants to try life on the kibbutz. Kibbutzniks of the classic Marxist persuasion cannot understand why homeless, penniless newcomers to Israel should want to turn their backs upon their Utopias where all men and women are equal and where the Ph.D. from Germany works in the fields side by side with the sandalmaker from Yemen.

If you press the Marxist kibbutzniks to state their views about the value of preserving the native folklore, culture and religious customs of the ethnic groups that come to Israel, they will answer you quite straightforwardly: "All that is not really important. What counts is that we establish here in Israel a classless society in which all social, economic and cultural differences will be abolished."

*The Religious View.* The religious view, of which I will attempt to give some samples in the chapter on *Kulturkampf,* also grossly oversimplifies the issue of integration. The rabbi-politicians of the Religious parties, who operate as the balance-wheel in Israel's coalition governments, insist that nationality and cultural differences are not crucial, because the basis for a united Israel can only be religion.

Dr. Joseph Burg, a leader in the Mizrahi — HaPoel HaMizrahi party and Minister of Welfare in the Eshkol Cabinet, has repeatedly stated his conviction that a Jewish State based on the laws of the Tora would be capable of unifying all Jews, regardless of cultural, national or religious background. Israel's religious leaders, who tend to disagree among themselves on many issues, proudly point to Israel's Army as powerful evidence in support of Dr. Burg's argument. In the Army, they say, a measure of religious unity has already been achieved. All soldiers, regardless of their personal attitude to religion — which they are free to express — are given kosher food, and they all go to services conducted by the military chaplains where they follow one prayerbook only. However, this is not the complete story. The Jews from the Oriental countries, reared in a centuries-old Sephardi tradition, do not feel at home in the equally Orthodox Ashkenazi synagogues of the European-descended Israelis, and the Yemenites in particular insist on following their own rituals which they have evolved in the course of many centuries of geographical and cultural isolation. In many instances, religion actually drives a dividing wedge between orthodox Sephardim and their equally devout Ashkenazi brethren.

*The Nationalist View.* The most articulate exponent of this approach is Menahem Beigin's Herut Party, which strives to unite Israel by the use of symbols and slogans of extreme nationalism. Beigin and his followers feel that labor, for instance, is putting undue emphasis on such "secondary" issues as wages, and not enough on national unity. They believe that the Jews who have come to Israel from the four corners of the earth would gladly rally around the symbols of Israel's strength and independence — the State, the Flag, and the Army, and that people of many different cultural and national origins would find common ground in helping Herut realize its aim to extend Israel's borders and to regain the Old City of Jerusalem from the Kingdom of Jordan. If war should come as a result of the extremist foreign policy advocated by Herut, the party's spokesmen argue, one beneficial effect certainly would be the goal all parties desire — unity behind the flag of Israel. But the destruction of what has taken so much labor to build, and the loss of life which would be an inevitable consequence of war, seems a high price to pay for unity.

*The Anthropocentric View.* There are others in Israel who believe that the Marxist, religious and nationalist approaches to the problem of integration are all guilty of oversimplification. A problem involving human beings, they point out, cannot be settled by slogans but calls for academic investigation in terms of human factors.

At the Hebrew University in Jerusalem, Professor Frankenstein is conducting studies in depth on the immigrants who have come to Israel from the Oriental countries. Prof. Frankenstein has described his approach to integration as the anthropocentric or "man-centered" view. His basic philosophy is that the crucial role of certain unchanging factors, namely, intelligence, sex, body build, personality type and hereditary influence, in the development of individuals and societies must not be ignored. Frankenstein's school of thought relies heavily on Jung's psychological theory of the "collective unconscious" of groups which hands down certain traits and talents from generation to generation. According to this theory, phenomena such as the predominance of Jews among the world's great violinists can be explained by the sadness in the Jewish soul which is best expressed in the music of the violin. The fact that some of the most single-minded thinkers in the history of man — Abraham, Moses, Jesus, Spinoza, Marx, Freud and Einstein — were Jews is attributed to a Jewish penchant to monistic or single-minded thought.

In the case of the Orientals, cultural and personality traits transmitted by the "collective unconscious", according to the anthropocentric theory, would be the introverted personality, the adherence to religious tradition and the patriarchal society which characterize the Yemenite and Sephardi Jews in Israel.

When Prof. Frankenstein and his adherents are pressed to come down into the realm of the "here and now," and asked, "Well, what kind of an Israel would you want?" they have no pat answer. Since the differences between the nationality groups are deeply rooted in the individual and collective "souls" of human beings and societies, they insist that integration or unification cannot be brought about by law or government policy. In line with their approach which centers on the individual human being, they will reply with questions of their own:

"What do we really want? Do we want to eat steak or *hummus?* Do we prefer European dress or Kurdish costume, Yemenite dances or modern horas, modern-type spiritual leaders or the Yemenite-style rabbi, coeducation or the Oriental idea that girls don't need to go to school, general education or Talmudic learning, Persian jewelry or American imitation gems, modern architecture or Arab-style houses?"

The "anthropocentrists" refuse to make subjective judgments. When asked whether the patriarchal, authoritarian family pattern of the Orientals is good and worthy of emulation or whether it should be abandoned in favor of more democratic ways, they ask: "Is it worse than the current vogue of (unrestricted) freedom for the growing child?"

The advocates of the anthropocentrist view do take a definite stand on the preservation of Oriental culture traits. They warn against the danger of allowing the treasures of Oriental folklore, custom, song, and religious ritual to get lost in the creation, by artificial means, of a new Israeli culture, based on modern Western notions.

They also caution against pushing the assimilation of the Orientals into Western culture. In view of the culture traits which have been transmitted from generation to generation in Oriental families, such forced integration would create inner conflicts. If, anxious to assimilate into sabra culture, Oriental youth would stage a wholesale revolt against the religious values that were part of the background in which they were reared, the result would only be suffering. Prof. Frankenstein recalls what happened when Oriental children were placed by Youth Aliya into non-religious kibbutzim where they were forced to abandon Sabbath observance. The change proved to have a traumatic effect on the youngsters, causing severe emotional disturbance in many of them. Today the Youth Aliya leaders make allowances for the background of the children, and place boys and girls from North Africa, Yemen and Iraq into special camps where they are taught by religious leaders of Oriental origin. And since the idea of communal ownership is foreign to them, these children receive cash payments for their work.

In the early years of mass immigration, the Israeli authorities, nearly all of whom were Ashkenazim, had little understanding or knowledge of the personality and psychological needs of the Oriental newcomers. They indiscriminately threw immigrants from Europe together with refugees from North Africa, Iraq and Yemen in the ma'abarot and immigrant villages. Many a settlement was actually destroyed by the clashes that developed between the ethnic groups. Today, integration in immigrant settlements is carried out deliberately, but by a gradual process such as described in the chapter "Melting Pot and Breadbasket."

In brief, the anthropocentric approach to the integration of the Ingathering is one of patience. What will be lost, it asks, if we proceed gradually in welding all the groups in the new Jewish State into one united Israel? Why should anyone want to hurry the process? The advocates of this approach also insist that the Ashkenazim should not look down on the Sephardi groups but should regard them as equals in every respect. Israeli culture, which will eventually evolve from the Ingathering, they point out, is likely to include some elements taken from the best of the customs and traditions of each nationality group, Ashkenazi and Oriental alike.

*The Sociological View.* This approach to the problem of integration is expounded by Professor S. N. Eisenstadt, who is the head of the department of sociology at the Hebrew University.

As opposed to the advocates of the other approaches, the proponents of the sociological view refuse to think of integration in terms of the "absorption" of Oriental immigrants by an established Ashkenazi and sabra society.

What is required, they argue, is that those actively concerned with integration exercise empathy and put themselves in the place of the Oriental newcomers before deciding "how to integrate" them.

To begin with, the Oriental immigrant should be considered not as an alien element to be "absorbed" but as a human being who must face certain given facts and problems when he moves to Israel with his family.

First and foremost, the Oriental is basically insecure. The very reason for his emigration to Israel is that he was haunted by oppression or fear of oppression in the country where he lived.

When he arrives in Israel, he makes a leap across centuries from the backward environment of the Arab world into a twentieth-century pioneer nation. This only serves to increase his sense of insecurity. He wonders what will become of him and his family. He is faced with the necessity of learning a new language and new ways of life which are entirely alien to him.

For some newcomers, the move to Israel means a loss of status. Not all the Oriental immigrants come from backward areas. Many Iraqi Jews held clerical and professional positions. Many of the Moroccans gave up flourishing business enterprises in large cities such as Casablanca, Rabat and Fez, and a large number of the newcomers from Egypt enjoyed wealth and prestige before the rise of Nasser.

If the immigrant is not among those assigned immediately to one of the development towns where he is provided with a home and a job at once, he must look about for housing and employment on his own. If this search does not bring results soon, he becomes convinced that he is a failure. His horizon limited to the search for a job and a flat, he may fall into the emotional rut of what sociologists call "reduction in interest." Forced to concentrate his interests on providing for his basic needs — food, shelter and status — his behavior will be crude, and he will become increasingly sensitive to slights and insults, real or imagined. He will think that others are depriving him of his rights and of opportunities to provide for the necessities of life. He will be inclined to exaggerate the frustrations that are part of everyday living, and will suspect the government officials, the policeman and the social worker of seeking to exploit him or of conspiring against him.

To make matters worse, the Oriental immigrant finds himself cast adrift, torn from the group which gave him a sense of belonging in his former home. In Israel, he misses his clan, his rabbi, his synagogue and his community which comprised his whole world in the alien, Moslem atmosphere of the country he left behind. His group life is narrowed down to his immediate family circle, but even there trouble begins when his children find out that, in the free society of the Jewish State, the father does not reign as a dictator in the home, and when his wife realizes that she can earn as much or more money than her husband by going out of the home to do housework or to take a job in a factory. Yehiel Wahab's monthly income of IL 25.00 as a yeshiva teacher compared to the IL 120.00 his wife gets each month as a maid does not enhance his sense of personal security and status.

The proponents of the sociological approach to the task of integration are convinced that their method of dealing with the problem represents the ideal solution.

The Oriental immigrant must be given a sense of security. But this cannot be done by Israel's bureaucratic institutions which, without intending to do so, only reinforce his inferiority feeling. What is needed is a voluntary mobilization of the entire population in a concerted effort to befriend the newcomers on a family-to-family rather than on a philanthropic basis. Old-established Israeli families should adopt an Oriental family as friends and equals. Kibbutzim should adopt neighboring ma'abarot or immigrant villages, exchange visits with the newcomers and invite them to their social gatherings and celebrations. The children of the "old-timers" should be encouraged to play with the "new" youngsters.

Congenial employment provides not only economic security but also social status. The Oriental need not remain an unskilled laborer or agricultural worker. There is a need for teachers, policemen, group workers and youth camp directors in the immigrant villages, and the villagers have come to demand that these positions should be filled by their own people rather than by outsiders.

Employment offices have an important role to play in the emotional adjustment of the newcomer. Interviewers should take great care not to discriminate against the dark-skinned newcomers and pass them over in favor of Ashkenazim in the distribution of better work assignments. Social workers must regard the newcomers as human beings and not as charity cases. There have been instances of immigrants attacking social workers with their fists and even with knives in resentment of the patronizing attitude of the men and women sent to care for them. Ashkenazi teachers, social workers and group leaders assigned to the immigrants should live in the same community as the people with whom they work. The newcomer is highly sensitive and considers it an insult if those who are assigned to work with him refuse to live in his neighborhood.

Those who are concerned with aiding the newcomer in his adjustment must not underestimate the importance of good family relations for the immigrant's ability to make the transition. Group workers and teachers should impress upon the children that their parents deserve respect even if they do not know Hebrew and are not familiar with modern ways, and teachers should make a special point of showing deference to the immigrant fathers in front of their children. Youth movements must not overlook the young people from the Oriental countries but make every effort to attract them.

Once the youngsters have been trained as teachers and group workers, they should be encouraged to carry on their educational activities in their home villages rather than seek employment in the cities in the belief that city jobs imply a higher social status. Indeed, it has been suggested that before they begin training at government expense, immigrants desiring to enter the field of education should be required to sign a contract to return to their home villages to teach.

*The Philosophy of Categorical Values.* Still another faculty member of the Hebrew University, Professor Nathan Rotenstreich, of the department of philosophy, applies the Kantian imperative to the integration of newcomers from the Oriental countries.

Cutting through the underbrush of trivial arguments on the effect of wholesale immigration from the Moslem countries on the culture and mores of Israel, the Rotenstreich school proceeds to separate what it considers the important from the secondary.

Rotenstreich's view is founded on the philosophy of the "categorical imperative" expounded by Immanual Kant, the eighteenth-century German thinker. Kant reasoned in terms of "categorical values," absolute ideals of morality for human society which are not subject to change. Rotenstreich's approach to the integration problem of Israel is based on the premise that Judaism has certain moral concepts which are eternal. These, he says, rather than such secondary features of acculturation as dress, food and etiquette, should be the standards by which to determine what behavior is desirable and what undesirable in the immigrants.

Such questions as whether, due to the Oriental influence on the evolving Israeli society, Israelis will develop a taste for hummus instead of steak, discard jacket and necktie, or learn Yemenite dances instead of the tango, are not in themselves significant to Israel's future development. But if a Yemenite family head persists in beating his wife and children because that was accepted practice in Yemen, he is violating the dictates of human decency and should be made liable to persecution by the law. If a Moroccan family is undernourished because the patriarch insists that all the food be given to him, the Israeli police should intervene. If an Iraqi husband takes a second wife because that was the thing to do in Iraq, he has violated Israel's law prohibiting polygamy. If a father, in order to obtain money, marries off his seventeen-year old daughter against her will to a man of seventy, he has acted counter to the fundamental concept which teaches that every human being is free to determine his or her own future. If an immigrant from the Atlas Mountains of North Africa sends his *Bar-mitzva* son out to sell papers instead of to school, he faces imprisonment under the compulsory primary educational law. It is one of the "categorical values" of Israel's society that every child has a right to education, to train his mind and to acquire the skills needed in adult vocational and occupational life.

This, then, according to the Rotenstreich school, should be the standard by which to determine whether a given person — be he Oriental, Ashkenazi or sabra — is a "good' member of Israeli society: does he act in accordance with the categorical moral values accepted by the new Jewish State or not? Rotenstreich feels that the level of the Israeli society of the future will rise or fall according to the extent to which these moral standards are observed and enforced in day-to-day living. It is therefore the task of the State of Israel to endow these moral values with legal force, and this, in fact, the State has been doing ever since its establishment in 1948, beginning with its draft constitution and continuing with every Knesset session, in army indoctrination courses and classes at public schools.

*The "Primitiveness" View.* "Primitiveness" is the catchword describing the philosophical approach to integration taken by Professor Ernst Simon, eminent Israeli thinker, educator and director of the department of education at the Hebrew University.

Any discussion on the integration of the Oriental immigrants starts out with the premise that thousands of these newcomers from Asia and Africa are "primitive," centuries "behind" Western civilization in their cultural development.

Dr. Simon calls for a more precise definition of the term "primitiveness." Primitiveness, he points out, really implies two distinct elements; "backwardness" and what he calls "primariness." Backwardness may be considered a shortcoming to be remedied, but primariness is not necessarily a cultural defect.

Ashkenazim automatically translate "primitiveness" as "backwardness" only and therefore are inclined to look upon the Orientals as inferior beings.

True, the newcomers have brought with them certain ways that are "backward" and that must be modified because they may be detrimental to health. For instance, it is an Oriental custom to sit on the floor at dinner and reach with the hands into one common pot for food. Newcomers following this practice should be taught to wash their hands with soap before and after eating, for hygiene's sake. They should also be made familiar with the elemental rules of health which they do not know but which every child of Western civilization follows as a matter of course; to cleanse their bodies and to brush their teeth each day, to sleep with windows open, to make use of bathroom facilities, etc.

"Primariness," on the other hand, implies folk characteristics and customs which can become valuable additions to Israeli culture and the preservation of which can help prevent the moral disintegration of the immigrant as he makes the transition to the new world he has found in Israel.

Religious customs, which these ethnic groups have developed through the ages, may appear quaint to Ashkenazim and sabras, but they must not therefore be branded as "backward." Professor Simon warns against attempts to undermine the Oriental's faith in the religious tradition he has brought with him. He criticizes the attempts made in Israel to persuade members of the younger generation of newcomers, either directly or indirectly, that they must get rid of their religious ways if they do not wish to be considered "backward."

In Israel, where much of Jewish religious expression is confined to strictly Orthodox forms, it is an easy thing for the Iraqi or Yemenite youngster, impressed by the arguments of doubters whom he meets in schools, secular youth movements and in the Army, to "throw the whole thing overboard" in his anxiety to be acceptable to his new companions. In a country where soccer is played even by small boys in the street and intercity and international "matches" attract as much public interest as the World Series in the United States, the temptation is overpowering to ride to the sports fields on Saturday, and buy a ticket for the game plus a bottle of gazoz (Israel's version of the soda pop) to sip while watching the best team win.

Once the youngster has broken the traditional law of Sabbath observance, both he and his pious father, knowing no religious alternative to "one hundred per cent or nothing" orthodoxy feel that he has moved outside the pale and might as well discard the whole thing.

And what, Professor Simon asks, does the Oriental

teen-ager then substitute for the tradition that preserved the moral integrity of his ancestors through centuries of oppression? The non-religious sabra has nothing to offer him beyond a lukewarm version of Zionist idealism, or empty Marxist slogans which have little relevance to life as it is really lived in present-day Israel, or plain café existentialism, living for today's kicks with no thought of tomorrow.

The wonder, according to sociologists, is that Oriental youth and their Ashkenazi contemporaries who have abandoned religious observance and have lost the faith taught them by their fathers, are, for the most part, good and law-abiding citizens despite the jeremiads about their lack of idealism. Juvenile delinquency is not a serious problem in Israel.

What is it that keeps these youngsters from flinging all moral and legal restraints to the winds? Professor Simon and his followers reply that even where conscious religious faith and observance are no longer present Israeli life is still essentially motivated by conformance to the ideals and values taught by Judaism which all have the same purpose: to make men deal decently and honorably with their neighbors and to inspire them to strive for social justice and the brotherhood of all mankind.

*The Gestalt Psychology View.* Hillel Barzel, Tel Aviv's deputy director of education and youth activities, interprets the task of integration from the vantage point of the *Gestalt* school of psychology, according to which the problems of human beings cannot be regarded from any single viewpoint to the exclusion of all others. People and their behavior cannot be seen in terms of economics, nationalism or religion alone. Man is a complex being, who must cope with many conflicting powerful psychological drives and impulses which are struggling within him for supremacy — the rational against the irrational, logic against emotion, old identification against new attachments, and the pull of inherited tradition against the urge to imitate the ways of other groups.

According to the *Gestalt* approach adopted by Barzel in his work with immigrants, the problems of the Oriental newcomer to Israel cannot be reduced to simple formulas. Religion alone will not provide a universal solution, nor will pat answers such as "all we need to do is overcome the newcomer's sense of insecurity," "just see that he abandons his backward ways and he'll do fine," or "teach him to abide by the moral values of Israel's society and he'll be a good citizen." The *Gestalt* school believes that the answer involves a highly complex combination of factors.

To begin with, any overall survey of Israel reveals an ever-changing scene with powerful forces seething and churning within. The flow of immigrants is not steady; it will slow down or speed up according to the shifting of political tides in the countries of Africa, Europe and South America. The character of the immigration waves is never the same; sometimes the dominant influence is that of more sophisticated elements from the cities, while during another period the mainstream may be from the rural, "backward" areas. Then, too, the ratio of immigration from the Moslem countries to the influx from Europe is not constant by any means.

As Jews from the Oriental countries get established in Israel, most of them, irrespective of temporary ups or downs, find that they have improved their lot by coming to the Land. The progress of these new Israelis is bound to have an effect on the immigrants that follow them from the Moslem world. If the latest newcomers from Morocco, for instance, find that those who preceded them to Israel have made a good adjustment and are on their way up, they will take a brighter view of their own chances for success. If immigrants arrive to find their precursors still in slum areas and ma'abarot; they will not look upon their own future prospects with such hope.

Barzel cautions Israeli authorities dealing with immigrant absorption against taking a rigid or dogmatic attitude and adopting any one approach to the exclusion of all others. Basically, he feels that Israel's approach should be an experimental one, combining the best features of each of the main schools of thought on the problem.

The Marxist parties — Mapam, Ahdut Ha'Avoda and the left-wing sections of Mapai — are quite right when they point out the necessity of providing all immigrants, regardless of national or cultural background, with a decent home, a job with a living wage, and an opportunity to educate themselves and their children. But this, Barzel insists, is not the whole answer.

The religious thinkers, and Ernst Simon, are wise in warning against the undermining of the religious beliefs and practices the immigrants bring with them to Israel. But it cannot be said simply that just as long as the newcomer keeps his religion, everything else will be *b'seder* (the Hebrew version of "O.K.").

The assertion of Herut that patriotism will make for unity is based on fact. Such patriotic displays as Independence Day celebrations are vital media for unifying the old-established Israelis and their newer fellow-citizens. The educational programs broadcast by *Kol Yisrael*, the State radio station, do much to foster a unified way of thinking on issues affecting the survival of the nation. But even this, Barzel asserts, is not enough.

The anthropocentric group's gradualist view of the integration process provides a sensible brake against those who would force the issue. But no one believes that the philosophy of gradualism or "no hurry" should be applied also to the development of immigrant housing and employment, and to the establishment of informal educational institutions for the newcomers, such as youth groups, and community centers for the adults.

The sociologist school's encouragement of voluntary efforts on the part of private citizens to bring Oriental and Ashkenazi families together is good advice, because bureaucracy often has little understanding for the personal factors that may constitute impressive barriers to successful integration.

The view advanced by the advocates of "categorical values" represents a fundamental ingredient of any effort at integration — an emphasis on the moral standards and ethical values without which no society can survive in the long run.

But regardless of the merit inherent in all approaches, planners of immigrant absorption must not fall victim to the mistaken impression that any one of these, without reference to the others, holds the magic key to the goal they seek to attain.

In the beginning, the State of Israel, floundering between extremes, made mistakes such as forcibly mixing ethnic groups in an attempt to set up a "melting pot." Experience has shown that drastic measures did not work, and the Israeli Government revised its integration program accordingly, providing for schemes of gradual meetings between the Ashkenazi elements and their brethren from the Oriental countries.

"We must get to know these lost and forlorn tribes who have re-emerged from the darkness of their dispersion into the light of our new history," the late President Itzhak Ben Zvi said. "We must train them and brief them in the pioneering spirit the better to equip them for the responsible task which awaits them, and do everything in our power toward their full and total integration into our body politic.

"The spiritual character of these immigrants or their

social and economic standards cannot be a matter of indifference to us. The determination of these will be to
us all a question of the first importance, and one of the
greatest national urgency."

President Ben Zvi called upon his nation to "train the
Orientals to become free citizens of the State, using one
language and adapting themselves to creative effort."

"We must bring to the fore their hidden and latent
cultural potential, on which we may all draw to enrich
the common treasure of our people as a whole," the late
President counseled. "When this is done, there is reason
to hope that this Jewry, too, will take a responsible part
in the reconstruction of our State."

# CHAPTER V

## MESSIAH COMES TO KIBBUTZ YAGUR

"We're not waiting for the Messiah. He's already here — at Yagur." Thus spoke Hanna Garber, — a member for the past thirty years of Kibbutz Yagur, one of Israel's largest collectives.

Nestled against the Carmel mountain range east of Haifa, with its modern two-story apartment houses, communal dining hall, community center, swimming pool, factory, cowsheds, poultry houses, tree-lined walks, lush flower gardens, wide lawns and two and a half thousand acres of farm land, Kibbutz Yagur looks more like an agricultural college than a pioneer settlement.

The 1500 haverim (members) of Yagur live in comfort — one might almost say in abundance. The tables in the communal dining hall are piled high with the tasty fruits, meats and vegetables of the land. The two-room apartment units are provided with the latest in Israeli furniture and appliances, including powerful radios that receive Arab as well as European stations. On Friday evenings, the kibbutzniks gather on the lawn for outdoor movies, and the atmosphere around the huge swimming pool on a Sabbath is that of a resort or country club.

104

Hanna's eyes shone as she talked of the life she had chosen in 1924 when, as a girl of fourteen, she left Russia for Palestine. Her thirty years as a builder of Kibbutz Yagur write a story of back-breaking labor in field and factory under the subtropical sun. It was a ceaseless fight for survival. In those early years she would follow her horse-drawn plow with a rifle strapped to her back, and fight alongside the men against the Arab raiders. Later, she commanded Hagana units in the struggle with British mandate police over illegal immigration, organized a hunger strike at the prison in Latrun, and saw front-line service in Israel's War of Independence. And after freedom was won she was nursery teacher to hundreds of Yagur's children. Today, a grandmother in her fifties, she is a leader in the councils of the Kibbutz.

"What do I mean when I say that Messiah has already come to Yagur?" she asked, and proceeded to answer her own question. "We live together here as brothers and sisters, sharing and sharing alike what we have, and meeting trouble together. If we have grapes and chickens, we all eat heartily. If we are short of food, whatever we have is distributed equally among our members. As long as we are well, we work. If a member gets sick, we care for him. As long as we are young, we work to the best of our strength and ability — for the common good. For those who are not quite so strong, we find work they can do. When we grow old, we are not forsaken in our declining years. At Yagur, it is all for one and one for all. We live together in peace as decent human beings should, if society is to survive at all in this age of the atom. We don't have to wait for the Messiah at Yagur. He's here already."

Six days a week, eight hours a day, the members of Yagur work at tasks in the fields, factory, kitchen, laundry, school, nursery, infirmary, office, or at other assigned chores. They begin their working day at dawn so they can finish by mid-afternoon, and in this manner gain "another day" for swimming, sports, reading, adult classes and cultural activity.

On Sabbaths, all except essential work comes to a standstill. On the day of rest, Yagur moves at a leisurely pace, the talk is quiet and unhurried, and a spirit of calm, relaxation and camaraderie pervades the kibbutz.

It is a rich and rewarding life for those dedicated to the ideal for which the kibbutz stands. The financial inducements can hardly be called great. It is true that the kibbutzniks receive all their basic clothing, as well as their apartments, furniture, radios, food, medical care, education and other necessities of life free of charge, but even so, the annual cash allowance of IL 65 — or a little over $20 — which each adult haver receives, does not go very far. At tea one Sabbath I asked Shalom Hetkin, who has been at Yagur since 1935, how the haverim spend their allowance. Shalom, who hails from New York where he taught English and did some writing, said that the IL 65 doesn't last very long even if you just want to go to nearby Haifa once every few months to see a movie or a play. His wife, who was a nurse in the States, said that all of her annual allotment could easily be spent on just one good dress. Hanna Garber spends her allowance on gifts for her grandchildren and occasional trips to Tel Aviv to visit relatives. Haim Varda, a landscape artist, who laid out the beautiful gardens of Yagur, uses his allowance to buy books, although the kibbutz library has 30,000 volumes.

In recent years, the kibbutz was faced with the question what to do about the restitution payments which some of its members received from Germany as survivors of Nazi persecution. These payments took the form of lump sums ranging from $2,500 to $10,000 in addition to monthly benefits of from $30 to $150 for loss of property, businesses or earning capacity. Only a few recipients of these indemnities left Yagur when they got their money. The rest agreed to turn over their restitution funds to the kibbutz treasury for such purposes as the construction of a community center. Each recipient was left enough money for himself to take one trip abroad. Haim Varda, a survivor of Dachau, went to visit his brother in Cleveland.

"I like life here in the kibbutz much better than the life my brother leads over there," he told me. "He's a landscape gardener, too. All he does is rush, rush, rush, and for what? When he comes home, dead tired, he sits down in front of his television set watching those horrible westerns, crime movies and ridiculous situation comedies. I'll take Yagur any time. I work from seven in the morning until three in the afternoon, and I have enough time every day to go swimming, to do some reading and to enjoy our cultural programs. We have no money worries. All our needs are provided for. Here at Yagur we have achieved peace of mind."

Shalom Friedman, Yagur's treasurer, recalled that when he first arrived from Russia in 1925, as a lad of seventeen, the kibbutz had only 23 members and a small 150-acre farm. It was only after the Arabs had evacuated the Haifa area during the War of Independence that Yagur expanded to its present size of 2,500 acres.

Today Kibbutz Yagur is a substantial business enterprise. Its tin plate factory produces $1,500,000 worth of cans each year, and the kibbutz farm has the same volume of production in dairy, poultry and agriculture.

While all the farm work is done by the kibbutzniks themselves, the can factory employs 30 hired laborers who live in Haifa. Like many other kibbutzim, Yagur has been compelled by a shortage of hands to modify its stand against the use of hired labor.

"But we are still against hiring labor for the farm," said Friedman, whom the kibbutz sent to the United

States in 1946 to take courses in agriculture. "The principle of all of kibbutz life is self-labor, and if we'd start hiring workers for the farm, our people would feel that they don't have to do their own work any more."

I asked Friedman whether increasing mechanization has tended to prejudice the principle of self-labor.

"It isn't much difference whether the kibbutz member works with his hands or with a hoe or at the controls of a tractor," he replied. "It is true, of course, that the attitude toward the principle of self-labor is changing. We can't help being affected by changing attitudes in Tel Aviv, Jerusalem and Haifa. Our people visit the cities, their people visit us, and we're bound to influence each other.

"Manual labor is definitely losing significance. The technological revolution has not passed us by. We have spent millions of dollars for the latest machinery from the United States, France, England and Germany. As a matter of fact, we here at Yagur use more farm machinery than farms our size in the States. Therefore, we have to study and learn to operate a mechanized farm and a factory full of machines. A large kibbutz like ours utilizes machinery more than the small individual farmer. Despite mechanization, we're always short of labor.

"But we refuse to exploit the skills of paid outside labor just so that we shouldn't have to work so hard. After all, we came to the Land and organized kibbutzim in order to reconstruct our lives, to cease being shopkeepers and become tillers of the soil instead. That is the reason why we have chosen and continued the kibbutz way of life."

The women of Yagur feel that mechanization has had an adverse effect on their position in the kibbutz. Hanna Garber regretfully conceded that the growing mechanization of farm and factory at Yagur has shunted the woman into the traditional feminine chores in the communal kitchen, laundry, tailor shop, office and nursery, jobs which, she feels, offer less status and less personal satisfaction than the position formerly enjoyed by the kibbutz woman when she still worked side by side with her husband at the plow or at the machine, and shared with him the task of guarding the settlement, or the dangers of the battlefield. As the pioneer woman loses her "emancipated" role, she feels a weakening of her influence in the kibbutz councils. As a result, Hanna explained, the women of the kibbutz no longer find communal life as challenging as in the pioneering days, when there was complete equality of the sexes in the struggle to convert the wilderness into green farmlands and to defend the settlers' hard-earned gains against Arab marauders.

"If the wife disappears into household work and then into her rooms with her children," Hanna continued in Yiddish, "the kibbutz is weakened ideologically. If the wife and mother does not take an active part in the leadership of the kibbutz, she exerts a negative influence on the next generation as far as its indoctrination in the idealism of our way of life is concerned."

True, the kibbutz gives its mothers the chance to take a more active interest in the education of their children than their sisters in the city, and to get intensive training for work as teachers in the kibbutz. But not every mother can be a teacher and, besides, there is no need for so many teachers in any one settlement. Therefore the kibbutz mother can find her place also on committees working on problems of education, health, culture, adult classes, meal planning and other day-to-day matters of communal living.

While at some other kibbutzim there have been prolonged discussions as to whether children should spend the nights with their parents or in the nursery or "children's house", Yagur has clung to the traditional kibbutz idea of separate quarters for parents and children.

"The mother can't work all day and then stay up all night with a sick child," said Hanna. The practical result of the kibbutz arrangement is that the children spend a few happy, relaxed hours with their parents at the end of the working day, first at supper in the communal dining hall, and then in the privacy of the parents' apartment until bedtime. The separation at night and during the working day makes the evening reunion all the more affectionate and rewarding for parents and children. They do not have sufficient time to get on each other's nerves.

I asked Hanna whether she missed preparing meals for herself in a kitchen of her own.

"I don't know how to cook," she frankly confessed. "I wouldn't know what to do in a kitchen if I had one. You see, it's perfectly possible for a woman to spend her entire life in the kibbutz without ever having to learn how to prepare a meal."

Hanna is a widow; her husband was killed in 1931 in an accident at work in Haifa shortly after the birth of their daughter. Hanna has no family at Yagur now. Her daughter left the kibbutz when she married an army officer, and is living in Haifa with her husband and children.

Yagur is losing members and no replacements seem to be forthcoming. Israel's population today is four times what it was in 1948, but Yagur's membership has remained stationary at 1500.

In response to suggestions for changes in the kibbutz setup to make the collective way of life more appealing to city youth and to immigrants, Friedman displayed an inflexibility typical of the old-time kibbutznik. To begin with, he pointed out, no basic changes can be made in arrangements in any one kibbutz without the approval of the entire "movement," the political association of which the kibbutz is a part. Thus, the kibbutz cannot, at its Saturday night "town meetings," propose and inaugurate basic changes in its way of living.

"I don't advise town people how to live," Friedman protested. "And I don't seek their advice on such matters as the equal distribution of property. By the same token, we at Yagur don't see why we should tailor our lives to fit their concepts. We have our own ideas on how best to arrange our lives."

Oriental Jews, Friedman felt, were reluctant to join kibbutzim. "They can't understand the communal principle involved, the idea that people should pool their resources and receive in return only their basic needs instead of daily wages," he explained. "They have to see money. They want to feel that the kitchen table at which they eat is really theirs. They don't understand that while no individual in the kibbutz may own a table by himself, the kibbutznik shares with his comrades a standard of living such as few of the unskilled and untrained newcomers from the Oriental countries will achieve within this generation."

Yagur worries about the loss of many of its boys and girls after army training. This is due primarily, not to a lack of idealism, but to "reasons of the heart." A kibbutz boy serving in the Army may meet a girl who, born and raised in Tel Aviv, is unwilling to give up the bright lights, the sidewalk cafés, the theatres, concerts and cinemas of the city for what she regards a humdrum, gray and unexciting existence on the farm. In such cases of "intermarriage" between kibbutz and city, the couple almost inevitably decides in favor of the city and the kibbutz is the loser. In those isolated instances where the city dweller yields and consents to "try out" kibbutz life, the experiment rarely lasts more than a few years and, again, the kibbutz loses out.

What does the absence of immigrant manpower and loss of youth mean to the future of this unique form of communal living?

"The future of the kibbutz," Friedman said, "depends on the future of Israel. If Israel should lose the idealism to which it owes its birth, the kibbutz may disappear in time. But if Israel as a whole regains its idealism, it will be easier for the kibbutz to survive within it."

* * *

The Sabbath I spent at Yagur I met Uri Paluska who had just turned thirteen. Yagur is not a religious settlement, and its members observe only a few of the customs associated with traditional Judaism, but on that Sabbath Uri was celebrating his Bar Mitzva.

Bar Mitzva is a good occasion to ask a boy what he wants to do when he will be grown up, and so I put the question to Uri Paluska of Kibbutz Yagur.

"I'm going into the Army," Uri replied, "And then I'll go to a border kibbutz." When pressed a little, he admitted that he could conceive of a situation where he might fall in love with a girl who would not be willing to live in a kibbutz. It hardly ever happens that a boy and girl from Yagur marry one another. They grow up together at such close quarters that they regard each other as brothers and sisters and search for marriage partners elsewhere.

Uri was an alert young man with many interests. Sitting by the side of the swimming pool that Sabbath afternoon, he asked me quite mature questions about politics in America, about my views on elections in Israel, the Middle East problem, the race for the moon, the world of sports and, of course the Eichmann trial.

Prior to the capture of Adolf Eichmann, the sabra youth of Yagur and of Israel in general had little interest in the Jews living in the Diaspora. Boys and girls raised in Israel could not understand the meaning of anti-Semitism or the feelings of human beings who are not free and able to defend themselves. They could not know what it is to be hated or to suffer from discrimination for no other reason but that one is a Jew.

The Eichmann trial first opened the eyes and the ears of Israel's young to the tragedy that overtook European Jewry in World War II. The youthful sabras along with their elders, listened to the testimony, the cross-examination, the questioning, and the summaries of prosecution and defense in the Jerusalem courtroom. Over their radios, they heard first-hand accounts from survivors of how the spirit of the Jews had been systematically destroyed by incredible cruelty and torture, and for the first time they were able to understand why the Jews of Europe, save for a few notable exceptions, should have been incapable of offering resistance to Hitler's storm troopers. Thus the trial of Adolf Eichmann brought the youth of Israel closer to world Jewry.

The Jews of the world, in turn, have good cause to admire the young people who are growing up in the kibbutzim of Israel. Although the collective farms hold only about three per cent of Israel's total population, 50 per cent of all the officers in the Israeli Army are kibbutzniks, as are 50 per cent of all the country's parachutists. Shalom Friedman proudly declared to me that Kibbutz Yagur alone has contributed as many jet pilots to the Israeli Air Force as Tel Aviv, which has a population of about half a million as compared to Yagur's 1,500. Friedman attributed this preponderance of kibbutz youth in the Army elite to two advantages the kibbutz youngster has over his contemporaries in the cities. First, young kibbutzniks are stronger and tougher than the sabras of the city, because they lead largely outdoor lives and, in Yagur, at least, start learning to do farm work at the age of six. Secondly, while many children in the city, particularly those from Oriental families, do not attend school beyond the compulsory eight years, all boys and girls in the kibbutz get twelve years of schooling.

Old-timers like Shalom Friedman are opposed to all higher education for kibbutz youth that does not specifically equip them for life in the collective.

"We do not send our young people to the Hebrew University or to the Haifa Technion to study the humanities or atomic science," Friedman asserted. "Their higher education has to be directly connected with skills they can use in kibbutz life, such as teaching, or technical knowledge directly related to our work on the farm or in the factory, or even medicine, which the youngster can put to use as a kibbutz doctor when he's through with his studies."

Thus far, not many kibbutz youngsters have left the collective to pursue higher studies of their own choice. But the limitation of career opportunities in the kibbutz in this age of technology is bound to keep away city boys and girls who might otherwise have considered answering the call to "be settlers on the land."

Take Yigal Becker of Ra'anana. He is only in his late teens, but he has already won a prize for an invention and hopes to enter Haifa Technion to study electronics. His parents own a three-dunam chicken farm and orange orchard.

"Why should I want to live in a kibbutz?" Yigal asked me. "Growing carrots holds no interest for me. It doesn't give me a chance to get ahead in my career. I've met kibbutz people who are chemists and musicians, but they've buried their talents in the soil."

The by-passing of the kibbutz by the new generation has forced upon the kibbutz a provincial and defensive attitude which has left its mark on the political party structure of the State of Israel. Except for the Orthodox kibbutzim, the kibbutz organizations, by and large, have abandoned the democratic, only mildly socialistic Mapai party of Ben-Gurion and Eshkol to form a nucleus for the left-wing Mapam and Ahdut Ha'Avoda parties. The prestige, influence and economic effectiveness of many of the older and larger kibbutzim have been greatly reduced by internal political divisions which have actually split some of the settlements in two.

Israel Bar Yehuda, who has lived at Yagur for the past three decades and served as Israel's Minister of Transportation, has on numerous occasions attacked the party of his boyhood friend Ben-Gurion, accusing Mapai of buying immigrant votes with promises of money, jobs and homes, of not exerting sufficient effort to make peace with Israel's Arab neighbors, and primarily of seeking to downgrade the role of the kibbutz in the Jewish State.

The children of the kibbutz absorb this rigid partisan attitude at an early age. Thus teen-aged Uri Paluska will read only *Lamerhav,* the organ of the Ahdut Ha'Avoda party to which Yagur belongs, and never *Davar,* the mouthpiece of Mapai.

This is the sort of political fragmentation which constitutes a chronic problem for the Israeli government.

\* \* \*

I stopped at Kibbutz Mishmar HaSharon which I had visited in 1949 and again in 1961.

Mishmar HaSharon, a garden spot of idyllic beauty in the fertile Sharon Valley midway between Tel Aviv and Haifa near the Mediterranean, is not a large collective. Its population is less than five hundred, including 220 adult haverim, 150 children, ten "senior residents" and fifty "youth visitors." But in 1963, its eight hundred acres of rich soil yielded nearly $900,000 worth of oranges, bananas, apples, avocados, mangoes, persimmons, pecans and grapes — an 18 per cent increase over the 1962 crop. The kibbutz farm makes use of the latest in agricultural machinery and scientific methods. Unlike Yagur, Mishmar HaSharon has no qualms about using hired labor on its farm, and is currently employing sixty Yemenite day workers who commute from the nearby village of Elyakkin.

Unlike most kibbutzim, which combine farming and industry for balanced employment and diversified income, Mishmar HaSharon has no factory. But it operates a bakery which services the entire Sharon Valley area.

My guide through Mishmar HaSharon was an old friend, Jacob Margalit, the secretary of the kibbutz. During his thirty years at the settlement, Margalit has served the kibbutz as a pioneer, a self-educated sage, soldier and expert on banana growing. Now in his fifties, Margalit is able to stand back and talk quite objectively about what Israelis term the "crisis of the kibbutz". He calls it "the crisis of society."

While nearly every other phase of Israeli life has forged ahead in the process of mass immigration, the kibbutz movement has stood still. The kibbutzim have shown no gains in total population or in numbers of new settlements in proportion to the growth of the country as a whole. In all of Israel today, there are 230 kibbutzim, including about 40 Orthodox collectives, with a total population of no more than 80,000.

Approximately one-third of Mishmar HaSharon's young people have left the kibbutz after army service. "Why," Margalit asks, "should this be so? What is happening to the kibbutz? And what is happening to Israel? Is it worth while to stay on the land, working without wages, receiving only basic needs in return for the hard life of a farm laborer? What is the purpose of the brotherhood in action which the kibbutz represents, if it does not attract the youth of the city or the immigrants and refugees in proportion to the phenomenal growth of Israel's population since the War of Independence? Every time one of our youngsters say 'Shalom, haverim' and leaves us, it hurts. And it makes us wonder what's wrong with us that we can't keep them."

Margalit is fortunate in that his own two older children — he's the father of five — did not leave the kibbutz when they married. His son is the only second-generation Mishmar HaSharon man in the thirty years of the settlement's existence to take a wife from the same kibbutz. His daughter, Tamar, married a youth leader from "outside," but she and her husband settled in Mishmar HaSharon and now have three children.

"Actually, the kibbutz encourages healthy family living," Margalit explained. "Our five children do not depend on us. Our married son has no reason to fight with his mother-in-law. We meet as kibbutz and family members, and as human beings. There's no place for family squabbles in kibbutz life. In fact, I can see our kibbutz eventually developing in units of' ten to fifteen large families, families of twenty, twenty-five people who are not economically dependent upon one another and are bound together only by ties of blood and affection."

Margalit is proud that not one of the original sixty men and women who organized Kibbutz Mishmar HaSharon thirty years ago has abandoned the ideal. At present, Mishmar HaSharon is entering the phase where its second generation is beginning to assume roles of responsibility and leadership in the kibbutz. The sons are taking over the burden of farm labor from their fathers. But, said Margalit, it will be another decade before the sons will assume complete control of Mishmar HaSharon.

What, I asked Margalit, would he say is the future of the kibbutz in Israel's changing society?

"That's all a matter of opinion," he replied. "It depends, of course, on the people who choose this way of life for themselves, and on our success in educating the younger generation in our spirit."

Unlike some other kibbutz veterans, Margalit is not opposed to strictly academic higher education for the young of the kibbutz.

"We are for a comprehenive education," he stated. "But we want it to be an education which holds up as the supreme goal the ideal of kibbutz life, in which men strive for justice, equality and mutual assistance, and the teachings of our Bible are carried out in daily practice, in which the commandment, 'Love thy neighbor,' will be a code to be observed in everyday life.

"Of course people have to study. Ask any Jew in Israel about his plans for the future of his children, and he'll tell you, 'I want my son to go to the university.' The kibbutz people feel the same way. I, personally, don't think that a youngster who leaves the kibbutz to go to one of our universities will ever come back. So maybe I'm waging a losing fight. But then we have to understand the basic problem: What is real education? Do we look on education as a screening process to sift out those three per cent of our people who are potential giants in the field of science and scholarship, or do we regard education as a way of producing happy, self-sustaining adults? Education must be used to build up the individual personality."

I asked Margalit why any kibbutz should wish to stand in the way of a youngster who wants to acquire a university degree.

"I suppose I can understand that view," he answered. "Because, as I've said before, there is always the chance that once a student's been away to school, he may be lost to the kibbutz. And if the kibbutz breaks up for lack of members, who besides ourselves will be there to mourn its passing?"

Finally, I came straight to the point. "Could it not be," I asked him, "that the kibbutz has outlived its usefulness? Holding only three per cent of the country's present population, is the kibbutz not out of the mainstream of Israeli life today?"

The kibbutz sage was visibly disturbed. He arose from his chair and strode back and forth, stopping at the window of his one-room cottage to look out on a verdant landscape of fruit trees, bushes and flowers.

"The kibbutz always represented a minority," he began pensively. "You ask whether we are outside the mainstream of Israeli life. Well, there was a time when that mainstream flowed through the kibbutz even though we were a minority. What, really, is our 'mainstream'? What people think of as the mainstream in Israel certainly is not a materialistic society. Only in Israel will you find the youth actually wanting to go into the Army, and Jews aren't a fighting people by nature, you know. There's a tug of war going on between the Halutzic ideal on one side and materialism on the other, and the Halutzic ideal stands for toil and service for the common welfare. What's the 'mainstream'? I really don't know."

Economic growth brings new problems to the kibbutz. "In the old days, when everyone was equal in poverty," Margalit reminisced, "it was easy to divide a loaf of bread. It's harder, much harder, to divide cake. When we have a lot to divide, we do it mechanically, equally, without regard to individual needs. It is an egalitarian society, but that does not necessarily make it a just society. Some people really need more than others. But attention to individual wants gives rise to new needs. For instance, we decided to buy small refrigerators for every dwelling unit, even though our members all eat together in the communal dining hall. Now once you have refrigerators, you want to fill them with things of your own. The kids want ice cream, for instance. I thought of the problems this might raise, and I opposed the refrigerators. Material progress is fine, but it has its disadvantages, as you see.

"Our farm has grown. What has been the result? The kibbutz gets more complex and the people no longer know every acre of the place. And an intimate knowledge of the entire kibbutz is absolutely necessary if there is to be complete personal identification with the settlement. If you don't know everything that goes on in the kibbutz, your ties to the other haverim get weaker. You become a victim of specialization. For instance, we had a frost recently, which did IL 250,000 damage to our crops, and imagine, the only members of the kibbutz to feel personally concerned about this disaster were those who happened to have been working in that particular sector.

"Prosperity has added a new item to our budget — trips abroad for our haverim. How are those travel privileges to be apportioned? Our treasurer proposed that we wait a year before we start these trips — on account of the frost, you know. It so happens that I opposed this delay. In the good years, we don't expand our budget. So there's no reason to cut it when there's a lean year. Our standard of living shouldn't depend on changes in our actual income. It is set by the movement of which our kibbutz is a part, in keeping with our movement's own concept of the proper standard of living in a kibbutz.

"That's the inconsistency which troubles us here in the kibbutz. Bigger quantities of material assets reduce the quality of our way of life. People are producing more but they are not happier for it. Our living standard rises. We gain confidence in our abilities as producers, but this does not make us stronger as individual human beings. So the kibbutz is getting to be the best argument against socialist ideology."

Margalit's obvious pessimism to the contrary, there has been a slight gain in the population of Mishmar Ha-Sharon, due to a modest influx of young immigrants and youth group members who are undergoing a training course on the kibbutz farm. This increase is only transitory, but there are always a few in each group who elect to stay at Mishmar HaSharon as full-fledged haverim.

Despite the alleged reluctance of newcomers from the Oriental countries to join kibbutzim, Mishmar HaSharon has succeeded in organizing an immigrant contingent of boys and girls between the ages of sixteen and eighteen. These youngsters come from North Africa, the Near East, and India, with a sprinkling from Europe and South America. Mishmar HaSharon is the first kibbutz to conduct an experiment of this type. The young trainees attend the kibbutz school, work on the soil and learn Hebrew, the language of the land.

"Mishmar HaSharon was my true gateway into Israel," a girl from Iran said to me.

"The kibbutz has taught me new standards of what is good and what is bad in our society," a boy from North Africa declared.

That the kibbutz is changing, for better or for worse, is a fact that cannot be argued away.

Though comprising only three per cent of Israel's population, the kibbutzniks now are responsible for one-fourth of the country's farm production. They are enjoying a standard of living equal to that of a skilled worker in the city, if not better.

Taking great pride in its own educational system — from kindergarten through high school — which is probably the best in the country, the kibbutz is abandoning its opposition to higher education at universities "outside," and the haverim are sending more of their sons and daughters to the Hebrew University in Jerusalem and to the Technion in Haifa.

It is interesting to note, too, that the kibbutz, which, save for the Orthodox settlements, has been largely indifferent to religion, is returning, to some extent, to a more traditional way of life. Marriages are solemnized by rabbis, the Sabbath is ushered in by Friday evening observances, and new ritual forms are being evolved for the celebration of the Jewish festivals.

Some Israeli observers have glibly written off the kibbutz as a vestige from a glorious but long-outdated past.

But the kibbutz, by and large, believes that it still has a very real purpose and place in Israel's society. Indeed, its spokesmen frankly warn critics and cynics that without the brand of Halutzic idealism represented by the kibbutz, Israel itself may not be able to survive.

# CHAPTER VI
# MELTING POT AND BREAD BASKET

Until 1955, Eliahu Cohen was a tailor in Marrakesh, Morocco. Today he is a farmer at Otzem, one of the fifty-eight moshavim (cooperative agricultural villages) of the pioneer Lakhish Project which covers the strategic thirty-mile strip of Israeli territory separating Jordan from Egyptian-held Gaza.

Eliahu, now in his middle thirties, is just one of 130,-000 immigrants who chose to become farmers in Israel and whose blood, tears, toil and sweat helped transform Israel's economy from one of shortages and rationing to one of surpluses and exports. These farmers — 33,000 families in all — have made Israel's barren soil blossom and yield an overabundance of fruit.

"Our food production today is enough to feed the third million which will be added to our population in the next decade," Prime Minister Levi Eshkol said. "Our task now is to stabilize and consolidate the 490 agricultural settlements we have established since the State was founded in 1948."

When the Cohen family came by truck from the port of Haifa to the newly established Lakhish Project, Egyptian *fedayeen* infiltrators from the Gaza Strip, ten miles to the southwest, were terrorizing the lonely countryside with raids in which Israeli farmers were wounded and killed. There were to be two hundred such incidents before Israeli troops put an end to these forays by destroying the Egyptian bases at Gaza, Khan Yunis and Rafa in the Sinai Campaign of 1956. And Eliahu learned that military training was to be an essential step in his transformation from a Moroccan tailor into an Israeli farmer.

Even in Biblical times, the Lakhish region was a battlefield. It was there that Joshua defeated the Canaanites and Rehoboam erected fortresses to guard the approaches to Jerusalem. In 587 B.C., the armies of Babylonia, led by Nebuchadnezzar, destroyed the ancient city of Lakhish and laid waste the surrounding countryside which until that time had brought forth a wealth of fruit, grain, wine and olives. Over 2,500 years later, in 1948, Nasser, along with thousands of Egyptian invaders, was trapped there, at the Faluja Gap.

In 1954, the Lakhish area at last became the scene of a campaign fought without blood and guns; in that year, the State of Israel launched "Operation Lakhish."

Conceived by David Ben-Gurion, Operation Lakhish had a multiple objective; to restore this region to the fertility for which it had been famous in the days of the Bible; to provide work, food and a livelihood for immigrants, mainly for those who had no special skills that could have been of use to them in Israel; to integrate immigrants from the Oriental countries who had to make the leap from existence in a primitive world to life in a new and growing nation; and in this manner to build up a chain of cooperative farms which would serve as a line of defense against Egypt from the West and Jordan from the east.

The Lakhish development consists, not of kibbutzim,

but of moshavim, cooperative agricultural settlements in which members possess their own homesteads, while agriculture and marketing, sales and purchases, are conducted as a single cooperative unit. But unlike the old-style Israeli moshavim, the settlements comprising the Lakhish Project are not independent from one another. All the villages in the project are grouped around one hub, Kiryat Gat, the administrative center, where there are schools, hospitals, factories, tractor stations, stores, theatres and cultural centers. It is there that the members of the various moshavim in the project meet. Each moshav is peopled by immigrants from one country or district only. Thus the Cohen family of Marrakesh and other Moroccan Jews from the Atlas Mountains live at Otzem, and immigrants from Kurdistan live at Noga, while Tunisians were settled at Zohar, Yemenites at Heletz, Jerba farmers at Telamim, Tripolitanians at Uzza, Iranians at Zarkhia, Rumanians at Karmon, Hungarians at Yad Nathan, Poles at Ge'ia, and sabras at Segula.

The reason for this arrangement was that when, in the early years, immigrants from disparate cultural and national backgrounds were thrown together to live at close quarters, the results had been disastrous. In the Lakhish development, the ethnic groups live separately, each in its own village. But the children of all attend school together at Kiryat Gat, Ashkelon and Nehora, and the adults from the various villages meet at adult classes, movies, hospital, shopping centers, tractor stations, factories and administrative offices at Kiryat Gat. Thus integration comes about naturally, gradually and with a minimum of friction.

I visited Eliahu Cohen and his wife Rachel at their two-and-a-half-room blockhouse at Moshav Otzem. Eliahu was relaxing over coffee and cakes.

"This is a big change from Morocco," he said, looking

out the window across the yellowing wheat fields toward the Mediterranean. "In Marrakesh, I had my own small tailor shop. We made a modest living and we didn't have to work too hard. But we Jews never knew what the next day might bring in Morocco. We had little to lose. It wasn't easy to learn to be a farmer here. But now I like the work and I want my children to grow up close to the soil."

Rachel, who was wearing a long, brightly-colored Oriental robe, did not agree. "I still think farm work is only for Arabs," she snorted. "Jews should live in the cities."

"No," her husband countered. "This is our land, and we have to work it and defend it by ourselves."

The planners of Operation Lakhish, aware that many Oriental Jews shared Rachel Cohen's antipathy to farming, had devised cooperative work projects to supplement the farmers' income to keep them from abandoning their farms during the early back-breaking and frustrating years which passed before they were able to see the fruits of their toil. When Eliahu first arrived at Otzem, he was paid a living wage for mixing the cement and carrying the wood to build his own farmhouse.

Today, Eliahu divides his time between his own plot of 2-1/2 acres and the cooperatively-owned 500 acres of fertile soil where vegetables, sugar beets, peanuts, sorghum, clover, wheat and cotton are grown. Eliahu's share in this cooperatively-worked field is ten acres. He earns about $20.00 a week. Of this amount, he spends $15.00. The food he grows for his table, of course, costs him nothing.

At Kiryat Gat, I met Avram Herr. Herr, who was born in Newark, N.J., and studied at the Oklahoma Agricultural and Mechanical College, is one of the planners of the Lakhish project. He revealed that the Jewish Agency had invested $400,000 in Otzem, which provides a living for eighty families from Morocco. Another $500,000 is still needed to make Otzem self-supporting.

The needs of Otzem, Herr said, are typical of the multi-million-dollar requirements of hundreds of similar agricultural settlements throughout Israel which have yet to be stabilized and consolidated after the manner of the moshavim in the Lakhish development. The Jewish Agency drew up a budget totalling nearly $200,000,000 for housing, farm buildings, machinery, tools, irrigation, livestock, citrus planting, electricity, roads, and other needs of the underfinanced settlements.

What happens when a settlement remains underfinanced is shown by the sad example of Kokhav, a village next to Otzem, which had been settled by Jews from Iraq in 1950. For a decade the seventy houses of Kokhav stood empty, abandoned because the settlers lacked water, livestock and remunerative work. Twenty villages throughout the land shared the fate of Kokhav.

Otzem has survived and done well because the planners of Operation Lakhish make sure that none of its settlements suffers from lack of capital, and because the members have been determined from the very beginning to stick it out.

The Cohens grow one-fourth of their food, mostly vegetables, potatoes and corn, in their own plot of land — the rest comes from the fields they own jointly with the other members. They have three sheep, two lambs and a poultry run. For their shopping they go to the cooperative stores at Nehora and Kiryat Gat. At Kiryat Gat, too, are the classes at which they study Hebrew, civics, and history and the special courses which are offered to women in child training, hygiene, cooking and nutrition.

The process of acculturation is further hastened by the new ideas which the children bring home from school, and by radio broadcasts from Station Kol Yisrael which bring a new world into the homes of the moshav members. The Cohens and other younger families welcome these influences. Middle-aged moshav members find the transition more difficult, and the new ways their children acquire create a gulf between the old generation and the new.

Eliahu Cohen is a member of the *Vaad*, the governing committee of Otzem. Each moshav in the Lakhish project has such a body which presents suggestions and complaints to Avram Herr and to the other advisors and instructors assigned to the moshavim by the Jewish Agency.

A rabbi, who came from Morocco with the Cohens, attends to the spiritual needs of Otzem, which is a religious settlement. On Friday evenings and Saturday mornings, Otzem's small red synagogue building is filled with worshippers chanting their prayers in the ancient ritual of their ancestors in Morocco. The Sabbath at Otzem is a day of complete rest, spent at worship and visiting relatives and friends in the settlement. Saturday night is movie night at Nehora and Kiryat Gat. There, the members of Otzem mingle with the men and women of the fifty-seven other moshavim that are part of the Lakhish project.

"Contacts such as these, and the personal relationships that develop from them, are important," said Mordecai Guber, chairman of the Vaad of Nehora. "In this way people get to know each other and see other aspects of life in Israel." Guber and his wife Rivka gave up their own farm, donating it to the Government, in order to settle in Nehora to help in the task of integrating the Oriental immigrants.

Eliahu and his farm neighbors spend one month of every year on active duty in the Israeli Army. When not on active Army service, they take turns at community guard duty. Eliahu and other immigrant farmers proved their mettle during the fedayeen raids and in the Sinai Campaign.

"They showed no panic. It was their first big test, and now we know we can rely on them to defend this area," said Guber.

Eliahu Cohen recently compared notes with another tailor from Marrakesh who had gone to Tel Aviv to take a job in a tailor shop.

"My friend in Tel Aviv was telling me that he earns over 100 pounds a week," Eliahu reported. "But living in the city is very expensive and he has no chance to save enough money to open his own tailor shop. Here, at Otzem, I have my own house, my land and my work. I can work my own field as I please. I can grow crops and make a profit. In a few years' time, I'll be independent."

* * *

Another moshav where Jews from Morocco have proven their willingness and ability to work the soil of Israel is Yad Rambam, a cooperative agricultural settlement near Ramle.

This moshav, too, is Orthodox, with a synagogue and religious school. All the members strictly observe the Sabbath, the dietary laws and generally pattern their lives on the precepts of the Tora.

Yad Rambam's 85 founding families came to Israel from Fez and Sifrou, Morocco, in 1957. Rabbi Isaac Benizi, spiritual leader of the Sifrou's Jewish community and director of the Société Em HaBanim School of 600 pupils, had gone ahead to prepare the way for his flock, made arrangements for their settlement in Israel and then returned to Africa to lead them to the Holy Land in person.

"I saw that there was no future for them in Morocco," Rabbi Isaac told me. Once his followers had decided to come to Israel, little white cottages were built by the Jewish Agency for them near Ramle, within the shadow of the Judean hills which mark the border between Israel and Jordan. When the newcomers arrived, they found finished homes waiting for them.

Like most of the Jews from the Oriental countries, the people of Yad Rambam observe the commandment to "be fruitful and multiply." The 85 families of the moshav consist of a total of 800 men, women and children, with seven to eight children in most families. Rabbi Benizi and his wife are only in their thirties, but they are the parents of eight.

Each family was assigned 30 dunams or about seven acres of land. Of these, ten dunams adjoin the family's cottage, ten are some distance away, and another ten are part of the cooperative orange grove. Until five years ago, the people of Yad Rambam worked the land on a cooperative basis. Now each family tills its own soil, but the farm machinery is cooperatively owned and the crops are marketed through Tenuva, Israel's cooperative agency for the sale of agricultural products.

Each family at Yad Rambam has invested $2,500 of its own money in the enterprise and signed notes for a thirty-year loan of $10,000 from the Jewish Agency. The land was leased without rent from the Jewish National Fund on Nahlat Rabbi Charles Eliezer Hillel Kauvas.

Recently the moshav sustained considerable financial loss on its 30,000 chickens and its dairy due to Israel's glut of poultry and eggs. As a result, the twenty-three children of Yad Rambam who graduated elementary school that year could not count on going on to high school, where tuition is $500 per year. The Israeli government is still in no position to provide free high school education for all. But despite their difficulties and insufficient income, the farmers of Yad Rambam refuse to abandon their moshav. The Tora, they say, teaches them that everyone who works on his own soil will always have enough bread to eat. Rabbi Benizi agreed that the change from city to farm life was very hard for his people, but, as he put it, *"en b'rera* — there is no other alternative. We must continue what we have set out to do."

"What is it that keeps you from leaving the United States and coming to Israel to live?" Rabbi Benizi asked me. "You say America's your home. It's the same thing with us. We are rooted to this land and to the homes we have built here."

\* \* \*

Only a decade after the reign of austerity rations of 800 calories a day, the fantastic success of Israel's agriculture has changed shortages into surpluses and rationing into open market. Israel's vegetable and fruit stands, groceries and supermarkets are colorful cornucopias of plenty.

The dramatic achievements of Israel's agriculture is due in large measure to those immigrants who are tilling the soil on the 490 farm settlements that have been established and expanded since the founding of the State of Israel. In partnership with Israel's kibbutzim and the private farms which already yielded good crops prior to 1948, the newer immigrant settlements have succeeded in doubling the area of Israel's cultivated soil to over a million acres, of which 350,000 acres have been made arable by irrigation.

The 130,000 farmers who work the soil in Israel's kibbutzim, moshavim and privately-owned farms produce three-fourths of the food consumed in the country, plus agricultural exports — mostly oranges and grapefruit — bringing $84,000,000 in foreign currency to Israel each year. Total agricultural production has grown in value from IL 172 million in 1948 to over one billion ($330 million) in 1963. The only agricultural products for which Israel must rely on import are wheat, fodder and fats, because Israel does not have sufficient land and water for wheat fields and herds of cattle.

Aided by intensive research, extension service education and modern methods of equipment, Israeli farmers have been able to develop new and better crops. Israel's Jaffa oranges are world-famous, and unsurpassed for size, juiciness, sweetness and vitamin content. Cotton fields, first planted in Israel in 1953, now cover 60,000 acres, and yield 47,700 tons of cotton each year in the value of IL 36 million thus supplying the demands of the large domestic textile industry. Israel's yield of cotton, corn, tomatoes and nuts is the highest per acre in the world. Next to citrus fruits, eggs and cotton, ground nuts, covering 12,000 acres, have become Israel's most important agricultural export item. In one recent year, sugar beets, grown on 14,000 acres, yielded 221,000 tons of sugar, worth IL 12 million.

Milch cow herds increased from 19,000 head in 1948 to 72,000 in 1963, and their milk yield is the highest per cow in the world. Israel's beef cattle and poultry are sufficient to provide all the country's meat requirements. Israelis are not big meat eaters. Due to the poultry and egg glut, chicken has become a staple in the Israeli diet.

Sheep multiplied from 20,000 head in 1948 to 188,-000 in 1963. Israel's fish catch is 16,000 tons a year. Israel produces 359,000 kilolitres of milk, 1,273 million eggs, 28,000 tons of beef and mutton, and 66,000 tons of poultry annually. Each year, too, she harvests 300,000 tons of industrial crops, 156,000 tons of cereals, 1,668,-000 tons of forage, 392,000 tons of vegetables and potatoes, 208,000 tons of fruit, 527,000 tons of citrus fruit, and 84,000 tons of melon.

This is the harvest of the land of milk and honey, achieved by the drainage of swamps, the removal of heavy rocks, the conquest of the sand dunes and the constant search for untapped sources of water.

That the soil of Israel can now supply the needs of a nation whose population has quadrupled within a decade and a half is due to the labor and devotion of the farmers who toil each day beneath the burning semi-tropical sun, to the efficient use which the kibbutz and moshav have made of their land, machines, manpower and knowledge, to the planning of Moshe Dayan and other ministers of Agriculture, who stabilized farm production, prices and manage the distribution of the surplus, to the ceaseless study of scientists and agricultural experts, and last but not least to the Jewish Agency which, with the help of funds supplied by the United Jewish Appeal, is financing the resettlement of newcomers from the world over. Each of these factors has truly helped turn the wilderness into a modern-day land of milk and honey.

# CHAPTER VII

## CENTER OF CULTURE IN THE MIDDLE EAST

If you were in Israel during the 1961-62 winter season, you were often asked, "Did you hear the Ninth?" If you were a baseball fan fresh from New York, you might have thought you were being asked about the ninth-inning score of the World Series. But in all likelihood the "Ninth" your inquirer meant was the Ninth Symphony by Ludwig van Beethoven which was played by the Israel Philharmonic Orchestra (I.P.O) as part of its twenty-fifth anniversary concerts that season in Tel Aviv's sparkling new Frederick Mann Auditorium.

To a music-loving people whose cultural roots go back thousands of years, the quarter-century milestone of the symphony orchestra of its old-new Homeland was as exciting as any World Series is to the lover of baseball in the United States. There are 28,000 season ticket holders all over Israel who regard their precious pasteboard cards as family heirlooms to be passed on to future generations. They make the I.P.O. self-supporting.

The Mann Auditorium seats "only" 3,000, but the Israel Philharmonic presents identical programs five or six times in Tel Aviv, twice in Jerusalem and twice in

Haifa for season subscribers, plus supplementary series and special performances with opera and ballet companies and guest artists from abroad for the general public. Each advertisement of open ticket sales brings long box office lines and almost immediate sellouts.

The audiences today appear in formal or semiformal dress, with an odd sprinkling of tieless, sweater-clad kibbutzniks and also soldiers, policemen and members of *HeN*, Israel's women's army auxiliary, in their khaki uniforms.

The story of the I.P.O., as the orchestra is affectionately known throughout the land, is closely interwoven with the turbulent annals of the State of Israel itself.

Originally conceived in the persevering mind of the late great European concert violinist Bronislaw Huberman, the I.P.O. arose in 1936 out of that tragic turn in our history which made refugees of some of the world's most brilliant Jewish composers, concert artists and musicians. Huberman strove mightily, as he put it, to "match the desire of the country (then Palestine) for an orchestra with the desire of European musicians for a country."

During his concert tours that took him all over the world, Huberman found time to write some 10,000 letters, personally enlisting for his project the support of lovers and patrons of music and of no less a performing artist than the late Arturo Toscanini, whom he lured to Tel Aviv to conduct the orchestra's memorable inaugural concert on December 26, 1936.

When the Italian perfectionist of the concert platform came to Israel — then Palestine — to meet the Palestine Orchestra, as it was then known, he was confronted by an agglomeration of concert artists from all over Europe. How were these many talents to be welded into one united orchestra?

The first rehearsal was preceded by well-nigh unendurable tension. Toscanini mounted the podium. "Brahms Second Symphony, Second Movement," he rapped out, and led the newly-organized orchestra through the work. When they were finished, the musicians cowered in terrified silence, waiting for the maestro's verdict.

"Not bad," Toscanini told them. "Not bad at all." Coming from Toscanini, this was praise indeed. The citizens of the then small town of Tel Aviv and music lovers from other parts of Palestine literally fought for tickets. The opening concert in the converted exhibition hall on the Levant Fair Grounds near the port of Tel Aviv was ecstatically applauded by an audience of 3,000 which called its new idol back time and again for standing ovations.

The Yishuv took the Palestine Philharmonic to its heart. More than 15,000 persons heard Toscanini conduct his first series of concerts in Palestine. The maestro took the all-Jewish orchestra to Cairo for the first of many concert tours of Egypt, Syria and Lebanon which were regular events until the War of Independence put an end to this musical neighborliness.

Neither Arab riots, nor World War II, nor the struggle against the British and the final battle for independence in 1948 could stop the Palestine Philharmonic. The orchestra never missed a concert except in 1948 when the mountain road to Jerusalem was cut off. Many times the players traveled to their engagements in armored trucks and were shot at by the Arabs.

During World War II, the Palestine Philharmonic gave a total of 168 concerts for the British forces in the Middle East, often at desert outposts in North Africa.

On May 14, 1948, when Ben-Gurion had finished reading the final words of Israel's Proclamation of Independence at the Tel Aviv Museum, the Israel Philharmonic Orchestra was also present in the historic chamber and greeted the new State with a moving rendition of *Hatikvah*, while tears coursed down the faces of the signers of the Proclamation.

When Israel went to war to safeguard her independence, the orchestra went out to the battle lines to play for the army of the Jewish State. In May 1948, Izler Solomon, conductor of the Columbus (Ohio) Symphony Orchestra, volunteered to conduct a front-line concert of the Israel Philharmonic. He received the first visa to be issued by the State of Israel. On the night of the battle for Lod Airport, Solomon led the orchestra in an outstanding performance at a military camp. In his audience were troops who, only hours later, were to capture this important center of communications. Leonard Bernstein directed the orchestra in an open-air concert in Beersheba for thousands of soldiers of the Negev Desert Command.

Arturo Toscanini and Bronislaw Huberman set a precedent for the world's greatest performers and guest conductors to include Eretz Yisrael in their concert itinerary. To list all those artists who followed the maestro's lead would mean to cite a veritable *Who's Who* of the musical world.

The dedication of the Mann Auditorium in Tel Aviv in 1957 was the start of a new era for the Israel Philharmonic, since the huge concert hall enabled additional crowds of Tel Avivians to hear the orchestra and its famed guest artists in their own city. Popular subscription concerts were inaugurated to enable workers in the lower wage brackets to enjoy the I.P.O. Nowadays, the orchestra gives one concert a month for the Israeli Army.

On its first tour of the United States in 1951, the Israel Philharmonic gave 54 concerts in 40 cities in eleven weeks, and was acclaimed throughout the country as one of the world's finest symphony orchestras. As Leonard Bernstein and the late Serge Koussevitsky opened the concerts with *Hatikvah* and the *Star-Spangled Banner,* many in the audiences wept.

In 1954, the Israel Philharmonic toured Europe, giving a total of 43 concerts in nine countries. It was in 1955 that the orchestra was summoned on one day's notice from Genoa to Rome to play part of Beethoven's Seventh Symphony at the Vatican Consistorium Hall. Attired in white tie and "tails," the 99 members of Israel's symphony orchestra performed for a distinguished audience of two — the late Pope Pius XII and the priest who attended him. Afterwards the Pope thanked the orchestra, talked to some of the musicians, posed for a picture with them, and then retired, leaving an aide to distribute Papal medallions to the performers.

The orchestra's program notes recalled that this special Papal concert resulted in large turnouts of Catholic Church dignitaries and laymen at subsequent I.P.O. performances throughout Europe.

In 1960 the I.P.O. went abroad again, on a world tour this time, giving 48 performances in Europe, North and South America, India and Japan.

Since 1936, the number of musicians in the orchestra has grown from 72 to 99. Twenty-four of the original members are still with the I.P.O. Fifteen have passed away, in addition to Huberman, the founder, who died in 1947. Today, nearly one-third of the orchestra is Israel-born or Israel-trained.

In order to promote the serious study of music and to encourage new talent, the Israel Philharmonic provides a dozen scholarships annually to gifted young musicians, commissions new compositions, arranges competitions, performs new Israeli-composed symphonies at home and abroad, and invites promising Israeli soloists to make their debuts with the orchestra. Young pianists such as Pnina Salzmann, Frank Pelleg, Varda Nishri, David Bar-Ilan and Daniel Barenboim went on from the I.P.O. to world-wide renown. Members of the orchestra are among the outstanding music teachers of the country.

Joseph Krips, conductor of the San Francisco Symphony Orchestra, and one of the Israeli orchestra's guest conductors, penned this tribute to the I.P.O.:

"You have really made music your life and not your profession; you give your heart and you get the hearts of people listening to you or working with you. . . . even your best performance is a step only to a still better one. And that's what makes you great — ability, devotion and ceaseless work. God bless you!"

The Israel Philharmonic sets the symphonic style for the Jewish State and has prompted the organization of many smaller ensembles, But the story of this symphony orchestra is by no means all there is to music in the Land of the Bible.

Kol Yisrael, the Government-sponsored radio station, of which I will talk in greater detail toward the end of this chapter, supports a symphony orchestra of its own which brings the classics as well as new Israeli compositions into 400,000 homes.

The Haifa Symphony Orchestra aspires to challenge I.P.O.'s leadership and brings its concerts to people living in the outlying settlements of the North.

The Combined Kibbutz Orchestra plays to kibbutzim throughout the country.

The Army has its own symphony orchestra, as does Gadna, the pre-military youth organization, which made a triumphant American tour. Even the police boasts of a band which performs to audiences in immigrant settlements; its repertory consists mainly of folk music.

Ramat Gan, a suburb of Tel Aviv, has a chamber music ensemble which has encouraged such "home" talent as the composers Paul Ben-Haim, Yehezkel Braun,

Ben-Zion Orgad, Nahum Sherif, Oedoen Partos, Joseph Tal, Mordecai Seter, Hanoch Jacoby, Menahem Avidom, Marc Lavry, Karl Salomon, Erich Sternberg and A. U. Boskovitch.

Choral groups are much in demand in Israel. Each year the country plays host to the *Zimriya*, a jamboree of singers from all over the world. At a recent *Zimriya*, nineteen Israeli groups and twelve choirs from abroad — over 800 voices, all told — gave twelve performances in the Mann Auditorium. Folk songs in many languages including Hebrew and Yiddish, of course, were presented by groups of all ages from Israel, the United States, England, France, Denmark, Finland, Italy, Holland, Switzerland and Yugoslavia. The choir from Yugoslavia, while representing the Jewish community of Zagreb, included a number of Gentile singers.

Musicals, operettas, ballets, jazz and rock-and-roll from abroad have found enthusiastic audiences in Israel.

The premiere of the New York Metropolitan Opera's production of "Cosi Fan Tutti," with a $6.50 top, drew a sparkling throng of Tel Aviv society as well as members of the Cabinet, the Diplomatic Corps and government officials. Conducting the Israel Philharmonic that night was Thomas Schippers, an artist still in his early thirties. The cast included Gloria Davy, the first Negro star of the Metropolitan Opera Company, Rosalind Elias, Cesare Valletti, Gimi Beni, Laurel Hurley, and Armand Ralph McLane who, I am told, has a Jewish wife and once sang cantorial melodies in Brooklyn.

Israel also has its own national opera company, which was brought into existence by the dedicated Edis de Philippe. But this newcomer to the musical scene is still handicapped by lack of sufficient funds, as is Haifa's Symphony Orchestra, many of whose members miss rehearsals because of other jobs they must hold in order to make ends meet. The America-Israel Cultural Foundation supplies partial financial assistance to the country's major musical ensemble as well as to the orchestra and bands organized by schools and settlements throughout Israel.

*    *    *

I sat in Tel Aviv's Mograbi Theatre and watched in fascination as the Inbal dancers portrayed the story of Ruth. And I had a feeling of being moved backward in time over thousands of years into the days of the Bible.

If there is any people on earth that preserved the customs and art forms of the ancient Hebrews, it is the Yemenites, one of whose gifted daughters — the fiery, inspired Sara Levi-Tanai — has single-handedly created and developed the world-renowned Inbal Dance Theatre.

Entranced and captivated by the delicate, refined spirituality of the Yemenite dance, and the haunting strains of ancient synagogue music blended with tunes from the Orient and from Spain, I commented to Sara Levi-Tanai that her people seemed to be the true bearers of the tradition of our ancestors who worshipped at the Temple of Jerusalem. For many centuries, the Yemenite Jews were virtually cut off from all outside influence excepting that of their Arab neighbors. Left almost untouched by the march of civilization beyond the confines of their own little world, the Yemenites, for a hundred generations, maintained with hardly any change an inward, pious way of life which centered about their little synagogues. The men, before and after work, devoted their spare time to prayer and study. Their daily life was permeated with the Word of God, and they would discuss the Tora and debate its commentaries without end. Even their dances expressed the ecstatic love of the Yemenite for the Tora.

The Yemenite woman mixed more freely than the menfolk with their Arab neighbors in the market place. From them, they learned Arabic love songs, and gradually the strains of these romantic tunes crept into the liturgical melodies of their husbands and sons.

Living in perpetual fear of massacres at the hands of the Arabs in whose midst they lived, the Jews of Yemen had to do their singing and dancing in tiny, crowded homes and synagogues, quietly and unobtrusively so as not to arouse the wrath of their hostile neighbors. This is the reason why Yemenite dance movements are so restrained and confined to hand and leg gestures and body twists, culminating characteristically in a raising of cupped hands as if in eloquent supplication to almighty God.

Inbal, which was founded in Jerusalem in 1949, literally removed the Yemenite song and dance from the deep-freeze in which it had been preserved for two thousand years, and resurrected it for the twentieth-century world.

The Yemenite troupers have won the acclaim of audiences and critics throughout America, Europe and the Far East. The world's approval of Inbal has greatly enhanced the pride of the Yemenites in their culture. But to Sara Levi-Tanai, Inbal's iron-willed creator and director, the daily work of creation and rehearsal means much more than acclaim from the press or the public. Presently, Mrs. Levi-Tanai is waging a one-woman struggle against those popular movements and critics who would distort the work of her troupe into hora-whirling and ballet-copying conformity with the "modern" taste.

While Inbal is appreciated particularly by the Tel Aviv intelligentsia and the outlying kibbutzim, villages, settlements and army camps, it is received with a good deal less enthusiasm by the average young person and the European-born Ashkenazim who prefer the classical ballet, Martha Graham's modern dance, or the latest Israeli folklore groups. Inbal's difficulty in capturing the hearts of the European-born Ashkenazis is symptomatic of the chasm that separates Oriental music and art from Western culture.

This does not seem to cause great concern among the critics in Israel. Yohanan Boehm, music critic on the staff of the *Jerusalem Post,* wrote: "There is nothing wrong in this (difference); the clash between European schools and Oriental music may yield some exciting results." Boehm sees new musical forms arising as Israeli composers are inspired by the encounter of cultures to write fresh and original creations that will be indigenous to the Land of the Bible.

I rode with the Inbal company in their bus to Kfar Saba where an audience acclaimed "The Story of Ruth" with enthusiasm. Teen-age sabra girls tittered around the stage door waiting for Inbal's singing and dancing star, Itamar Cohen, to emerge.

Overseas audiences are no less enthusiastic. The Jewish community of Winnipeg, Canada, lionized members of the troupe at home parties and, at midnight, the Jews turned out one hundred strong to see the company off at the railway station. Alexander Kroll, Russian-born manager of Inbal, likes to tell the story of an Inbal fan in Winnipeg who, swept off his feet by the troupe's performance in his city, boarded a plane and flew west to Edmonton to see the same show again the next night.

All this world-wide acclaim does not turn the head of Sara Levi-Tanai. The sabra daughter of Yemenite immigrants who came to Jerusalem half a century ago, Mrs. Levi-Tanai said she would rather work with her young singers, dancers and musicians in her basement studio in a Tel Aviv apartment house than tour the world.

"Here, I am able to create," she said as she tore herself reluctantly away from the rehearsal of "The Story of Ruth." "On tour, I feel out of my element."

An intense, handsome, middle-aged little woman with strong features and tanned skin, Mrs. Levi-Tanai spoke to me in English, acting out everything she said with gestures from the dances that are part of her very life. She began her career as a teacher in a kindergarten where she taught children the dances of the Yemenites. Inbal started with a small group of young Yemenites in Jerusalem soon after the War of Independence in 1948.

I asked Mrs. Levi-Tanai whether her family had approved of worldly entertainment such as the theater.

"My father and I were a thousand years apart," she replied. "But when I saw him dance and sing with the Scroll of the Law on *Simhat Tora,* I beheld the roots whence I came." She proceeded to demonstrate how the Yemenite Jews dance with the Tora as with the love of their youth.

"I always loved the theater," she mused. "It took me many years to discover myself. I decided that I wanted to be in the theater. And I want this Yemenite theater to express fully what is in me. It was a slow process which still goes on. But I am sure where I want to go. I know very well — too well — what I want. And no one will turn me aside from my chosen path.

"What is it I want? I want to express myself as an artist, I want to express myself as a Jew, and I want to express myself as a Yemenite, and as an Oriental. What is most important for me is that I should be able to express my ideals through the dance and the theater. And if the theater is good, it is good for Israel. If it is genuine and has true merit, it will live on as a form of art long after I am gone. And others will come along and continue it as part of the artistic and cultural life of Israel."

As Mrs. Levi-Tanai sees it, Inbal has an important part in the integration of the Ingathering, in the process of acculturation of the Jews from the Oriental countries into the new State of Israel.

"I want to see a true integration of the Orientals and the Ashkenazim," she said. "But not at the expense of the rich culture which the Oriental Jews have brought with them. At present, the Ashkenazim, the Jews from Europe, are dominant nearly everywhere in our country. Inbal represents the one way in which the people of Israel can be shown the wealth of charm, beauty, refinement and spirituality that is contained in the culture of the Yemenites. But before the Jews from the Orient will be able to depict their culture to the Europeans, they must first truly know and understand it themselves. Our Oriental people do not really know what they have."

"The Story of Ruth" represents a new trend in Inbal's development. Until recently, Inbal performed only programs consisting of groups of Yemenite works. With "The Story of Ruth" and its immediate predecessors — "The Song of Deborah" and "The Yemenite Wedding" Inbal has gone into theatrical ballets with a central theme.

"We find new things every day — new movements and steps, tunes and tones, rhythms and instruments, costumes and ornaments. The unveiling of historical sources serves to whet the imagination and enriches creativity," said Sara Levi-Tainai.

A group with a profound sense of religion, Inbal approaches the challenge of interpreting a story from the Bible with a good deal of trepidation, dedication to detail, and a real sense of responsibility. In each composition the Biblical version is closely adhered to.

"Our ear is attuned to the words and sounds, and our eye is receptive to the images and the visions that are contained in the pages of the old-new Book," the program notes state. "We cannot say that the Bible makes our task an easy one. The work is difficult and exacting, arduous and elusive, but it exerts a pull on us with the beauty, delicacy and warmth which pervades the subject. In 'The Story of Ruth' we followed closely the original love story which enchants all by its charm and simplicity."

The choreography of the performance, on the other hand, created by Mrs. Levi-Tanai and Anna Sokolow of New York, reveals the effect of the new, free atmosphere of Israel on the tradition of the Yemenite dance.

Three athletic young Yemenites leaped about the Mograbi's stage with an abandon unheard-of in their former home.

"When we came to Israel," Sara Levi-Tanai explained, "We felt free. We no longer feel bound to the constricted culture of our Yemenite forefathers. And we want to express this freedom by action. We blossom forth. We no longer need to dance in narrow spaces and be quiet for fear of our neighbors. Our movements are no longer shackled by fright. So we spread our arms outward now rather than only upward to heaven, and we fly off in every direction. We are free. And yet, we keep the spiritual and traditional element as our basis, for our tradition is rich and spiritual and expresses the true beauty of Jewishness, the modesty of our women. Only here we have more air and space and freedom."

I asked her whether the Yemenite dance as performed today really had its origins in the days of the Bible. "We can't be sure, of course," Mrs. Levi-Tanai replied. "But we believe it did. Of course, this is just an assumption, but I believe it is indeed so."

Mrs. Levi-Tanai spoke of the modern trends and controversies in the Israeli art world. "No one knows just what is Israeli art. I feel I am an Israeli artist. And I feel I am an Oriental and a Jew. I can't rid myself of the feeling that I am an Oriental. I am a Jew. I am an Israeli. I feel this countryside of ours and I feel that a strong, rich Jewish tradition must be the foundation for every Jewish artist. To begin with, the Jewish artist has to feel Jewish. And a Jewish artist who is an Israeli and also an Oriental has much to give. This special Oriental-

Jewish-Israeli art form has a right to be recognized. We will make our contribution to the building of an Israeli culture. We have our treasures. Thus far other Oriental groups — those from North Africa, for instance — still don't identify with us. But I already see Inbal as an exponent of Oriental art, music and dance. Inbal as it is now is only the beginning. If we can discover the true artists among our Oriental peoples and bring them out to the public, Inbal will realize the great potential which it holds."

\* \* \*

The theater plays an important role in Israel. Most outstanding among the country's theatrical companies is *HaBima*. Fast-growing rivals are the dynamic *Ohel* and *Zuta* theatres. Recently, a new, modernistic theater building was dedicated in Haifa, on the slope of apartment-house-studded Mount Carmel.

In *El-Hamam,* a centuries-old Turkish bath in Jaffa, Hayim Hefer played a leading role in a controversial night club show — which he wrote himself — lampooning Israel's Arab minority. This production set off a heated controversy among knowledgeable theatregoers.

A Polish-born impresario by the name of Yosifon, who directs Histadrut's *Telem* shows in immigrant settlements, accused Hayim Hefer of characterizing the Arabs as illiterate and childish, and portraying them as sensualists, wife-beaters and homosexuuls.

Hefer, a Polish-born *Palmah* veteran who is regarded as an authentic interpreter of the Israeli spirit, contended that his sketches were not meant to attack the Arabs but were aimed solely at Jewish complacency vis-à-vis the Arab problem in the State of Israel. His sketch, he explained, poked fun at the Israeli military government and its planned attempt to educate the Arabs so that they may get a better understanding of Jewish ideals. While the debate wore on, audiences of two to three hundred young people filled El-Hamam every night at IL 2.50 per ticket.

\* \* \*

The People of the Book revere every form of literature. The business districts of Tel Aviv, Jerusalem and Haifa are full of bookstores and news kiosks. No other country with a population of 2,500,000 can match Israel's array of 25 daily newspapers with headlines screaming in black and red from newsstands, side by side with a host of weekly and monthly journals, Israeli and foreign, in virtually every language, catering to the varied tastes of a truly cosmopolitan population drawn from every continent.

Deserving authors and publishers receive help from the America-Israel Cultural Foundation, which gives support not only to musical projects but also to such varied cultural undertakings as museums, art galleries, art colonies, literary associations and archaeological publications.

Some cynics say that Israeli culture is a "cinema culture." It is true that the motion picture theatre enjoys considerable popularity in the country. Movie fans line up for tickets hours in advance in front of the box offices of 24 cinemas in Tel Aviv, fourteen in Haifa, thirteen in Jerusalem, and in nearly every village. These theatres offer shows from many lands, but the most popular, of course, are from the make-believe world of Hollywood. Hollywood seems to be the source of ideas and ideals, values and knowledge — good, bad and indifferent — for young Israelis.

There is even a "beat" culture, complete with beard-

ed boys and Bardot-coiffed girls. Israeli youth today —
particularly the sabras — seem to prefer the jazz music
from America to the marching songs of the Palmah.

*     *     *

Late every Friday afternoon, as the Sabbath approaches,
Kol Yisrael ("the Voice of Israel"), the government-op-
erated radio station, begins its Sabbath program with a
broadcast of the *Lekha Dodi,* the traditional hymn with
which Jews for centuries have ushered in the weekly
day of rest.

As mothers in thousands of homes prepare to light the
Sabbath candles and bless their children, the official
broadcasting station of the State of Israel carries the
Friday evening service, followed by folk songs, sermons,
Biblical discussions and liturgical chants. Thus the Is-
raeli radio brings the synagogue into the home.

Later, there is a recorded concert by Kol Yisrael's own
orchestra or the Israel Philharmonic.

Kol Yisrael broadcasts intermittently throughout the
day of rest, enriching the Sabbath atmosphere with Hebrew songs, synagogue music, concerts, operas, light classics and "music off the beaten track."

According to the Rabbinical interpretation of Jewish
law, the operations involved in transmitting broadcasts
and in turning on a radio come into the classification of
work forbidden on the Sabbath. Yet Israel's Orthodox rabbinate does not insist that Kol Yisrael remain off the air
on Friday night and Saturday. Instead, it tolerates this
"violation" of Rabbinic law because the operation of Kol
Yisrael on the Sabbath may well serve to save human
lives in an emergency, and the preservation of life super-
sedes even the law of Sabbath observance. In this little
country, surrounded by hostile Arab neighbors, the radio
is the only means of communication through which all

the people can be warned of surprise attacks which an enemy may well deliberately plan for the day when Israel is at rest.

Israel is still a country on the alert, where hourly newscasts put an abrupt stop to dinner party conversations or parlor chit-chat. Veteran Israelis have never forgotten the news bulletins of life-and-death importance that were broadcast by Kol Yisrael during the wars of 1948 and 1956.

The radio in Israel has a prominent place in the government's program of cultural integration for immigrants. Lessons in the Hebrew language are broadcast, as are programs in English, French, Rumanian, Hungarian, Polish, Spanish, Yiddish and Ladino to acquaint the newcomers from many different countries and backgrounds with the way of life of their new Homeland.

Short-wave programs are beamed at South America, South Africa and Europe. Some three hundred broadcasting stations in the United States carry transcriptions from Kol Yisrael programs.

Kol Yisrael broadcasts in Arabic to neighboring Moslem countries. These programs do not attempt to compete with the hysterical propaganda rantings carried by stations in Cairo, Damascus or Ramallah. Rather, they are designed to appeal to the thinking Moslem who secretly listens in to Jerusalem and Tel Aviv for factual accounts of what really goes on in the dis-United Arab Republic.

Probably the station's only real concession to government ownership is that news commentaries and documentary broadcasts refrain from criticizing the government's foreign policy even if they do not necessarily feel compelled to make statements in its support. Beyond that, the people insist that even though Kol Yisrael is operated by the government, it must retain its independence. In line with this attitude, Kol Yisrael's staff of veteran radio experts gives ample time to candidates of every political persuasion at election season. Its documentary crews tackle the most controversial and delicate political issues without regard for government policy, presenting both sides — or all sides — of every question of current interest. A recent engineers' strike was analyzed from every conceivable angle. Kol Yisrael tape recorders were taken into Jerusalem's ultra-Orthodox Mea Shearim district to ferret out the views of the Neture Karta which still refuses to recognize the State of Israel. An interview with Rabbi Amram Blau, the leader of this splinter group, and his family, was broadcast by the station uncensored, complete with the blasts of Blau and his extremist followers at the State and the Government of Isreal.

The Israeli Army has its own radio station — *Gale Tzahal* — whose evening broadcasts draw many young civilian listeners.

The radio commercial has not yet found a firm foothold in Israel. Kol Yisrael is supported by fees paid by radio set owners ($7.50 per year). In a recent experiment, some advertising was accepted in order to support light programs. This step elicited a warning from the *Jerusalem Post* that "we need more and brighter radio, but not at the expense of setting our national sights low. The answer (to this need) is not to (seek to) appeal to the lowest common denominator, but to develop and expand broadcasting that entertains as well as educates and is free from both the soft and the hard sell which accompany cheap music, vulgar songs and 'gimmick shows'."

What impact will television have when it comes to the Holy Land?

UNESCO, asked to make recommendations with regard to the establishment of a TV station in Israel, proposed the appointment of an independent television authority responsible to the Israeli government. The cost

of the organization as envisioned by UNESCO was estimated at over $3,000,000, operating expenses at $1,593,-
760 per year. The UNESCO research staff has established
that the Israelis do want television and would be willing to pay the taxes and license fees to support the station which will be educational and non-commercial.

According to the UNESCO report, Israelis have an
aversion to the introduction of such programs as "The
Untouchables" and "Route 66" which they consider horrible, and to the dissemination of murder, violence, sex
and mayhem that is one of the less desirable features
of American television programming.

My own bet for top rating is a program which had an
avid audience even before television was seriously considered in Israel, a broadcast which supplies a type of
suspense all its own. I mean, of course, "The Bible Quiz."

# CHAPTER VIII

# "KULTURKAMPF"

On the gentle slopes of Har Shalom — "Hill of Peace" — just thirty minutes by bus from cosmopolitan Tel Aviv, is the city of Bene Berak. Atop the hill, overlooking the Mediterranean Sea to the west and the Judean hills to the east, stands the impressive edifice of the Yeshiva of Ponevezh. This institution of higher Talmudic studies is a symbol of the spirit that predominates in Bene Berak. Nearly three-fourths of the city's population of 60,000, including the mayor, is Orthodox.

On the Sabbath, beginning with twilight Friday, an atmosphere of peace and tranquility descends on Har Shalom. Until after sundown on Saturday, Bene Berak is fenced off by chains, barriers and guards from the busy traffic of the main highway which links Tel Aviv and Petah Tikva, and there is not one truck or car, or even a bicycle, to mar the day of rest in the streets of the city. On the Sabbath, the people of Bene Berak move about on foot.

By mid-morning of a Saturday, the streets of Bene Berak are crowded with Sabbath strollers, and with Hassidim returning from their synagogues, enveloped in their long, fringed prayer-shawls. The Hassidim are garbed in full Sabbath dress: silken black kaftans and fur *shtreimels*, the headgear adopted by their ancestors from seventeenth-century nobles in Eastern Europe. There are slight variations in this attire depending on the allegiances of the wearer. The Hassidic *rebbes* of the European Jewish communities of Ponevezh, Satmar, Vishnitz, Ger, Lubavitch and Bobov each have disciples in Israel, who have set up yeshivot and synagogues of their own in the new Jewish State. Sporting more colorful Sabbath garb are the "Orientals" from Yemen, Tripoli, Morocco and Iraq. The streets in which they mingle with their brethren from the world over are named after the prophets, rabbis and Talmudic sages who have left their mark on the history of the Jewish people.

Bene Berak's Mayor Reuben Aronowicz, a bearded scholar who lives modestly in a one-family house in back of the farm of Meir and Cilla Goldberg, survivors of Eichmann's death factories, estimates that the population of his city is 70 per cent Ashkenazi, and thirty per cent "Oriental." He told me that at least 70 per cent of the people of Bene Berak are religious, and that the city had well over a hundred synagogues and *shtiebels* (prayer rooms).

I talked to the Mayor about the religious conflict between the observant and the non-observant of Israel, in which some see the dangerous beginnings of a *kulturkampf*, a war for supremacy between two cultures, two philosophies of life. Reuben Aronowicz did not seem alarmed. "Eventually peace will come in Israel between the religious and non-religious, and between the Ashkenazim and the Orientals," he said. "Bene Berak is an example of how all people can live together in peace. Of course, it will take time, patience and understanding, but all the Jews here basically want to be Jews, and those who are not religious now will return to religion in time." He was not disturbed by reports of pressure from non-Orthodox elements in Israel for changes in Rabbinic law and for restrictions on the role of Rabbinical courts in the country. "That's just Nelson Glueck [President of the Hebrew Union College — Jewish Institute of Religion, the seminary for Reform rabbis in the United States] talking. There'll be no change in the law."

Mayor Aronowicz disapproves of the tactics of the extremist Neture Karta, who seek to enforce religious observance by acts of violence, such as hurling rocks at automobiles attempting to pass through Bene Berak on the Sabbath. "That's not the right way," he said. "We may shout 'Shabbos' at the drivers of cars passing by on the main highway, but we certainly won't throw stones at them." On the other hand, he refuses to stamp the entire extremist group as meshugo'im, a "lunatic fringe."

"They are very pious," he said, "and they are extreme in their views. But some of them are very wise." The Neture Karta, whose members reside mainly in the Mea Shearim section of Jerusalem, refuse to recognize a Jewish State not established by the Messiah. The group will not accept Hebrew as a language for everyday use, and its schools teach in Yiddish. Its leader, Rabbi Amram Blau, brands Zionism as disobedience to God, and the official Chief Rabbinate as clerical minions of the State of Israel who are spreading a false doctrine.

\* \* \*

"The kulturkampf is already on in Israel," said Dr. Zerah Warhaftig, Israel's Minister of Religions. "A kulturkampf, you know, is not necessarily fought out with sticks and fists," he said. "But it is a fight just the same and it is going on here right now."

When I asked him to define the aims of the religious, the Polish-born lawyer, who is a lay leader in Mizrahi-

HaPoel HaMizrahi, Israel's strongest religious party, replied: "The religious believe that the State of Israel should embody a fulfillment of Jewish tradition in everyday life." The development of any other way of life in the Jewish State, he said, would be tantamount to "the creation of a new tradition which would be contrary to the law of the Tora."

At least to one not so pious, Dr. Warhaftig appeared to be using the term *kulturkampf* rather loosely. David Ben-Gurion bent all his efforts to averting the dreaded "clash between the cultures" and few among the non-Orthodox would be as quick as Dr. Warhaftig to assert that Israel is in the midst of a *kulturkampf* right now.

Any *kulturkampf* going on, the non-Orthodox maintain, is a strictly one-sided battle fought by the religious leadership. The general public has no desire to fight about religion. By and large, the vast amorphous non-Orthodox majority of Israelis does not worry excessively about the role of religious law in the State. There are, of course, instances when the non-religious Israeli feels the authority of the Rabbinical courts interfering in his personal life, as when he is refused permission to marry the woman of his choice on the basis of Biblical law because he is a Kohanite and she is a divorcée. But except in such relatively rare cases, where they affect him personally, the non-Orthodox Israeli does not consider Rabbinical restrictions infringements on his freedom to live as he pleases. Restrictions on public transportation on the Sabbath disturb only the poor. While the cooperatively-owned bus systems and the State-operated railway do not run from sundown Friday until sunset Saturday, it is possible to travel almost anywhere on the Sabbath by *sherut* (jitney cab), private taxicab or automobile. These non-public forms of transportation are convenient and efficient, and although fares are higher than on public vehicles, the thousands of Israelis who travel on the

Shabbat — their only day of rest in the week — do not find the additional expense prohibitive today. Kashrut is a matter of personal choice. It is not a subject of acrimonious debate. With meat as expensive as it is in Israel, most Israelis concentrate on fish, vegetables, cheese and fruit that are available in plenty in the stores and supermarkets.

Deputy Premier Abba Eban feels that the non-observant Jew scarcely notices the minor restrictions imposed on his way of living by such laws as those of Sabbath observances. And even if he does, he still willingly submits to them for the sake of continued peace in Israel. At a time when mass immigration and the Arab threat create ample complications, the non-observant, by and large, do not wish to bring added trouble to the new State. The League to Prevent Religious Coercion in Israel, led by Prof. Rom Moav, a veteran of the War of 1948, receives little organized support. Although he is outspoken in his opposition to the law compelling Israelis to accept Rabbinical jurisdiction in matters of marriage and divorce, which he feels discriminates against women, Moav himself, who teaches botany at the Hebrew University, admits that he has little liking for political activity and public demonstrations. He has repelled a number of potential followers by his insistence that civil marriages and pig-breeding be officially permitted in Israel.

Fighting a lone *kulturkamp* against Prof. Moav is Rabbi Shelomo Lorincz, a representative of the Orthodox Agudath Israel party in the Knesset, who said, "We should have a League to Prevent *Anti*-Religious Coercion, because it's anti-religious coercion, not religious coercion, that's the trouble in Israel."

Dr. Warhaftig believes that the influx of religious immigrants from the Oriental countries, combined with the influence of various Orthodox elements still arriving from Europe, is lending added strength to the religious movement in Israel. But the trouble is that, despite the piety they hold in common, the religious "Orientals" and the Orthodox Ashkenazim are kept apart by differences in custom, ritual and cultural background, so that the Orthodox leaders in Israel, who are predominantly of Eastern European origin, frequently find themselves unable to get much help from the "Orientals" in strengthening religion in the Jewish State.

Dr. Warhaftig stressed the great need for rabbis and religious teachers in the immigrant towns of the Negev, where anywhere from sixty to ninety per cent of the population is of Oriental origin.

Dr. Warhaftig has little use for efforts to introduce Reform Judaism into Israel. "A Jew can't be 'more' or 'less' Orthodox," he insisted, and suggested that if the Reform movement in America or elsewhere should feel a desire to strengthen religion in Israel it could do so by giving support to existing religious — meaning, of course, Orthodox — institutions there. The religious problem in Israel, he felt, simply boils down to the question of belief or lack thereof. Defining Reform Judaism as a product of assimilation, he asserted that there is no room for assimilation in the Jewish state. He spoke with pride of the 12,000 students now attending a total of 185 yeshivot in Israel, whom he regards as future pioneers in the field of religious education.

\*   \*   \*

Rabbi Maurice A. Jaffe, executive vice-chairman of Hekhal Shelomo, the Chief Rabbinate's religious center in Jerusalem, told me that he did not see the religious issue in Dr. Warhaftig's terms of a "clash between cultures." In his opinion, religion is on the upsurge in Israel. Israelis of all ages, walks of life and national backgrounds, he asserted, are turning to religion to fill a "vacuum" in their lives. He attributes this development to general disillusionment with Communism, to the search for moral values in a strife-torn world, to a quest for human dignity after the Nazi insult to humanity, and to the growing number of Orthodox immigrants from the Oriental countries.

Rabbi Jaffe spoke of the demand for additional synagogues throughout the country, including requests for synagogues from hitherto "irreligious" kibbutzim such as Ein Harod, Givat Brenner and Degania. He told me that Israel now has 6,000 to 7,000 synagogues, and another estimated total of 2,000 temporary places of worship during the High Holiday season. He estimates that 80 per cent of Israel's population attend religious services at least on Rosh Hashana and Yom Kippur. Israel has 100 religious settlements, Rabbi Jaffe reported, and there are in Israel a total of 50 high schools of religious orientation which he claimed could double their enrollment if they had the funds needed to double their classroom facilities. He recently visited the United States to enlist investments in the Hekhal Shelomo Foundation which gives sorely needed financial support to religious institutions in Israel.

The fact is that, in the Jewish State of today, the overwhelming majority of the population is not "religious" in terms of synagogue attendance and personal observance. But the Jewish holidays are observed throughout the country as national festivals so that the individual, even if he does not mark these occasions in accordance with religious practice, is still deeply conscious of his Jewishness.

"We don't have to go to the synagogue," the non-Orthodox maintain, "because we live the Jewish religion. We live in the land of the Bible, and we speak the Hebrew language. And while we may choose as individuals to travel or smoke or engage in sports on the

Sabbath, we do observe the Sabbath as our national day of rest."

Unlike the American Jew whose communal and social life frequently takes him to the synagogue and keeps him in touch with his rabbi even if he himself is not Orthodox, the average non-Orthodox Israeli Jew has little contact with the synagogue or members of the Rabbinate except when he is compelled to appear before a Rabbinical court on personal business such as marriage, divorce or inheritance. The rabbis in Israel, from the Chief Rabbis down, do not serve as leaders and spokesmen of the community, nor do they engage in debates on religious issues of substance, except to defend the religious *status quo* whenever it is challenged.

*     *     *

Israel's Chief Rabbinate is more liberal than many an Orthodox rabbi in the United States with regard to the interpretation of Jewish law concerning marriage and divorce.

One example of the willingness of Israel's rabbinate to interpret these laws of the Tora in such a manner as not to cause undue personal hardship and suffering is the way in which it has dealt with the problem of the *aguna,* the wife whose husband is missing and who cannot remarry until such time as she has met the specific requirements of Rabbinic law with regard to proof of her husband's death. Many presumed widows of men declared missing in wartime action or last seen in a Nazi concentration camp cannot contemplate remarriage because they cannot submit actual proof that their husbands are dead. In order to provide relief for these women within the framework of Rabbinic law, the Israeli rabbinate has resorted to a legal fiction based on Talmudic sources.

However, many Israelis feel that the Jewish law as

such is obsolete and are opposed in principle to the jurisdiction of the Rabbinate over such personal matters as marriage and divorce in the case of citizens who do not regard the laws of the Torah as binding. Knesset member Mrs. Beba Idelson declared in a recent Mapai campaign pamphlet that "this linking [of marriage and divorce to Rabbinical jurisdiction] raises an inconsistency between the status of the Israeli woman under the civil law and her traditional position in the Rabbinical court. The Rabbinical courts do not even consider seeking solutions for individual problems raised by present-day life such as marriages between Kohanites and divorcées, mixed marriages and marriages contracted before civil authorities. In the course of time, there will be basic changes in this area. The women of Mapai are particularly aware of this and demand thorough-going reforms..."

Divorce in Israel is not a rare phenomenon by any means. It is estimated that of 100 marriages in Tel Aviv, 25 end in divorce; so do between 15 and 20 out of 100 marriages in the rest of the country. Religious leaders attribute the high incidence of divorce in the Jewish State to hurried, ill-considered marriages between young people of widely divergent cultural and national backgrounds and to the "free spirit" of Israel. "Where religion has lost its hold on most people," they assert, "materialism takes the places of holiness. The wife may say, 'If you give me all I need, I'll be your wife. If not, I'll find someone else who can satisfy me.'"

"The sex code is changing all over the world," said Rabbi I. I. Rackovsky, a Jaffa attorney and counselor at Rabbinic law licensed to practice at the Rabbinical courts, "and Israel is part of that world. Had Israel kept its specific religious character, our values would be different from the constantly changing concepts in other countries."

When asked his views on Mrs. Idelson's plea for a

change in the religious status of women, Rabbi Rackovsky demanded: "Why should we change three thousand years of Jewish tradition for the benefit of two people who want to marry outside our Law?"

Chief Rabbi Issar Yehuda Unterman received me in his austere office in Tel Aviv's modernistic Bet Rabbanim. Warm, friendly and unassuming, Rabbi Unterman, who was born in Poland, held a pulpit in Liverpool, England, for twenty years before being called to the Chief Rabbinate of Tel Aviv. Eighteen years after his arrival in Israel, he was elected Ashkenazic Chief Rabbi of all Israel.

I posed to the Chief Rabbi the question which former Premier Ben-Gurion put to a convention of the Rabbinical Council of America in Israel, namely, how Jews, as citizens of the State of Israel, could live together on the basis of freedom of conscience as specified in the State's Proclamation of Independence which had been signed by all parties, from the extreme Orthodox Agudat Israel to the Communist group. How could the observant and the non-observant each live in keeping with their beliefs without giving offense to the Orthodox but also without placing restrictions on the freedom of the non-Orthodox?

While he declined to answer this question directly, since Ben-Gurion had not addressed it to him personally, the Chief Rabbi allowed that it was "quite possible to live in peace and to cooperate with non-religious elements on national, social and civic matters without friction."

"What people do in the privacy of their homes is no one else's affair," the Chief Rabbi told me. "If I have a non-religious neighbor who desecrates the Sabbath by cooking, smoking or engaging in work, I will not interfere with him. We will still be good neighbors and if I can help him I will do so willingly.

"However, our community is Jewish. We live in a Jewish State. Our nation claims that it is realizing the

Messianic hopes of the Jewish people. Therefore our Orthodox community would like to see that, in public life, our country should not offend the sensibilities of religious people and not create an atmosphere alien to religion. Whether or not a person goes to the synagogue is his private affair. But if he creates an alien atmosphere, that affects me directly. In Israel, we are entitled to a traditional Jewish atmosphere."

I discussed with Rabbi Unterman the decline of religious observance among the youth of the Oriental immigration wave. According to estimates of Sephardi religious leaders, 70 to 90 per cent of these young people are no longer Orthodox.

The Chief Rabbi blamed this wholesale defection on the fact that they had been "living in the religious atmosphere where they did not get the chance to develop an immunity to influences from a non-religious environment." Ashkenazi youngsters, the Chief Rabbi explained, are better able to resist these influences because, unlike the Orientals, their parents in Europe have had extensive experience in living in non-Jewish and non-religious environments.

Like Dr. Warhaftig, Rabbi Unterman deplored the lack of religious schools in immigrant towns and villages. He pointed out that where boys and girls from the Oriental countries attend religious schools, they have proven to be "devoted, religious Jews," capable of defending their beliefs in any situation.

"The members of the young generation promise to become devoted adherents to traditional Judaism," he said. "I am confident that within a decade, the religious situation will be much better than it is at present." He was certain that the youth of Israel will not find sports and games an adequate substitute for religion in the long run. The young people, Rabbi Unterman said, feel that without religion there is a void in their lives. Already the percentage of youth receiving their education in religiously-oriented schools is growing compared with that enrolling in the general, non-religious schools.

I asked the Chief Rabbi his views on "one hundred per cent or nothing" religion, or, more specifically, the charge of the non-religious in Israel that whereas in America and elsewhere, Jews can adopt Conservative or Reform Judaism if they do not feel at home in the Orthodox synagogue, the Israeli Jew has no other religious alternative but to remain within Orthodoxy.

"I think that is a healthy state of affairs," Rabbi Unterman replied. "Pseudo-religion would not be accepted in Israel." He was referring to the possibility of the introduction of Reform or Liberal Judaism in the Holy Land.

He told me of an American Reform rabbi who had admitted that, after a lifetime of service, all that he had achieved was to effect an easier transition to mixed marriages and assimilation.

"In America, Jews go to temple because the Gentiles go to church," the Chief Rabbi said. "But for us in Israel, the observance of our religion never depended on the religious practices of others."

My interview with Chief Rabbi Unterman took place on a Friday. That Sabbath was a sizzling summer day. I took a *sherut* (jitney cab) to the Bilu Synagogue on Tel Aviv's King George Avenue. There, in a well-filled, fairly modern house of worship, several hundred persons had gathered for Sabbath services. A Bar Mitzva boy led the entire service, accompanied by a fine boys' choir whose reverent rendition of the prayers seemed to justify the Chief Rabbi's faith in the coming generation.

Shmuel Baruch, Vice-President of the Religious Council of the metropolitan area of Tel Aviv-Yafo (population 400,000), told me that on an average Sabbath morning, 70,000 Jews in that area attend services in the city's 700 synagogues — an average attendance of 100 worshippers per synagogue. On Rosh HaShana and Yom Kippur, the estimated total attendance was 200,000.

*   *   *

One Friday night I was invited at a private home to a traditional Sabbath dinner. There were candles, a white tablecloth, and the host recited the *kiddush* over wine and *halla*. Also present were a young schoolteacher in her twenties and her thirteen-year-old sister. The girls had not been brought up in a religious atmosphere and did not consider ceremony imperative, but they admitted that, when they saw for the first time how beautiful *Erev Shabbat* could be in a Jewish home, they felt profound regret that their parents had failed to show them this aspect of Jewish living in their childhood.

"It's too late for us to return, Rabbi, but save our youngsters." This plea was voiced to Sephardi Chief Rabbi Yitzhaq Nissim by Shelomo Levi, a member of Kibbutz Ein Harod, when the rabbi visited that famed Mapai collective.

The members of Kibbutz Degania, Israel's oldest collective settlement, showed considerable interest in religious observance when members of the Rabbinical Council of America, in Israel for a convention, visited the kibbutz. Degania, which had not held a Sabbath service for fifteen years, arranged to participate in worship with the modern Orthodox rabbis from the United States, and the haverim cheerfully assisted the rabbis and their wives in preparations for the day of rest. In the discussion that ensued between the rabbis from America and the men and women of Degania, the members of this non-religious collective expressed pleasant surprise at the modern, clean-shaven, youthful American rabbis who wore bright sports shirts, carried cameras and were no different in dress and outer appearance from other tourists from the United States. "They don't look like rabbis," said the Mapainiks of Degania, who have been accustomed to associate the term "rabbi" only with the black-coated, bearded religious leaders of the Ashkenazi community.

"You see, it's not the synagogue that repels me," said one of the youths of Degania. "It's the people who stand behind the synagogue in Israel."

At Kibbutz Yagur, on the other hand, the haverim seemed as opposed as ever not only to Israel's religious leadership but also to religion as such. When I visited Yagur on a Friday night, I saw religion and ceremony shunted aside, observed only by a handful of aged parents in their own separate kosher dining room and in a little chamber set aside for prayer where a bare *minyan* out of a total population of 1,500 gathered to welcome the Sabbath.

As in other non-religious kibbutzim, Friday evening at Yagur differs from other nights only in that a movie is shown on an outdoor screen set up outside the communal dining hall. On Saturday morning, only the oldsters went to pray. The younger members who had no essential kibbutz chores to perform went off to the pool for a swim.

Israel Bar Yehuda, Minister of Transport and member of the Knesset since the founding of the State, has been a member of Yagur for over thirty years. That Saturday morning I asked him to define Yagur's attitude toward religion.

"Religion is fixed and unchanging," Bar Yehuda replied. "Religion implies blind belief, and we cannot accept that. We have our own ideals here at Yagur. We're trying to find more meaningful ways of living together as brothers, working for the common good, and building up the land."

Bar Yehuda, who is secretary of the Ahdut Ha'Avoda party, is among those who believe that basic changes are in the making in Israel's religious life. These changes, he asserts, will come about as the result of the increasing defection of young Orientals from traditional observance — and by 1975, these may well represent two-thirds of Israel's population — and the growing number of Sephardi rabbis in Israel who are more tolerant and flexible in their religious views than their Chief Rabbi Yitzhak Nissim.

Bar Yehuda recalled that, in dealing with certain religious problems as a member of Israel's Cabinet, he had occasion to make a study of religious rulings handed down by Sephardi rabbis. In the course of this research, he discovered that, as early as the seventeenth and eighteenth centuries, rabbis in the Oriental countries had actually attempted to modify traditional laws of marriage and divorce to meet the requirements of their times. He offered an interesting explanation for the difference between the attitude of these rabbis and the inflexibility of their Ashkenazi counterparts.

"Consider for a moment where the most fanatical rabbis come from," he said. "They come from Poland and Hungary, the European countries where the Catholic clergy was strongest and exercised an unyielding hold on the people. In the course of the centuries, the rabbis there took on the authoritarian spirit of the priesthood. But the Oriental rabbis come from the Moslem world where the clergy as well as the people were easy-going and individualistic in spirit. The Sephardi rabbis, therefore, were not influenced by authoritarian patterns of thinking, by the Moslem clergy, or by the Ashkenazi rabbis, with whom they had little contact."

\* \* \*

Rabbis and religious leaders in the Diaspora, Orthodox and Liberal alike, watch the development of religious life in Israel with interest and concern.

Dr. Moses H. Hoenig, a former president of the Orthodox National Council of Young Israel in the United States, has said that "there definitely is in Israel a religious awakening, a thirst for the Word of God, and this trend will become a full-scale movement if only Orthodox Jewry will know how to respond to this miraculous homecoming of its perplexed brethren to Tora and Judaism." In an issue of *Viewpoint,* Young Israel's organ, he called upon Orthodox leadership in Israel to stop the bickering within Orthodox parties over political issues which definitely will not serve to imbue youth with respect for religion; to introduce decorum and dignity into the synagogues of the Holy Land; to organize religious youth clubs which will create a climate and environment for a religious and spiritual revival and which will attract young people and intellectuals, and to establish contacts with American students at the Hebrew University and the Haifa Technion.

Rabbi Raphael Grossman of Long Branch, New Jersey, member of the Rabbinical Council of America, which is composed of "modern Orthodox" rabbis, has come to feel that the existence of a religious political party in Israel is not an unmixed blessing.

"If the rabbis would put their energies into seeking votes for Tora instead of votes for their party, Judaism would do better in Israel," Rabbi Grossman told me. He believes that the few concessions gained by the Religious Party would be surpassed by gains conceded voluntarily by the public as a result of good will generated by the departure of the rabbis from Israel's political scene.

Rabbi Jaffe of Hekhal Shelomo, on the other hand, believes that a religious party performs a vital function in behalf of Judaism in Israel. "Religious people have a right, as citizens in a democracy, to send rabbis to the Knesset," he said. "If they don't send their own people to the Knesset to protect their interests, religious people know that nobody else will help them."

Orthodox rabbis in Israel point with pride to the government's introduction into the public schools of courses in "Jewish consciousness."

The decision to introduce this new subject into Israel's non-religious schools has an interesting inside story. Several years ago, left-wing Israeli youth groups were invited to the World Youth Congress held in Moscow. There, the sabras, who spoke Hebrew but were ignorant of religion, were literally mobbed by Soviet Jews who ecstatically welcomed them as emissaries from the Jewish homeland. They pulled the young Israelis into the synagogue and gave them *aliyot* and other ceremonial honors at services. When the visitor youngsters stood upon the *bima* in prayer shawls and yarmulkes borrowed for the occasion, some, to their embarrassment, did not know the appropriate blessings and prayers and burst into tears. To their added consternation, the Moscow worshippers verged on hysteria in welcoming their young Israeli visitors.

This emotional confrontation of the Marxist youth from the Holy Land with Moscow Jews who clung to the tradition of Judaism, caused the leaders of the left-wing Mapai, Mapam and Hashomer Hatzair youth clubs to stop and think, particularly when the delegates returned to Israel and filled the publications of their groups with letters and articles questioning whether, by ignoring religion, they had not neglected an important aspect of life.

The first concrete result of the incident in Moscow was the inauguration of compulsory classes in "Jewish consciousness" in Israel's non-religious chools. Rabbis and educators in Israel agree that the "Jewish consciousness" study program is far from perfect. The religious claim that not enough is taught. Teachers must come to grips with their own religious — or non-religious — tenets as they try to teach their students about Judaism with vary-ing degrees of conviction and belief. And due to the varying religious backgrounds of the teachers, students are apt to get a grab-bag of interpretations of Judaism ranging all the way from atheist to Hassidic, depending on who their teacher happens to be. But the chief thing is that the young Hebrews are being taught that they are not only Israelis but also Jews.

Exponents of liberal Judaism agree that most Israelis would welcome religion in their lives but believe that Orthodoxy cannot fill the needs of the modern Israeli in search for some form of religious expression.

"Most Jews do believe in God, but they have been un-able to translate that faith into acts of prayer or ob-servances because the only such acts they knew were those of the ultra-Orthodox pattern and these they were unable to accept," asserted Simcha Kling, writing in the *Reconstructionist,* which is the organ of the Recon-structionist movement in American Jewry.

Dr. Mordecai M. Kaplan, founder of Reconstruction-ism, has written of the astonishing "contrast in the career of Israel between her great intellectual strides and her disheartening spiritual backwardness." Listing the mirac-ulous military, political, economic, technological, cultur-al and social achievements of the State of Israel, Dr. Kaplan said that the Jews who, in ancient times, had shown religious maturity exceeding that of all other peo-ples, and had a unique impact on the spiritual growth of all mankind, today display unequalled powers of growth, maturation and progress in every aspect of hu-man living — except religion.

As examples of this spiritual retardation, Dr. Kaplan cites the now familiar complaints about restrictions on personal freedom imposed by religious law in the State of Israel on all citizens. He brands *halitza,* the ceremony of release from the husband's brother, without which a childless widow cannot remarry, as "absurd, scandalous and degrading," and claims that the ban on marriages between Kohanites and divorcées in Israel leads to illicit cohabitation and to absurd situations in which Israelis must go abroad in order to be married in civil ceremonies.

Dr. Kaplan blames Israel's "spiritual lag" on its "all-or-nothing" type of religion, which he labels as a characteristic of the immature mind that "cannot conceive even of the possibility of religion under freedom or of religion without supernaturalism."

He feels that the development of a mature religion is essential to Israel and to the future of the Jewish people because, as he puts it, "without religion based on a mature religious concept of freedom, freedom itself is bound either to turn into anarchy or to give way to tyranny; without religion based on a mature religious conception of the pursuit of happiness, the pursuit of happiness itself is bound either to degenerate into licentiousness or to be treated as sin . . . . Without a unifying purpose which only mature religion under freedom can provide, Jews in the Diaspora are bound to lose interest in the Jews of Israel, even as those in Israel have already begun to lose interest in their brethren in the Diaspora, to the detriment of the Jewish people as a whole."

In a book entitled *Israel's Odyssey*, Abraham Mayer Heller stresses that the differences of opinion between the religious and the non-religious lie solely in the areas of worship, ritual and in the question of the binding force of religious law on the individual. Orthodox and non-Orthodox have no quarrel with one another over the ethical content of Judaism, or the "duties of man toward his fellow-man." He reports that "the standards of human behavior are no lower among those who are not identified with the official religious camp in Israel than among those who are," and cites in support of his view the irreligious kibbutzim which are constantly at work to improve relations between man and his neighbor in their effort to evolve a more perfect social order.

The late Hayim Greenberg, Labor Zionist writer, scholar and thinker, included a chapter on religion in Israel in his book *Israel — Its Role in Civilization.* In this essay, he pointed out that the State of Israel at present considers every citizen to be under the jurisdiction of one of three religious bodies — Jewish, Christian or Moslem — in questions of personal status and inheritance. If he refuses to submit to the authority of the religious court competent for his religious affiliation, a citizen of Israel has no way of legalizing his marriage or procuring a divorce, or of settling the estate of a deceased relative. Israel's draft constitution, which was never put into final form, for fear of precipitating an open conflict between the religious and the non-religious, does not provide for secular bodies similar to American divorce or orphans' courts.

This tripartite system of religious civil courts, Greenberg continued, poses several questions. To begin with, there is no such thing as one single "Christian community" in Israel. Why, then, should a Protestant, a Greek Catholic or a non-practicing Christian, be forced to abide by the decision of a Roman Catholic ecclesiastical court on such questions as, say, divorce? And what about Jews who adhere to other forms of Judaism than Orthodoxy? Would marriages or divorces authorized by non-Orthodox rabbis in Israel or anywhere else in the world be considered valid by the Jewish religious court, which is Orthodox?

Greenberg predicted that the Orthodox religious authorities in Israel would not renounce their present legal status without a violent struggle, for they do not want the State to accord official recognition to a Jewish religious community that is not Orthodox. They cast doubts on the scholarly qualifications of non-Orthodox rabbis and warn that the recognition in Israel of forms of Judaism other than the Orthodox would give rise to disunity and open religious strife in the Jewish State.

A separation of Church and State in Israel, Greenberg explained, need not preclude the functioning of ecclesiastical courts in matters of personal status for those citizens who would want to live under their jurisdiction. A marriage or divorce sanctioned by an ecclesiastical court under such circumstances would be recognized also by the State.

However, Greenberg felt, as do most Israelis today, that the time is not opportune for a showdown. In view of the crucial and complex problems of security, immigration and development with which Israel must come to grips, most of Israel's political parties give national solidarity priority over a forced settlement of religious issues.

Howard M. Sachar, the American Jewish historian, points out that as a result of compromises made by the non-religious parties to stave off open warfare, "the Religious Bloc, which has failed to win more than 13 per cent of the popular vote of any Knesset election, managed to exercise a disproportionate influence over the public services of the State."

In *The Course of Modern Jewish History*, Dr. Sachar writes:

"On Saturday, no restaurant or theater (in Israel) remained open; railways and bus lines were at a halt from Friday night to Saturday night; citizens in the interior, most of whom could afford neither automobiles nor the price of a taxi, were unable to reach the seashore on their one day of rest. The importation of non-kosher food into Israel became a statutory offense. . . . In marriage, divorce and other intimate matters of personal status, a woman, according to Israeli statute, was technically as much a chattel as in Biblical times. . . . The rabbinate

justified this rigidity by stating that an imposed Orthodoxy was a safeguard, in a Jewish State, against the feeling
of alienhood which had been the age-old burden of the
Jews in a non-Jewish society. Now that Judaism had roots
of its own, they argued, after so many centuries of flight
and persecution, traditional religious practice took on the
habiliments of solemn obligation. On the other hand, the
critics of Orthodoxy — a majority of the Israeli population
— wondered how one would respect a religion which required police enforcement."

Dr. Sachar, a former professor of history at Harvard
University and director of the Hiatt Institute in Jerusalem, sponsored by Brandeis University, stresses that "the
propaganda of the Religious Bloc obscured the fact that
many of the country's leading intellectuals were embark-
ing on a serious quest for faith and were sharply questioning whether Israel's future lay with pure secularism.
They had seen their faith in socialism and international
brotherhood shattered by the wars of the twentieth century, and were awakening, as a result, to the simple, un-
dialectical humanism of the ancient Jewish tradition."
However, he emphasizes that "one must not confuse religion in its pure meaning with the legalistic rigors of
Orthodoxy."

Professor Sachar foresees the emergence of "a synthesis
of the secular and religious viewpoint. . . . The majority
of Israelis seemed willing to regard the Bible as a majes-
tic distillation of a national literature. They respected
and observed the holy days as popular festivals and celebrations. Even in the socialist settlement a more mellow
attitude toward the religio-patriotic tradition was increasingly apparent; the ceremonials of Judaism were
cherished now as the custom and folklore of a historic
people."

I had interviews with two prominent representatives
of the aliya from the United States; Murray Greenfield,

who founded the Association of Americans and Canadians in Israel, and Dr. Israel Goldstein, the veteran world Zionist leader who is also rabbi emeritus of New York's Conservative Congregation B'nai Jeshurun.

Both men, in separate conversations, expressed a common complaint made by many American olim who leave Israel to return to the United States; namely, that the Jewish State does not offer much in the way of religious life as they knew it in America.

"I miss going to my kind of *shul* on the Sabbath," Greenfield told me. "The rabbi in Israel is not a community leader like the American rabbi. He never speaks out except to complain about violations of the Sabbath. I was a Sabbath observer in New York and I want to feel part of a religious group. Here, I can't."

Greenfield attempted to organize a congregation to meet the spiritual needs of a like-minded group of American Israelis, including the novelist Meyer Levin. They became involved in a complicated legal hassle over renting a hall in Kfar Shmaryahu.

"What would happen if a group of Yemenites would want to organize a synagogue?" Levin demanded. "The Ministry of Religions and everybody else would knock themselves out providing financial assistance, land, facilities, prayerbooks, a Tora Scroll and everything else they might need. But if a group of Americans wants to start a congregation to worship as we do in the United States — as Conservative or Reform Jews — we run into every obstacle. The rabbis oppose us."

Rabbi Goldstein, for lack of a Conservative congregation, "goes slumming," as he puts it, in Mea Shearim, stronghold of extreme Orthodoxy. "The sooner religion is divorced from politics in Israel and the sooner the heterodox groups in Judaism have the same rights in Israel as the Orthodox groups, the more secure will be the place and the appeal of religion in Israel in all its manifestations, and the sooner will Israel, so abundant in democratic institutions and procedures, be able to free itself from its theocratic label. The qualities of religious orthodoxy should not be strained. It should fall as the gentle dew from heaven upon the lives of those who espouse it," he said.

Rabbi Goldstein deplored the fact that, unlike the American synagogue, the synagogue in Israel does not function as a spiritual and cultural center for the community. He urged more rabbis from the United States to come to Israel in a new religious pioneering movement.

\* \* \*

A few blocks from Rabbi Goldstein's Jerusalem office at the Jewish Agency headquarters, the World Union of Liberal Judaism purchased three buildings, and, despite opposition from Israel's Chief Rabbinate, built a Reform temple.

Speeding high above the Mediterranean in a New York-bound El Al jet plane, I met one of Israel's future Reform rabbis. He is Samuel "Shmilik" Keheti, a Yemenite from Jerusalem. He was going to America to attend the Hebrew Union College, the Reform rabbinical School in Cincinnati.

Keheti told me that 80 per cent of Israel's youth are not religious. "The Orthodox way does not come to the heart of our youth," he said.

"Shmilik," who is in his late twenties, was the natural leader of a small group of Israeli students on the plane. Pounding on his Oriental drum, he led the exchange students in Israeli folk songs, a jazzed-up mixture of Palmah martial music, Hassidic melodies, synagogue liturgy and the ancient chants of the Yemenites.

"Shmilik," I asked him, "is this the way you'll go about starting a youth synagogue in Israel?"

"This is our secret weapon," Shmilik nodded. "We'll get together on Friday nights for a jam session. When we'll get tired, we'll start discussing religion, and the meaning of God and religion in our lives."

He believes that Reform Judaism in Israel will be less radical than American Reform. But there will be neither yarmulkas nor separate seating of the sexes in Israel's Reform temple, and members will be permitted to ride on the Sabbath. Later on, the Reform leaders will join the advocates of civil marriage and divorce.

"We should keep those laws that are written in the Bible," Shmilik said. "But you must remember that before the destruction of the First Temple, Judaism was the most progressive religion in the world. The Shulhan Arukh is not a code of law for us in modern times. The rabbis must sit down and try to change the law to fit the needs of present-day life. If they can't take the lead in religious life, they should quit right now. If they want to take the lead, they should also have the power to change the religious laws that have become obsolete."

Shmilik, formerly the principal of a technical school in Jerusalem, is a Jerusalem sabra. His parents came to the Holy City fifty years ago. His wife, Geula Winkler, comes from an Ashkenazi family. She was born and raised in Mea Shearim.

The Yemenite Reform rabbi-to-be verified our reports that nearly 90 per cent of the young immigrants from the Oriental countries give up Orthodoxy when they come to Israel.

In Dimona in the Negev, Rabbi Avraham Almaliah had bemoaned to me the lack of interest in Judaism among the young, primarily those from Northern Africa. Rabbi Almaliah, who comes from Morocco, gives classes in Talmud three times each week, but barely manages to draw a minyan for worship.

He was bluntly critical of the Ashkenazi-dominated

Rabbinate and yeshivot for not encouraging the migration of religious young people to Dimona and the other "development towns."

If the religious youth went to the Negev like the secularist young people, we'd make a success of religious life here," he said. "As it is, the youth in Dimona have no example to emulate; they look on their parents as old-fashioned, and take their cues from the youth leaders, who're secularists."

Rabbi Almaliah is impatient with the Ashkenazi-dominated Chief Rabbinate, which includes only a tiny minority of Oriental rabbis quite out of proportion to the number of Orientals and Sephardim now residing in Israel. Today, the Orientals comprise 55 per cent of the country's total population. Above all, he disapproves of the long-drawn-out and complicated divorce procedures enforced by the Rabbinate, which, he feels, inflicts cruel suffering upon the women.

A few days after my talk with Avraham Almaliah of the Negev, I was in downtown Tel Aviv with Rabbi Eliahu Shrem, Sephardi chief rabbi of the city's Merkaz Mishari district.

Wearing a gray flannel suit, and no beard, Rabbi Shrem, who is about Shmilik's age, could walk down either Tel Aviv's Ben Yehuda Street or New York's Madison Avenue without ever being recognized as a rabbi.

He differs from the bearded, black-coated Ashkenazi rabbis of Israel not only in appearance but also in basic ideology. A fourth-generation Jerusalem sabra, representing the seventh generation of a long line of Sephardi rabbis, the young rabbi, who is in charge of eight Tel Aviv synagogues, is the spokesman for a yet unseen but nonetheless explosive force seething beneath a camouflage of religious unity.

Rabbi Shrem spoke of the two basic underlying trends within Israel's Sephardic community which threaten the unbending "one hundred per cent or nothing" stance of the Ashkenazi rabbinate.

The first force working within the Israeli Sephardi community is its dark-skinned youth. In their anxiety to become more sabra than the sabras, these young men and women are rapidly casting off the religious tradition of their pious parents. The other force is operating within the Sephardi Rabbinate.

Admittedly, Eliahu Shrem cannot speak for the entire Sephardi Rabbinate whose head, Chief Rabbi Yitzhak Nissim, is probably the most inflexible of all in his views. But this young Tel Aviv rabbi represents a tradition of religious tolerance which has characterized the Oriental rabbis for many centuries and influences the thinking of many Sephardi leaders in Israel today.

At the present rate of immigration from the Moslem countries, and with "internal immigration," the high birth rate in Oriental families where ten children are not uncommon, it is obvious that eventually, and in the not-too-distant future, the Orientals will greatly outnumber the Ashkenazi element in Israel.

If the new generation of Orientals could be kept close to the Orthodoxy of their fathers, their growing strength, added to the present power of the Ashkenazi Rabbinate, could perhaps lead in time to the fulfillment of the dreams and prayers of those who yearn for a "Tora-true" State in Israel. But if alienation of Oriental youth from Orthodoxy continues at its current rate, the religious parties obviously cannot hope to gain from the increasing numerical dominance of the newcomers from the Moslem countries.

The Oriental rabbis, with the notable exception of Chief Rabbi Nissim, are chafing under the dominance of the Ashkenazi Rabbinate in politics and are expressing dissident thoughts on the interpretation and enforcement of Tora law. They resent the fact that, of the 62 rabbinic officials in the Bet Rabbanim, only seven are Sephardi, and that the religious party, which relies heavily on the Oriental vote, has not named a single representative of that segment to its executive committee of fifteen.

But, even more important, many Sephardi religious leaders like Rabbi Shrem have little sympathy for the "one-hundred-per-cent or nothing" approach of the Ashkenazi rabbis and teachers. Rabbi Shrem believes that vacillating youth and unbelieving adults should be courted by the rabbis "with kindness and patient education." He himself goes out to youth centers, non-religious kibbutzim and villages of Oriental immigrants to persuade the young and their parents that the religious way is the best path to personal happiness and the service of God. On the first day of each Hebrew month he conducts Rosh Hodesh receptions in various Tel Aviv synagogues and utilizes these occasions for talks to young and old.

Rabbi Shrem believes that the rabbis of Israel should emulate the "Tora Cavalcades" organized by the Conservative movement in the United States, and go out into the villages, moshavim, kibbutzim and development towns to bring the message of religion directly to the people. This approach has already been utilized in Israel by the Habad movement or the Lubavitcher Hassidim as they are familiarly known, and with interesting results. Habad rabbis report that even in the most Godless kibbutzim of the far-left Mapam party, young settlers involve Habad lecturers in all-night discussions on questions of religious philosophy and the nature of God. Kibbutz youth who proudly identify themselves as atheists turn out in large numbers to hear the followers of the Lubavitcher Rebbe, and ask them to return for continued talks.

"As far as I'm concerned," Rabbi Shrem said, "I will go to the most irreligious kibbutz and talk to the members, even if they should laugh at me. I believe that if we educate them with love and understanding, we will ultimately make an impression on them."

I asked him whether he meant that Israel needed Jewish missionaries to go among the Jews.

"Yes," he replied, "we must go into every corner of the land and explain the truth of the Tora. The godless are honest and dedicated in their fight for their doctrine. We must fight for our truth with equal dedication."

And yet Rabbi Shrem is by no means intolerant of those who will not accept Orthodoxy.

"I try to live according to the Tora," he said. "But I also welcome others when they come to the synagogue, regardless of whether or not they are observant. Even if someone is only partially observant, he should not be turned away. We should try to teach him to be more religious, for, from the moral standpoint, the Tora is indeed perfect. But we can't force people to be religious."

He is sympathetic to the needs of the unsynagogued young. To put it crudely, soccer is practically a religious rite among the sabras, and most of the games are held on the Sabbath, Israel's only free day. Rabbi Shrem told me that he would permit youngsters to attend these games on the Sabbath as long as they did not ride there. "It is better for them to walk to a soccer game than to stand around and gossip on street corners."

Many of Israel's Ashkenazi Rabbinate believe that in conflict between the Tora and personal needs the person must be changed to conform to the law. Rabbi Shrem's approach is more conciliatory.

The Sephardi tradition has always been more liberal than that of the Ashkenazim. For centuries, the rabbis in the Oriental countries had autonomous jurisidiction, also in matters of civil law, over their communities, as opposed to the religious leaders of Europe who had to cede jurisdiction in these matters to the secular authorities at an early date. Faced with the constant challenge of applying the civil law of the Tora to contemporary affairs, the Sephardi rabbis preserved a more realistic attitude to the interpretation of Biblical and Talmudic legislation. As early as forty years ago, the late Sephardi Chief Rabbi Ben-Zion Uziel wrote a treatise on artificial insemination.

As for the Yemenites, they never adopted the Shulhan Arukh, the code of Jewish law set down by Joseph Caro and Moses Isserles in the sixteenth century, but refer directly to the Bible, the Talmud and the works of Moses Maimonides.

Since their rabbis lacked the encyclopedic scholarship of their Ashkenazi counterparts, the Sephardi laymen, unlike the Ashkenazim, did not feel the need to strive to outdo one another in strictness of observance.

"We will use our influence to separate religion and State in Israel," declared David Sitton, chairman of the Council of the Sephardic community of Jerusalem. Sitton is now editor of a new Sephardi community journal whose Hebrew title, translated into English, is *In the Battle*. He revealed to me the depth and passion of the rift within the Religious Bloc, which might, in time, result in the elimination of the Rabbinate from Israel politics.

"In the Diaspora, the Jews fight for the separation of Church and State. Why not here?" he demanded. "Mark my words. A few years from now, the Sephardi rabbis will be fighting for just that in Israel."

The Sephardi community flaunted the Religious Bloc in the elections of 1961 by throwing its weight to Ben-Gurion's ruling Mapai party.

Sitton bitterly assailed Sephardi Chief Rabbi Nissim. "Nissim's against the Sephardi way of life," he declared. I noted that he did not refer to the Chief Rabbi by his title. "He was a merchant from Baghdad, and the Religious Party made a chief rabbi of him to use as a tool against Ben-Gurion. The entire Sephardi organization is against Nissim," Sitton said.

Sitton expressed particular resentment at what he feels is Chief Rabbi Nissim's indiscriminate use of the *herem* or religious interdict on the sale and purchase of milk from kibbutzim where pigs are bred, against the American-Israel Paper Mills of Hadera for operating on the Sabbath in order to maintain the continuous movement of paper rolls, and against the intermarriage of Jews with Indian Jews of the Bene Israel sect. The Bene Israel ban was not lifted until it became a national issue in 1964.

In response to these advocates of the removal of the Rabbinate and religious leadership from the political scene, *Hatzofe,* the official organ of Israel's Religious Party, puts forth the platform of those who want Israel to be a State based on the laws of the Tora:

"The main aim of the religious party is to create a State based on Judaism. A religious regime in Israel would prove that the Sabbath does not interfere in any way with the economic development of the State and, indeed, contributes to its moral strength."

The aim of the Religious Party, stated in its election advertisements, are as follows:

1. A strengthening and expansion of the authority of the Rabbinical Courts, based on the legal framework of the Tora.

2. Proper deference by State authorities to the Rabbinate in general and to the rabbis of State institutions in particular.

3. More financial assistance from the Government in the development of religious institutions.

4. A national Sabbath Law, and a five-day work week to facilitate Sabbath observance in accordance with Tora law.
5. An explicit ban on pig-breeding.
6. The granting of university status to yeshivot.
7. The abolition of indiscriminate autopsies, which Jewish law regards as a violation of the dignity of the dead.
8. Legislation to restrict the activities of missionaries.

\*   \*   \*

At present, the religious controversy in Israel appears to be at an impasse. I feel that the solution of what now seems an insuperable problem may well come from Israel's Oriental segment and their tradition of "live and let live," as opposed to the intransigence of most of the Orthodox Ashkenazim. As the religiously-inclined Israelis of Oriental origin will learn in the course of time to make use of their numerical power at the polls and wield a greater influence in government and in other phases of life in the Jewish State, they may come to serve as a bridge between the religious and the non-religious and lead the way to the reconciliation that is essential to the continued growth and development of Israel.

# CHAPTER IX
# THE POPE COMES TO ISRAEL

Pope Paul VI reaffirmed the Jewish roots of Christianity when he made his historic pilgrimage to the Holy Land, including a visit to the two-thousand-year-old synagogue of Capernaum on the northern shore of the Sea of Galilee, or Lake Kinneret.

Here amidst the ruins of the synagogue where the founder of Christianity is said to have preached nearly two thousand years ago, the spiritual head of the Catholic Church paid homage to what he later characterized as "the common affinity of Jews and Christians for the Old Testament as the source of Divine revelation."

Pope Paul who, together with his predecessor, John XXIII, had urged the Ecumenical Council Secretariat to adopt a statement condemning the religious roots of anti-Semitism, said prayers for peace and for good will among men at the places sacred to Christianity which line the northern shore of lovely Lake Kinneret, and also at Mount Tabor, in Nazareth and in Jerusalem. The Pope's journey covered the whole of the Galilee, and the highway down through Lydda airport, near Tel Aviv, and then on to Jerusalem.

Considerable significance was attached to the cooperation between Israel and Jordan necessitated by the Pope's crossing between the two countries at Taanakh.

In some quarters, the Pope's visit to the Holy Land aroused hopes for the coming of peace which, however, were officially discounted by a statement from the Vatican stressing the purely religious nature of the Pontiff's pilgrimage to Jerusalem, Nazareth, Amman and the Sea of Galilee.

It was on a mountaintop overlooking the storied Sea of Galilee that Jesus of Nazareth preached the Sermon on the Mount in which he blessed the poor, the peacemakers and the pure of heart.

Why cannot the Israelis and the Syrians, facing each other across the Sea of Galilee, make peace with one another? Why cannot Israel and Jordan, which cooperated in opening the border crossing at Taanakh for the Papal party, end their cold — and warm — war sputtering since 1948? Israel reiterates that she is ready at any time to sit down at the peace table, but the Arab neighbors at their conferences reply with repeated threats to exterminate the Zionist state.

This much is certain; there is no doubt but that the Pope's historic pilgrimage from Rome to Jerusalem already has given added impetus to Christian tourism to Israel.

Even as they hoped for good things to come from the Pope's visit, the Israelis heaved a collective sigh of relief that Israeli security measures had succeeded in making the Pontiff's journey proceed safely and without untoward incidents from beginning to end.

Five thousand Israeli policemen were assigned to protect Paul VI during the day he spent in the Jewish State. All along the Papal route, roads were cleared and non-official traffic stopped. All correspondents, as well as radio and television personnel, save for the official crew from Italy, traveled in buses chartered by the Israeli Government. Only the radio and television technicians from Rome were permitted to use their own transportation facilities and to move about freely to film the journey. From each stop, Italian television films were flown by helicopter to Lydda airport where Italian jet fighter planes waited to speed them to Rome. From Rome, the films were relayed by Telstar to television broadcasting networks in America and elsewhere.

In all the planning, top priority was given to the Pope's safety. Correspondents were told precisely what they would and what they would not be permitted to do. No one complained. Sobered by what had happened in Dallas only six weeks before, the reporters did not insist on the "freedom of the press" to create the sort of chaos which allowed a Jack Ruby to enter a police station unimpeded and make a mockery of law and justice.

Israel's security measures for the Papal visit, and the transportation, filing, mailing and helicopter-jet and air mail facilities for the press were examples of the manner in which a government can give every assistance to a free press while, at the same time, assuming full responsibility for the protection of a most important personage.

In the flag-draped courtyard of the Museum of Antiquities in Megiddo, Zalman Shazar, President of the State of Israel, welcomed Paul VI, the head of the Catholic Church.

"With the utmost respect and fully aware of the historic significance of this event, which is unprecedented in the annals of the generations," said the President, "I have come in the name of the Government of Israel and in my own, to welcome the Supreme Pontiff, the spiritual father of the Catholic Church throughout the world. I have come to greet him with the age-old blessing: 'Blessed be thou in thy coming!'

"From Jerusalem, our capital City of David, I, and the members of the Government of Israel with me, have made our way down to Megiddo, the city Solomon built, so that we might welcome him as soon as he would step upon the soil of our land, this Holy Land. It was with profound interest that we have learned from his utterances that this pilgrimage is a journey of prayer, to seek mercy for all mankind suffering from pain and hunger and conflict, thirsting for peace and prosperity, freedom and justice.

"Surely the devastation of my people during this last generation is a bitter warning of the depths of bestiality and loss of the Divine image to which ancient prejudices and racial hatreds can demean men if a purifying spirit does not come into being while there is yet time to dam up these perils forever. At the same time, progress and science, the pride of modern times, which have rendered man the master over so many of nature's forces, expose him to perils of destruction that would have been inconceivable to the generations that went before us. The hearts of men everywhere yearn for a great moral revival to forestall evil, to root out hunger and hate and tyranny, to secure peace, and to strive toward the realization of the vision of our Prophets: 'I will take away the stony heart out of your flesh, and I will give you a heart of flesh' and 'Nation shall not lift up sword against nation, neither shall they learn war any more.'

"This countryside about us is living witness to the fact that prophecies are being fulfilled — those of the ingathering of our people here from all the corners of the earth and the renewal of their independent life as in days of old. From Megiddo, there stretches before us the Valley of Jezreel, with scores of new settlements founded on labor, equality and justice. And in every village and town of our land that is being rebuilt there are signs of the fulfillment of the promise of new life. Thus our belief is strengthened that the vision of our seers of universal peace and social justice will come true also. Mankind will be redeemed from its distress, the world will be built in righteousness, and our own eyes will behold this. Blessed be our illustrious guest upon his arrival in our midst!"

The Pontiff, clad in a white gown topped by a bright red cape, warmly thanked the President and greeted him with "Shalom, shalom!" Then he distributed medals to the Israeli leaders and expressed his prayerful hope for peace in the world.

At the end of his visit to Israel, the Pope told Israeli officials at the Mandelbaum Gate that it had been "an unforgettable day" for him.

"We wish to express our satisfaction with the visit and our gratitude for the welcome we have been accorded," he told them. "We extend our blessings and good wishes to you as we conclude our visit. It is with satisfaction that we consider that our Catholic children living in this country shall continue to enjoy the rights and liberty to which all men are today considered to be entitled. And wholeheartedly we lift our eyes on high and pray that God's blessings may be lavished upon you, on our Christian children round about us here, and on everyone everywhere whose thoughts are of peace and reconciliation."

President Shazar, in his farewell to the Pope, reassured him of Israel's intentions to seek peace with its neighbors. Just before leaving, the Pope commented, in French, to Avraham Gilboa, Israel's Chief of Protocol: *"Un peuple vivant et plein d'energie"* ("A lively people, full of energy").

The Pontiff's emphasis on the fact that the Jews were the "People of the Covenant" and his references to Abraham, Isaac and Jacob were regarded as a reaffirmation of the trend within the Ecumenical Council toward rectifying the historical relations not only between Christian and Christian, but also between Christian and Jew.

Israel's newspapers stressed the Pope's recognition of the freedom accorded to the Catholic Church by the Government of Irael and of the protection afforded by the State of Israel to the holy places of Christianity. Newspapers representing every shade of political and religious opinion, from the organ of the far-left Mapam party to that of the extreme right-wing Herut acknowledged that the visit of the Pope to the State of Israel had been an event of great historical significance. The Mapam paper went so far as to regret the absence of normal diplomatic relations between Israel and the Vatican, and to state that the Pontiff's visit "carried much political meaning."

The Pope, who was constantly smiling and extending blessings to all within his sight, impressed reporters profoundly with his kindliness, humility and charm. Thousands waited for hours to catch a glimpse of the distinguished pilgrim. An atmosphere of friendliness and goodwill prevailed between Jews and Catholics as the Pope traveled about the Jewish State from early morning until the evening.

Among the participants in the official Israeli ceremonies honoring the Pope at Megiddo and in Jerusalem was Dr. Zerah Warhaftig, the Minister of Religions, whose department superintends the holy places of all religions. He told me that the Pope's pilgrimage implied "recognition by the Vatican of the moral and legal authority of the Jewish State for the care of the Christian holy places."

"The fact that the first voluntary trip (abroad) made by any Pope was to visit the Christian holy places in Israel took place now that a Jewish State governs them, implies such recognition," Dr. Warhaftig said. "The Pope said that he was satisfied with the attitude of Israel to the principle of freedom of religion with regard to the Christian communities, and this statement, coming from the Pope, has value."

Dr. Warhaftig expressed the hope that the Pope's visit to Israel would bring about a decline of anti-Semitism.

Widespread resentment was expressed throughout Israel — except in some of the extreme Orthodox circles — over the refusal of Sephardi Chief Rabbi Nissim to participate in the official welcoming ceremonies at Megiddo.

Originally, Rabbi Nissim had insisted that the Pope come to meet him as an equal at Hekhal Shelomo, headquarters of the Chief Rabbinate in Jerusalem. Next, he offered to meet the Pope on equal terms on Mount Zion. The Pope, of course, came neither to the Hekhal Shelomo nor to Mount Zion, but Eugene Cardinal Tisserant, Dean of the College of Cardinals, entered the Chamber of the Holocaust on Mount Zion and, in a gesture of good will of the Catholic Church toward the Jewish people, lit six candles in memory of the six million Jews slaughtered by the Nazis.

Many regarded the absence of the Chief Rabbi from Megiddo as a sign of the alienation of Israel's religious leaders from the secular State. The heads of the State of Israel were left to greet the head of the Catholic Church, while the chief representative of Jewish religious authority was conspicuously missing.

An editorial in the *Jerusalem Post* pointed out that "by this withdrawal, Chief Rabbi Nissim has, in fact, placed a division between the religious and lay representatives of the State. Such a division has in the past been desired more by the non-religious than by the religious. . . . Usually, it was the religious authorities who protested whenever the civil authorities wished to go their own way. Rabbi Nissim has scarcely set the right example."

Jerusalem's Chief Rabbi Eliahu Pardess, on the other

hand, attended the official farewell ceremonies at the Mandelbaum Gate.

As for President Shazar, he had the feeling that the Pope was as aware of the historic significance of their meeting for Christianity as he, the President, had been of its meaning for Judaism.

"I knew that I was there not only as the President of Israel," the President said. "Standing there with me in spirit were all the generations of our long past, those of our ancient glory and those who suffered humiliation, persecution and massacre.

"Herzl stood with me there in Megiddo and in Jerusalem, and so did Sokolow, and my father and grandfather and all the twelve million Jews of our own day. I felt that I was speaking in the name of them all when I quoted the words of the Prophet Micah: 'Let every nation walk in the name of its God, and we will walk in the name of the Lord our God forever.'

"I stressed 'forever' to indicate that this was not merely a transient passing thought," the third President of the State of Israel said. He explained that he had chosen this particular Biblical passage because it best expressed Judaism's own ancient doctrine of coexistence and religious tolerance — the only way to that peace which the Pope so ardently desired.

The President felt that he had to mention the European holocaust in his welcoming address "regardless of (Rolf) Hochhuth (author of *The Deputy*)." He said that he spoke of the murder of the Six Million "in its meaning of a bitter warning, illustrating what can happen if ancient prejudices and racial hatreds are not dammed up in time."

President Shazar predicted that the Pope's visit to Israel would result in "a relationship of mutual respect and understanding, as well as the absence of hostile or unfriendly feeling on either side."

"I believe that a most important fact has been established," the President said, "and that, as time passes,
it will grow in importance, provided that we continue
to preserve our identity. Without Statehood we could
fall back again to a position of inequality and humiliation.

"I came away from my meeting with the Pope a
better Zionist and a better Jew, more deeply rooted
than ever in our heritage," said the President of Israel.

# CHAPTER X
## THIS IS JUSTICE

Meir, Cilla and Moshe Goldberg sat close by their radio in their farmhouse in Bene Berak listening to Adolf Eichmann mouthing the Nazi "Big Lie" over Station Kol Israel.

Meir and Cilla Goldberg, who miraculously survived the death factories which Eichmann had created and directed, and their teenage son Moshe, talked excitedly of what was taking place in the Jerusalem courtroom where Adolf Eichmann was facing Jewish judges and the attorney-general of a Jewish State in one of the most dramatic encounters in history.

While more "objective" observers elsewhere grudgingly conceded that the twentieth-century Haman was a match for the legal mind of Attorney-General Gideon Hausner, the Goldbergs had only contempt for Eichmann's denials of the charge that he had been directly associated with the torture and annihilation of the six million martyrs of their people.

"Eichmann knows nothing, sees nothing, and did nothing," Mrs. Goldberg cried out in frustration over the failure of the prosecutor to wrest a confession of guilt from the accused.

Her husband, who bore the tattoo mark of Auschwitz on his arm, took a longer view of the Hausner-Eichmann duel:

"You can be sure that when Eichmann was riding high he never dreamed that he would have to face a Jewish court. If he ever thought of what might happen if his *Fuehrer* lost, he might have pictured himself being charged with war crimes in some Allied country, but he certainly never imagined that a State of Isreal would arise, hunt him down and bring him to trial in Jerusalem. This," said Meir Goldberg, "is justice."

It was no more than justice that the Goldbergs and 200,000 other survivors of Eichmann's diabolic labors of extermination should have found a haven in Israel. Indeed, Israel's very establishment as a free and independent nation was bound up in a manner with this unbelievable tragedy. For it was the gassing, burning, shooting, starving and torture of six million innocent men, women and children, and, more specifically, the plight of the remnant which survived, that awakened the conscience of the world to the half-century-old struggle of modern Zionism for a Jewish State.

It is a living demonstration of justice to see how the Goldbergs and hundreds of thousands of the fraternity of the tatooed numbers have rebuilt their shattered lives and regained their human dignity in the State of Israel.

The Goldberg family lives peacefully and with a sense of security and well-being in a farmhouse Meir built with his own hands on a half-dunam of land which he bought in 1952 for the equivalent of $250. They raise chickens, sell eggs and eat the fruits of their apple, orange and plum trees. Meir, a roofer and all-around construction workers, has been employed by the Remet Construction Company ever since the family's arrival in 1947 with a group of illegal immigrants.

Moshe, their only child, was born on May 14, 1948 the day of the signing of Israel's Declaration of Independence, so that his Bar Mitzva in 1961 coincided with the Bar Mitzva anniversary of his country. Moshe's coming of age was celebrated at a synagogue in Bene Berak by a congregation of survivors of the Nazi concentration camps — a collective act of defiance of Eichmann who was then sitting in a glass cage in Jerusalem only seventy miles away, on trial for his life.

Mrs. Goldberg told me that she actually saw Eichmann visit a concentration camp near Stuttgart. At the time she had not known who the Nazi officer was, but learned his identity some time later. Eichmann had come with Dr. Mengele, the infamous deviser of medical experiments on Jewish prisoners. Mrs. Goldberg had been asked to testify at the trial but had declined because she felt that she would not be able to control herself if she were to come face to face with the man she called "the Devil." Were she sitting as a judge in Jerusalem, she said, she would have Eichmann put out naked in sub-zero winter weather even as she had been by his guards. She had no desire to see him hanged, but wanted him to feel upon his own body the sufferings she had endured at the hands of his henchmen.

The Goldbergs were bitter at the humane treatment accorded Eichmann in court. They resented that the State of Israel should have supplied him with a suit, a tie and slippers in which to stand trial. Mrs. Goldberg never forgot how a three-man Nazi "medical commission" had forced her to run naked before them as they separated the physically unfit from those they judged fit for slave labor.

Because she was considered an impressive physical

specimen, Cilla was selected by the Nazi doctor to live rather than die in the gas chambers. She was one of the 500 women picked to work on highway construction projects. Thirty thousand other women in her transport were marched to extermination. For sixteen hours a day, with barely enough food scraps to survive, Cilla sweated in hip-deep mud to help build a 30-mile military highway.

When she would return to the camp after a day's work, she would ask not who had been killed that day but who was still alive. With her own eyes she had seen women tortured and shot, and babies snatched from their mothers' arms and torn to pieces by Nazi sadists.

In 1945 Cilla was liberated by the Russian Army and hospitalized. She and Meir first met in Germany after both had been released from the hospital. They were married in Germany and set out for Palestine in 1947 on the refugee ship named the *Exodus*.

The actual story of the good ship *Exodus* differs from its film version. She was stopped in Haifa harbor by British warships and turned back to Hamburg. At the port of Hamburg, representatives from the Hagana and the Jewish Agency went out in a small boat to meet the *Exodus*. They pleaded with the weary, sick and homeless passengers to remain on board and refuse to be evacuated to displaced persons' camps in Germany.

"You are the soul of the Jewish State," the Hagana representatives shouted through a megaphone. "Go on strike. If you give in and let them take you to the DP camps, Bevin's navy will send all the other refugee ships back to Europe also. But if this shipload refuses to disembark here, the British blockade will be broken."

The refugees voted to stay on the ship, threw their food overboard and went on a hunger strike until the British yielded. After a voyage of three months on the

high seas, the *Exodus* reached Palestine once again
and unloaded its passengers at the port of Haifa.
The landing operation had to be performed quietly
and with speed because it was strictly illegal, in blatant
defiance of the British White Paper. The refugees were
whisked away from the harbor and dispersed all over the
country, to cities, villages and kibbutzim.

The Goldbergs found themselves in Tel Aviv, standing in a rainstorm on my wife's doorsteps on HaYarkon
Street. Wet, hungry, cold, and with only the clothing they
wore on their backs — they had left all their possessions
behind in the hurried landing — they were taken in, given
clothes and cared for by Dora and her family. Dora found
a job for Meir in the building industry, and the Goldbergs
saved and scrimped to buy their plot of land and build
their farmhouse.

Had Eichmann seen the Goldbergs' farmhouse and
the new and upright life they have made for themselves in this Jewish nation, he probably would have been
unable to bear it. It is the age-old chronicle told anew
of the survival of the Jewish people through four
thousand years of Pharaohs, Amaleks, Hamans, Tor-
quemadas, Hitlers and Eichmanns.

Every Saturday morning Meir Goldberg takes his
son to the synagogue. He is not religious, but he wants
his son to see what it is to be a Jew so that if, God forbid,
another Eichmann should rise some day, Moshe Goldberg would know the heritage for which he is being
persecuted. This is the way Meir has to look at life.

The Goldbergs received restitution payments from
Germany in a lump sum and still get IL 64 a month
as an indemnity for the spinal and knee ailments Cilla
incurred as the result of Nazi beatings.

This is the story of one simple farm family in Israel
whose life is intimately bound up with the testimony
that was heard in the court in Jerusalem in those spring

days of 1961. As the Tel Aviv—Jerusalem bus carried us up the winding mountain highway away from the green fields and the terraced valleys with rich crops of cotton, tobacco, tomatoes, vineyards and orange groves, our hearts filled with a song of new life.

As the bus labored up the steep climb on the Road of the Heroes, it passed rusted, wrecked armored trucks which littered the side of the highway as mute reminders of the sacrifice of the young men of the Hagana who had defeated the Arabs and saved Jerusalem so that people like the Goldbergs would be able to live again in dignity and freedom in the Holy Land, and redeem the honor of decent men everywhere thirteen years later in the capture and trial of Adolf Eichmann.

* * *

The voice protesting innocence was the voice of Eichmann. The hand was the hand of Eichmann, stained with the most horrible crimes ever to have been committed against humanity.

The hand formed a terrifying claw as it reached out within the glass-cage in the Jerusalem courtroom, the gesture of a wild beast, stressing yet another point in his redundant denials of responsibility and guilt in what his adversary, Attorney General Hausner, termed "the slaughter of the innocents."

It was a blood-curdling drama that unfolded in the brightly-lit chamber before a tense audience of Nazi death camp survivors, relatives of concentration camp victims, tourists and 400 newspaper reporters from all over the world.

At one point, at the mention of the Ghetto of Lodz, someone rose from among the audience and screamed, "Devil! May your name be blotted out! I was in the Lodz Ghetto that October 1941!" The vigilant police rushed him out of the courtroom. It was Nissan Herszkowicz, a cobbler, who had lost his wife and five children in the Nazi mass shootings, and had come to Jerusalem to make a new life for himself, to remarry and to raise a new family. He is the father of two Sabras now.

After weeks on the stand to protest his innocence, the Pharaoh of Auschwitz succeeded only in infuriating the entire land of Israel with his dogged denials, his stubborn refusal to plead guilty to any of Hausner's charges, and his serpentine weaseling out of nearly every trap set by Israel's Attorney General.

Eichmann's defense was so simple that I think the court, the press and the public missed the point entirely and played into the claw of the man-monster. It was based simply on Hitler's own crude strategy of the "Big Lie," which *der Fuehrer* himself had blatantly described in *Mein Kampf:* the bigger the lie, the easier it will be to believe, he had said, and if you repeat the big lie often enough, people will eventually believe at least part of it. For weeks and weeks, Eichmann clung tenaciously, with a claw-like grip, to his own "Big Lie"; namely, that he had known nothing, seen nothing and done nothing in the mass murder of the Jews, Poles and others who went to their deaths in the concentration camps. He placed the blame on Himmler, Heydrich, Mueller and others in the Nazi hierarchy, insisting that he, Eichmann, had only carried out orders as a small cog in the machine in which he had functioned as an ordinary transport officer.

The net result was to sidetrack the prosecution's argument against Hitler's Minister of Death, and even to raise some doubts in world opinion about Eichmann's guilt. Even in Jerusalem, Tel Aviv and Haifa I heard people admit grudgingly, "By Jove, the bastard is making a bully fight of it. He is standing up to Hausner." A noted Israeli editor said to me in private: "You know, you have to give the devil his due. He's still a Nazi through and through. He refuses to give in."

As the trial degenerated into what the *Jerusalem Post* at one point headlined as "The Battle of the Documents," it seemed that Hausner had slid down from the peak of his classic oration of indictment into a monotonous, repetitive, boring and inconclusive discussion with the unspeakable defendant about the validity and value of the Nazi files. On this file-clerk level, Eichmann was at his best, lecturing the court on the maze of Hitlerian organization charts, and bewildering the world with his protestations of innocence. The Attorney General might have done better if he would have told the accused in court one day: "No more questions."

As the voice of Eichmann boomed out in the evening rebroadcasts of each day's trial highlights from 7:10 to 7:30, listeners throughout the land could hear Eichmann the Aryan, addressing a Jewish judge as "Your Honor."

Sitting in the courtroom and watching the black-suited, hawk-faced figure with the horn-rimmed glasses jump from his seat and snap to attention a hundred times each day to answer the Attorney General's charges and questions, I could not help comparing his enforced attitude of respect to a Jewish court with his brutal destruction of Jewish dignity and of six million Jewish lives during the Second World War. Here I saw how Israel has reversed positions in our own lifetime. This trial was the ultimate in the turning of tables. But while Eichmann had trod upon the Jews as on many insects, the Jews of Israel treated Eichmann with justice and fairness. According to a report carried in *Editor and Publisher,* not one of the 400 correspondents from all over the world who covered the opening phases of the trial believed that the proceedings could possibly have been fairer or more just than they were.

Philip Gillon, editor of the weekend supplement of

the *Jerusalem Post,* said at the time that the trust of the people of Israel in its judges was so great that even if the court would have acquitted Eichmann, the people would have accepted the verdict without protest.

However, as Gillon also admitted, it is doubtful that, in such a case, Eichmann would have been able to get out of Israel alive. Indeed, as someone put it, the worst punishment for Eichmann would have been to let him go free, without a police escort to stand between him and the people of Israel. As the trial wore on, all sorts of "oddball" suggestions for punishment made the rounds of the streets. One proposal was to place Eichmann in the Tel Aviv Zoo in his glass cage to keep him safe from would-be killers, so that tourists from all over the world might be able to see the man turned beast. One macabre mind had it that Eichmann should be placed into a cage with a lion and a tiger and his tongue paralyzed that he might know what it is to live in the constant fear of death. A somewhat more constructive recommendation, by a teen-age girl, was that he should be taken on a never-ending tour of Israel to see how the Jewish people managed to survive and build up a State of their own.

Actually, save for some very articulate survivors of the concentration camps and close relatives of the Six Million, the spirit of vengeance was not conspicuous in the land. Many of the people I met, including a number who had been in concentration camps themselves or had lost their families there, shrugged their shoulders and sighed helplessly. "Could the execution of this one monster bring back even one of our dead from the crematoria?" asked Dora, who lost her mother and father and a brother and many aunts, uncles and cousins in the Nazi slaughter of Vilna's Jewish community.

Said the *Jerusalem Post:* "There is no redress or expiation. There is only atonement — not for the criminal or the sinner, but for the man who had yet to sin." And the paper expressed the hope that the Eichmann judgment would put the fear of God into all the little men of the future who, out of fear of higher-ups, would so demean themselves as to bring horror and death to their fellow men.

The fundamental purpose of the trial had been achieved: that is, to impress indelibly upon the minds of the world, of Israeli youth and of Germans of all ages, and to inscribe permanently into the books of history, what Hitler and his followers did to six million innocent human beings.

While the trial fulfilled its stated purpose, which was to make sure that the world would never forget how the Nazis dishonored mankind, it had an even deeper meaning in Israel in that it served as "the unforgettable demonstrator of the ties that link Israel with Diaspora Jewry . . . and of the historical necessity and justification for the State of Israel," as the *London Jewish Observer and Middle East Review* expressed it at the time.

For, from my repeated questioning of young Israelis, there is no doubt that the trial taught them a never-to-be forgotten lesson about the past of their people.

The trial has helped them understand why the Jews of Europe did not revolt in Israeli fighting fashion. They heard witnesses testify how the Nazis broke the spirit of the prisoners by starvation, torture and false promises.

But it has also left them somewhat confused. If the Nazis really did this to our people, they reason — and it has never occurred to them to question Eichmann's guilt — then Israel should have nothing to do with Germany. So why, then, they ask, does Israel accept German reparations and restitution payments, do business with Germany, and allow German Opels and Volkswagens on its streets?

As Patrick O'Donovan wrote in the *London Observer,* there is in Israel a passionate desire for justice, not just for Eichmann or even for Israel itself, but for the dead.

In a more profound sense, Israeli observers viewed the Hausner-Eichmann duel as a clash between two worlds — the free world society based on law and justice, ethics and morality on the one hand, and totalitarian society, founded on total loyalty to one *Fuehrer* and total surrender of individual responsibility on the other. This, according to Leni Yahil of the *Jerusalem Post,* explained why Eichmann had been able to persist in his denial of guilt. But that may be too subtle an explanation for the Nazi mentality. A simpler reason would be that Eichmann had been taught by Hitler how to use the "Big Lie" and hence was able to say in court: "I have no regrets, for I do not regard myself as guilty."

Hitler's "Big Lie" seemed to me a shameless affront to the integrity of language. When I heard Eichmann refer to his system of extermination as "absorption," I actually felt sick. For in the Land of Israel "absorption" means the rehabilitation of survivors of the death camps and the rescue of victims of oppression from the Moslem and Communist worlds. To Israel, "absorption" signifies new life. To Eichmann, "absorption" meant death.

Reporters from the world over, including Germany itself, agreed with the Israelis regarding the historical significance of Eichmann's capture in Argentina, and his trial and execution in Israel.

The German newspaper *Koelnische Rundschau* of Cologne declared that the Jerusalem trial "had become a monumental warning against inhumanity of any kind and in any country." Frankfort's *Allgemeine Zeitung* said: "There is no conceivable punishment which would be in line with the monstrosity of the crime. The sinister man the Israelis caught in Argentina can never deputize for us Germans in carrying the burden of our recent history and its darkest chapter."

Regarding the relation of Eichmann's crime to the guilt of the German people, Yosef Neuman, Secretary of the Israel Organization of Former Nazi Prisoners, who had lost 80 close relatives including his parents in Auschwitz, said: "We don't want revenge, for that would mean annihilating hundreds of thousands of Germans. It would mean treating the German people like they treated us. We want only justice. We only want the murderer executed because he is a murderer."

But there were others in Israel who questioned whether the death penalty would be justified even in this case. Professor Hugo Bergman, Czech-born and German-trained philosopher and one-time Rector of the Hebrew University, declared:

"No country, no State, no authority, no individual executioner, has the right to put another person to death. The commandment 'Thou shalt not kill" applies with equal force to the State and to the individual. This is all the more true in a Jewish State." Instead of the death sentence, Dr. Bergman recommended life imprisonment for Eichmann "to give him time to repent."

Opposition to the death penalty for Eichmann came also from a representative of the Sabra generation that did not know Hitler and had not lost close relatives in the Holocaust. Ido Gilboa, secretary of the Hebrew University Students' Association, regarded Eichmann's trial mainly as a reminder to the world of the Nazi terror. He opposed death for Eichmann because he felt that the punishment was only of secondary significance but mainly because he reasoned that if Eichmann were to be sentenced to a life term in prison instead, the memory of Hitler's mass murder scheme would remain alive longer.

As for Eichmann himself, he was quoted as saying to his prison chaplain that he would hang himself in public as a lesson to all future anti-Semites. He admitted that Hitler's murder orgy was one of the most heinous crimes in the history of mankind and that the leaders of the Nazi party were deserving of punishment.

Eichmann had his wish. After an eminently fair trial and appeals to the Supreme Court of Israel and President Ben-Zvi, which were heard and rejected, Adolf Eichmann was hanged. His body was cremated and his ashes were scattered over the sea from an Israeli army plane.

With the trial and execution of Eichmann, has Jerusalem completed its mission of justice simply by informing the world of the horrors of the Nazi regime?

There is another side to the coin of righteousness. Rabbi Harold M. Schulweis of Beth Abraham Congregation, Oakland, California, declared that the Jewish people have a moral mandate to seek out those Christians in Europe who risked their lives to save Jewish men, women and children from death at the hands of the Nazis, and to commemorate their heroic acts forever in a *Mosad Haside Umot Ha'Olam,* a "Foundation to Honor the Righteous of All Nations." Such a foundation, Rabbi Schulweis said, was "a holy imperative for the Jewish people and Israel to create a testimony of Godliness established in the Holy Land by a people whose career is founded on the belief that man was made in the image of God." It will be a testimony that will give the lie to the half-truth that man is capable only of hate and destruction; a building which will stand side by side with that of *Yad VaShem* where the documents of Nazi genocide are stored.

Who knows the names of all the valiant men and

women who helped Anne Frank and her family while they hid out in an Amsterdam attic for two years until the Nazi murderers found them and sent their protectors to concentration camps? Who knows the identity of all the righteous Christians who paid with their own lives for their acts of Godliness?

Shall evil be recorded and made known, and goodness lie buried silent in neglect? What of Anna Simaite, the librarian who saved hundreds of Jewish children from the Nazi ghetto in Vilna and forged passports that enabled many adults to escape? Anna was captured and sent to Dachau, then escaped and lived for years in Toulouse as a penniless dishwasher until one of the children she had rescued wrote her from a kibbutz in Israel: "My dear mother, when will you finally come to us?" Now Anna Simaite lives with "her children," in Petah Tikva.

What of Eduardo Focherini, editor of the Catholic daily in Bologna, Italy, whose rescue of Jews brought death to his own seven children in a Nazi concentration camp?

"A Jew," wrote Rabbi Schulweis, "must know how and what to remember. A Jew must know what to tell his child. A Jew must know what to tell the world."

Christians, too, Rabbi Schulweis said, need heroes to exemplify their ideals of faith, love, charity and kindness. The guilt which weighs heavily upon the Christian heart must be expiated, and the Jews must help remove that burden of guilt.

If a child is told each day that he is bad, that he is a good-for-nothing, he will fulfill that expectation. And if the Christians are made to feel that the Jews expect them all to be anti-Semites, they may, Heaven forbid, unconsciously select Adolf Eichmann as their model.

Former Premier Ben-Gurion, too, has cautioned

against misplaced accusations. "We must not visit the crimes of the fathers upon the children," he told the German Press Agency.

Rabbi Schulweis' proposal, published in the *B'nai B'rith National Jewish Monthly,* brought him countless letters of approval and offers of support from the Christian world.

"Yes...a Christian (too) must know what and how to remember. He must know what to tell his child. What is a Christian to tell his child of the cancer of Naziism that grew in the hearts of Christian Europe? What is he to tell his child of the apathy of the Christian nations in the face of this evil? Indeed, what is he to tell his child of the extent to which Christian history over the centuries is defiled by anti-Semitism? The answer to these questions must be the same answer (that is given by) Rabbi Schulweis to the question he puts to the Jews, and that answer is — the truth..."

So far, all that has come of Rabbi Schulweis' suggestion is a file of laudatory comments. That nothing more has been done is one of the tragic symptoms of the rivalry and lack of overall leadership which unfortunately characterizes our Jewish organizations.

# CHAPTER XI

# DEAD SEA YIELDS LIFE

The Dead Sea, the lowest point on earth, has come to life as a major source of the world's supply of potash.

For the past three decades, the Dead Sea Works Company has operated a complex industrial enterprise in temperatures of 125° in the summer and 70° in winter to draw potash and bromine compounds from this salt lake 1300 feet below sea level. The company is now pushing a $50,000,000 expansion program for which it has obtained loans of $25,000,000 from the World Bank, $10,000,000 from banking interests in New York, and $13,500,00 from an Israeli stock issue. It is expected that by 1967 the total output of potash from the Dead Sea will have risen from 14,000 tons to 590,000 tons per year.

In this eerie Arava valley, which looks like some lunar landscape, Israel at long last has discovered a great natural blessing.

In addition, a source of natural gas was found only twenty miles to the west, and now a pipeline brings the gas from the Zohar gas field to the Dead Sea Works, assuring an ample, easily accessible and economical fuel supply for the company's expansion program.

209

This gas field at Zohar, the Canaim gas wells — which were discovered in November 1963 — and the Heletz oil field on the Mediterranean side of the Negev desert are rich in hydrocarbon resources for a potential petro-chemical industry which, according to Ben-Gurion, could provide a living for a population of a million in the Negev, Israel's southern wilderness, by 1970. To this end Israel is planning to invest half a billion dollars in the Negev during the 1960's.

At the Dead Sea, nature and history have come together to produce a modern-day miracle. This area holds practically limitless mineral reserves. Locked in the Dead Sea are an estimated 43 billion tons of magnesium bromide, and chlorides of sodium, magnesium, calcium and potassium. These salts, which the burning sun crystallizes out in huge evaporation pans on the shores of the sea, are of great value in the chemical and fertilizer industries. And history has brought it about that there should be masses of immigrants in Israel now to reap this invaluable harvest and to populate the towns yet to be born as the Negev comes to life.

Engineers from America and Holland dealt with the challenge of building up forty miles of dams and dykes to protect the evaporation pans in the shallow parts of the Dead Sea from the rains that pour down from the hills in the winter. Plans included additions to the bromine plant and a magnesite factory which makes use of rock mines alongside the Dead Sea and of by-products obtained from the potash. There is a new plant, too, for the processing of the estimated 22 billion tons of magnesium chloride to liberate magnesium, a light, hard metal which shows powerful resistance to heat. This process requires electrolysis, for which the gas fields nearby have proven excellent sources of cheap energy.

Supervising the salt works at the Dead Sea plant from his modest, radio-equipped office is Abraham Shamir, a middle-aged engineer and retired Israeli army officer. Shamir, who was born in Rumania and came to Palestine in 1935, now presides over a civilian army of four hundred and fifty employees. They work in three shifts, because the plant can never stop churning salt water into potash and its by-products. If operations would ever come to a halt, Shamir explained, the iron pipes and vats would be ruined overnight by corrosion from the combination of salt and oxygen. There is a standby Diesel oil power plant which can be put into operation at a moment's notice if the electricity should fail or the natural gas pipelines break. The Dead Sea air is so heavily laden with salt that the power must be turned off periodically in order that the salt deposits may be removed from the wires. All equipment, pipes and vats coming into contact with the salt water must be replaced every three years. Wherever possible, these iron utensils are now being replaced by corrosion-resistant asbestos. The fresh water required to wash salt deposits from the evaporation pans must be procured from artesian wells drilled in solid rock and gravel dirt wadis.

All plant employees, with the exception of a few security officers and repair experts, commute to work from Beersheba, Arad and Dimona, the "bedroom" towns of the Negev. The bus ride over hairpin turns and steep climbs in the jagged mountains rimming the Dead Sea down to the sea itself, 1300 feet below sea level may take anywhere from half an hour to an hour and a half. In the summer, the heat is so intense that if the buses and cars used to transport the workers were not kept in the shade when not in use, the passengers would roast in them as in an oven.

These are only a few of the handicaps and problems with which Abraham Shamir and his associates must contend each day.

Shamir is well qualified for the arduous tasks entrusted in him. He studied engineering at colleges in Italy and Czechoslovakia and later at Columbia University. When he first came to Palestine, he worked as a boiler attendant at the Dead Sea's northern plant which was subsequently captured and destroyed by the Jordanian Army in the War of 1948. After the outbreak of World War II, Shamir joined the Royal Engineers of the British Eighth Army. In 1948 he became a lieutenant-colonel attached to the general headquarters of the new Israeli Army. Retiring from active service in 1953, Shamir became manager of a plastics factory in Rehovoth, remaining there until 1955 when the Dead Sea Works were reopened by the Israeli Government, and Mordecai Makleff, his former Chief of Staff in the Army, who was appointed president of the company, requested him to come to Sdom as manager of the salt works.

"Once we breathe the salt air of the Dead Sea," said Shamir, "we must come back. There is a fascination to this wilderness, and this work, so vital to Israel, presents a real challenge. This is what keeps us on the job. I might also add that even when it is 125 degrees in the shade here in the summer, it's more comfortable than on a humid day in Tel Aviv when the temperature is 90. Here in the Negev, the air is dry."

Despite the labor shortage in the country, Shamir told me, there is little personnel turnover at the Dead Sea Works. Employees receive 20 per cent more pay than workers with comparable jobs in the cities, in addition to low-cost housing. Originally, General Makleff built quarters for the employees at Sdom, adjoining the potash works. However, due to the unfavorable climate, the workers could not bring their families there. Realizing that it would be difficult if not impossible to keep a permanent employee force under these conditions, Gen. Makleff conceived the idea of "bedroom towns" further away where employees could take up permanent residence with their families. This was the origin of the town of Dimona which was founded in 1956. The newest Dead Sea employee community is Arad, to which Shamir, who now makes his home in Beersheba, is planning to move.

When the expansion program is completed, 1,400 additional workers will be employed at the Dea Sea plants. Employee morale is high and labor-management relations, according to Shamir, are excellent. Here, too, I saw Jews from the Oriental countries working side by side with Ashkenazim in complete harmony, another instance of the joining of Jews from many lands to form one united Israel.

How the Dead Sea took on new life and became an essential component of Israel's future growth is a story that defies belief. It is a strange turn in history that the place where, according to the Book of Genesis, Lot's wife turned to salt when she looked back upon the ruins of Sodom and Gomorrah, should now yield up life-giving chemicals to refresh the farmlands and to help the earth supply bread and fruit to hungry millions in many parts of the world. Thirty-five-ton trucks bring the potash from the Dead Sea to Elat for shipment to the Far East and to Beersheba, from where it is taken to Haifa harbor by rail. From there, three-fourths of the potash goes to Western Europe. The rest is shipped to South America, to Africa, China and Japan, and to countries behind the Iron Curtain, including Russia whose potash reserves, although they are the largest on earth, cannot supply all of the 800,000 tons of potash she needs each year.

While potash and petro-chemicals alone have a fabulous dollar-earning and job-creating potential for Israel, they represent only the beginning of a seemingly endless chain of subsidiary industries deriving from the operations at the Dead Sea plants as well as from the petroleum fields of the Negev.

There is bromine, a story in itself, which is extracted from the potash in a factory at Sdom. The concentration of bromine salts in the Dead Sea, over 4,000 milligrams per litre, is from 50 to 80 times higher than that found in ocean waters. Bromine is used in the production of ethylene dibromide for high-test gasoline, as well as in the manufacture of chemicals for photography, pharmaceuticals, soil fumigation and pest and weed control.

The potassium chloride from the Dead Sea is utilized as a basic material and processor in the production of soap, glass, enamel, chinaware, paper, dyes, plastics, and dynamite.

Magnesium chloride is used in the light metal industry, photography, bricks and as a corrosion preventive.

Petrochemicals have already yielded 2,347 by-products, as chemists constantly open new areas in the development of synthetics and plastics. This, of course, is a "natural" for Israel, which has the needed brain-power and the support of investors, domestic and foreign, willing and able to pour millions of dollars into petrochemical industries of which some will be set up near the Dead Sea at Arad.

The minerals of the Dead Sea lay unknown and unexploited until the 1920's, when Moses Novomeysky, a Jewish mining engineer from Siberia, experimented successfully with solar evaporation of the salt water at Sdom. Novomeysky enlisted the help of Israel B. Brodie, a prominent New York Zionist, in raising $300,000 to underwrite Palestine Potash, Ltd., the forerunner of the Dead Sea Works, for which he obtained a 99 year concession from the British Mandatory authorities. Among the first stockholders in the enterprise were Supreme Court Justice Louis D. Brandeis, Judge Julian Mack and Aaron Strauss, who made their investment on a "sporting" basis, willing to risk loss on the chance that their money might be of some help to the Zionist movement. These men realized that whoever controlled what was obviously great untapped wealth would gain control also over the destinies of the Holy Land.

Brodie's son, Gerson H. Brodie, who is president of the Denver-Golden Research Corporation in Denver, told me that the Dead Sea could supply the world's fertilizer needs for the next two thousand years. The younger Brodie, who acts as an oil advisor to Israel's petroleum interests, said that the combination of Dead Sea minerals and the oil and gas fields of the Negev eventually will give rise to a great chemical and petro-chemical industry in Israel's southern desert in size and scope comparable to America's Du Pont enterprises.

The first potash and bromide plants were constructed in 1930 and 1931 at the northern tip of the Dead Sea where the River Jordan enters, bearing water from the Sea of Galilee up in the north. In 1937, another potash plant was built at Sdom, the southern end of the Dead Sea.

During World War II, the Dead Sea was Britain's only source of potash and chemicals for the production of explosives. In the War of 1948, the Army of the Kingdom of Jordan captured and destroyed the northern Dead Sea plant. A handful of devoted workers and defenders, led by Moshe Langowsky, who had never left the area since 1927, staved off sporadic Jordan attacks on the southern plant and saved it for Israel. War damage and lack of road communications — the Army of Jordan had cut off the Jerusalem road — left Dead Sea industries idle until 1955, when a new asphalt-cement two-lane highway was built between Sdom and Beer-sheba. When the highway was ready, the Dead Sea area came alive again. Fresh water wells were bored in the hills and wadis, new equipment was installed, and the Dead Sea enterprise was reorganized by the Government of Israel with monies from Israel Bonds and other development funds and from private investors.

The Dead Sea industrial complex, which owes its rebirth primarily to Israel Bonds, is the most dramatic testimonial to the Bond drive. In 1955, when funds from Israel Bonds first brought the Dead Sea factories back to life, only the most fervent among Zionists would have invested in Sdom. Now, the industries of the Dead Sea are considered a prime investment by the World Bank.

Here, too, Israel is glad to have foreign capital share in her resources. The Dead Sea magnesite plant which manufactures the raw material for refractory brick, will be expanded to a 75,000 ton-a-year capacity by a partnership formed for this purpose by the Dead Sea Works and two American corporations, Harbison-Walker of Pennsylvania, and Continental Ore of New York.

At nearby Oron, another corporation, Phosphate, Ltd., is mining calcium phosphates, soda ash and concentrated phosphate fertilizer for export, mainly to the Far East. On the road to Elat, at Timna, King Solomon's mines are producing 6,000 tons of copper annually for export to Brazil, Portugal, Japan and Germany.

As for Elat, Israel's harbor at the Red Sea, it has grown from a site of two mud huts in 1949 to a seaport with 10,000 inhabitants, boasting modern hotels for an ever-growing tourist trade and holding seemingly limitless potential for industries such as fishing, shipping and manufacturing.

*    *    *

The older of the two development towns to have risen from the barren wasteland of the Negev is Dimona, founded in 1956.

Here the traveler in the Negev desert is suddenly confronted with blocks and blocks of newly-completed apartment houses, unfinished buildings in various stages of construction — a new city with a population of 26,000.

At the entrance to Dimona are two sprawling textile plants, Dimona Fibres, Ltd., and Kitan Mills, the largest in the Middle East, employing more than 1,000 men and women from the four corners of the earth. Both plants, which began production in 1961, expect to expand their output and to be in need of additional labor.

At present, much of the reservoir of labor on which Dimona Fibres and Kitan Mills expect to draw is still in Africa and Europe. National immigration plans call for the settlement of 1,000 newcomer families in Dimona each year. Immigrants assigned to Dimona are brought there directly from Haifa harbor or Lod airport and placed in new apartments that same night. The very next day the breadwinners are sent to work at the textile mills or on construction projects. Also living in Dimona are 200 workers who commute to the Dead Sea Potash Works and another 100 who are employed by Oron's Phosphate, Ltd. As a result of the southward drive of industrialization, sparked by the enormous influx of foreign capital investment, Dimona expects to acquire other factories in the near future.

I paid a visit to Haim Amiel, who had arrived from Algeria a short time before with his family. Crowded into a two-bedroom apartment were Haim, his pregnant wife, and their eight children, the youngest an infant in the mother's arms and the oldest married at 19, with two tots of her own. Each room is crowded with cots, and other beds stand on end during the day to be laid down at night.

Amiel, who was a waiter back in Oran, earns IL 7.50 a day as an apprentice at the $4,000,000 Dimona Fibres plant. His job is to lug bales of cotton to the textile machines. His married daughter and her husband are also working at the mill to contribute to the family income until they will receive an apartment of their own. The children run around barefooted and in thin clothing, some of the younger ones without pants.

"What can I do?" Haim, who is in his early 40's, shrugs in resignation, but not in despair.

"I prefer Israel with all its difficulties, I'd rather be here than live surrounded by Arabs who want to kill us. We came to Israel for the sake of our children, for their future. We'll adjust, and in a year's time we should be happy and contented."

Noah Naton, personnel manager at Dimona Fibres, who came to Israel from his native Holland several years after World War II, explained that while Haim Amiel had had to start at a low base pay, he had a chance to move up to better-paid jobs where he could make the equivalent of $10 a day, including productivity incentives and overtime.

As an apprentice, Haim was trained in the operation of the plant's latest spinning machines which had been purchased from Germany on reparations arrangements and from Japan on long-term loans. Within three months, Haim, or any apprentice with average intelligence and manual dexterity, becomes a productive worker and can rise to a top pay of $60 per week (before taxes and deductions for union dues, health insurance and compulsory payments toward the immigrant absorption loan). As head of a large family, Haim benefits from tax deductions for each child. He also gets bonus payments for every child beyond the first four.

This is the way Israel seeks to encourage what is called "internal immigration."

At Dimona Fibres, Haim works together with Jews from the world over. Standing at a machine near him I saw a woman from India dressed in a flowing sari.

I asked Naton about his experiences with regard to the acculturation of the plant's immigrant workers.

"We do not regard our workers as Algerians or Europeans or Yemenites or Indians," Naton replied. "We consider them all Israelis. There is no discrimination. Some of our employees from the Oriental countries think that there is prejudice against them. It's probably the oppression they've suffered in those countries that makes them suspect discrimination here. Actually, everyone here at the plant, regardless of his background, is treated alike and given the same opportunity to advance to top pay." Raphael Ozalb, the chief engineer, is an immigrant from Turkey.

Naton himself exemplifies a new type of immigrant to the development towns of the Negev, young sabras and young Europeans who are answering the call to "go South, young man!" When Dimona was first founded, 88 percent of its population was Oriental; this percentage has dropped with the arrival of newcomers from Europe and the coming of sabras and other residents from Tel Aviv, Haifa and Jerusalem to fill supervisory and technical positions. Naton and his wife came from Tel Aviv, and they are making the break by degrees. They took an apartment in Beersheba where they are still living. Naton commutes to his job in Dimona by Egged bus, a 45-minute ride each way. When a sufficiently large apartment will become available there, and life in the new development town will be a little less "frontier-like," he will make the final move to Dimona.

"We're much happier in Beersheba than we were in Tel Aviv," Naton told me. "We only miss the Israel Philharmonic concerts at the Mann Auditorium. Aside from that, we have everything here, and more. There is a special kind of spirit in the Negev. You really see something grow before your eyes. When you help build up new things like this plant and this town, you feel that you're truly building up Israel. Then, too, the dry climate here is better than the humidity up north. All our friends who made the move from Tel Aviv to Beersheba feel the way we do. They would not leave the Negev."

The "old-established" Israelis who have moved to the Negev regard it as their task to help train and educate the immigrant newcomers in Dimona in the Hebrew language, Israeli customs and ways, and to inform them about factory work habits, social benefits and workmen's rights.

Polish-born Menahem Schechter, who came to Israel in 1948, is secretary of Dimona's Histadrut Council. On the day of my visit, he was presiding at the dedication of the new Histadrut headquarters and social center in the town. Integration, he said, proceeds much more quickly at Dimona than it does in the larger cities, because Orientals and Ashkenazim have no other alternative but to work side by side in the textile plants and on construction jobs.

A significant aspect of Dimona's story is the presence of several ex-kibbutzniks, who left their kibbutzim after five to 25 years of communal living to become pioneers in the Negev.

One of these former kibbutzniks, who preferred to remain nameless, said he definitely preferred Dimona to his old kibbutz. After 20 years at the kibbutz, he felt the need for some incentive to make a new life for himself. "True," he said, "in theory, everybody owns a share in the kibbutz. But actually, nobody owns anything there."

When he decided to leave the collective, he, his wife and their young son had no possessions or assets except $2,500, which they had received in restitution payments from Germany, and which the kibbutz had allowed them to keep. It was not enough to buy an apartment in Tel Aviv, where apartments cost from $7,500 to $40,000. When the family turned to Histadrut for advice, they were told to go to Dimona.

In Dimona they could buy an apartment with a down payment of $850 and monthly installments of $22. The father is now employed as a white-collar worker, and he likes his job and his new life in the small town because it affords him an opportunity to get ahead as an individual.

"After twenty years on the kibbutz, I was fed up," he told me. "Many others feel the same way, and they're leaving, too. The wives are especially disgruntled because they have to work in the communal kitchen, laundry and perform other domestic services for the whole kibbutz, and they don't have the clothes, the entertainment and the comforts they've seen in Tel Aviv. Plenty of young people are leaving the kibbutz and settle either in Tel Aviv or in the development towns down here."

My informant believes that this exodus from the kibbutz to new frontiers may bring about far-reaching changes in the kibbutz itself.

"Maybe it'll make the kibbutz adopt a more individualistic way of life — more like a smallholder's moshav, perhaps . . ." he mused.

\* \* \*

Newest and most exciting of the developments in the

rebirth of the Negev is Arad, Israel's latest planned industrial community. Founded in 1963 with 170 families, or a total of 800 inhabitants, its aim is to have a population of 50,000 by 1980.

Arad, located in the midst of the Zohar-Kidod gas fields of eleven producing wells, is being built on the site of the ancient Canaanite city of Tel Arad which flourished during the Early Bronze Age, some 5,000 years ago. Its rocky, sandy soil holds a wealth of potash, vari-colored marble, and quarrying stone.

One of the main purposes of Arad is to serve as a "bedroom town" for the men who are employed at the Dead Sea Works in Sdom, seventeen miles away. But it seems that Arad has other assets that should make it attractive also to those not connected with the Dead Sea industries. Situated 2,500 feet above sea level, the town is blessed with dry, clean air and with sunshine 340 days out of every year. Kupat Holim, the Histadrut's health insurance fund, investigated Arad's possibilities as a resort for asthma sufferers. Cure seekers may well be drawn to Arad by hot mineral springs at nearby Abu Kek. And, of course, there's the Dead Sea, where vacationers can bathe the year round. The Federmann-Miami Investment Company, which owns the King David Hotel in Jerusalem and the Dan Hotels of Tel Aviv and Haifa, proposed to build a 60-room hotel on the hilltop overlooking Arad, which affords, among other things, a spectacular view of the Dead Sea far below.

More than 1,500 tourists take the bus trip from Tel Aviv to Arad each month to watch the new city rise from the sandhills. The visitors see an administrative center built in a low, square, frontier style, new apartment houses with 463 spacious dwelling units in the making, 30 temporary asbestos homes for the pioneer families, a police station with apartments for three

policemen and their families on the floor above headquarters, and a bustling potash plant. And the guide is
quick to show the plans for Arad's future, which call
for marble quarries and knitting mills to be operated
by Histadrut, and chemical plants and other concerns
to be run by private enterprise.

To induce Israelis from the cities to settle in this
desert town, the planners provided Arad with the trap-
pings of urban civilization from the very outset. It already has an elementary school, a health clinic with resident doctor and nurses, a synagogue, two grocery stores,
a post office, a bank and a library. For recreation, there
are playgrounds, clubhouses for youth and adults, athletic fields, and a large restaurant, which also serves
as a kind of town auditorium for movies and other entertainment presented once every two weeks.

I met Daniel Gavron, Arad's public relations officer
and tourist guide. Daniel and his wife like Arad and
insist that they feel neither lonely nor isolated there.
Every evening they meet their neighbors in an un-
ending series of discussions, study groups, socials and
parties.

The Gavrons, who are in their late twenties, are from
England. Daniel was born and raised in metropolitan
London. Why, I asked them, did they choose to come
to Israel, and to Arad, of all places?

Daniel, a slender young man with a goatee and shell-
rimmed glasses, told me his story. He and his wife An-
gela had been enthusiastic members of the Zionist
movement in London ever since they could remember.
Their goal had always been immigration to Israel and,
more specifically, to settle in a kibbutz. When they
arrived in Israel, the Gavrons stayed in a kibbutz but
had to leave after two years, because Eytan, their five-
year-old son, could not adjust to the kibbutz system
of communal child raising. They then tried out a

moshav. Eventually, they decided to become pioneers in the Negev.

"We wanted to be in a young and growing place," Gavron explained. "We feel we're doing constructive work for Israel here. It's a nice environment for the kids, too. In Tel Aviv, traffic's so chaotic that no parent would think of buying a bike for a boy. Here, it's perfectly safe for Eytan to ride his bicycle. No, we don't feel that moving away from the city was a sacrifice. True, we miss the concerts and the theaters of Tel Aviv. But to make up for that we get together every week to listen to records, and the radio plays lots of good music. And then we have our own celebrations of Pesah, Purim, Hanukka, Sukkot and Shevuot. Mind you, I'm not religious, but here we observe these holidays as cultural events, folk festivals, you know. And our social life is most enjoyable. Oh, there's lots of work, too, for all of us, down at the Dead Sea, and right here in construction and any number of services. Most of us are young, with small children, so the women are all busy housewives, but many of them are working as teachers, nurses or in offices just the same."

How will Arad get the 50,000 people it wants by 1980? With the Israel Government, Histadrut and Israel Bonds committed to the Arad experiment, the secret of its planned growth lies in careful timing and coordination in the expansion of industry and housing as well as of population. Prospective residents must pass a selection committee which accepts them only if new apartments and jobs are ready for them.

In this controlled timetable of growth, there can be no unemployment. In fact, there is in Arad a chronic shortage of labor which is alleviated by hired desert Bedouins and workers from Beersheba who are brought into the town by bus each day.

Zalman Mizhari, Histadrut's Absorption official, our host on the tour, explained that the Government and Histadrut induce industrial concerns to come to desert development towns such as Arad by extending attractive benefits including free land, fast tax write-offs, property tax moratoriums, and low-interest, long-term loans in amounts of up to 80 percent of the cost of factory and equipment. Histadrut aids many pioneering firms by going into partnership with them. Lured by these incentives, many Tel Aviv industries are selling their real estate to land speculators at a minimum of IL 100,000 per dunam (or a little over $33,300 per quarter-acre) and moving to the new Negev towns where the land, owned by the Jewish National Fund, is leased free, immigrant labor is abundant and development loans (financed by Israel Bonds) are available on liberal terms.

The population of Arad represents a cross-section of Israel in miniature. Its inhabitants are a good sample of Israel's Ingathering of exiles from the entire world. In Arad, each charter resident was a volunteer and was selected from a list of applicants including only "veteran Israelis," meaning men and women who were not entirely "green" but had been living in Israel for several years. Unlike that of other Negev towns where Orientals predominate, the population of Arad represents a fairly even balance between Orientals and Ashkenazim. The planners of Arad hope to be able to maintain a 50-50 Oriental-Ashkenazi ratio.

Daniel Gavron told me that many of his friends have married into Oriental families.

"Actually, here at Arad, you don't feel there's any difference between the Orientals and the Ashkenazim," he said. "The few Anglo-Saxon families here don't just go off by themselves for a social evening. At every social, they mix with others from other countries and other cultural backgrounds. And, of course, we all speak Hebrew.

"If we have any problem of prejudice, it's not with the Orientals. It's with the Bedouin workers who come here every day. Frankly, we treat them like aliens. And yet they've lived in this desert since the time of Abraham, and, according to the Bible, they're descendants of Abraham, too, through Ishmael."

The Bedouins who work at Arad have proven quick to learn skilled trades in Histadrut schools. They are simple, unobtrusive, friendly and peaceful. They have learned to speak Hebrew and use the bank of Arad. They benefit from the country's health program and are multiplying rapidly as their infant mortality rate plummets. As Israeli citizens, the Bedouins of the Negev have the right to settle at Arad if they so desire, and to apply for the same low-cost housing loans as any other Negev settler, but it is hardly likely that many of them will abandon the nomadic desert life they have led for centuries and settle in modern city dwellings instead.

I asked Gavron how the Bedouins, who are Moslems, feel about the Jewish state that has risen in the land they call their own.

"I think they're largely indifferent to the State of Israel," Gavron replied. "Their loyalty is to their tribe, and their only concern is to find waterholes and pastures for their sheep."

Colonel Yitzhak Pundak, Government-appointed town manager of Arad, has no doubt that Arad will be a city of 50,000 by 1980. "If Beersheba can do it, so can Arad," said white-haired Pundak, a veritable dynamo of drive and energy. "Within a year, they'll be bringing immigrants straight to Arad from the boats and planes, as they do now in the older development towns, to mix with the old-timers here. There should be plenty of jobs for them in our own industries, and at the Dead Sea..."

Archaeologists from the Hebrew University, digging through the rocks in and around Arad, have found vases, stones and other artifacts from ancient Tel Arad, dating from 3,500 B.C. to 800 A.D. These remnants of an ancient civilization are now on view to tourists visiting this newest of desert development towns in the Negev.

Said the *Jerusalem Post:* "Modern Arad realizes that its present-day industry had its precursor in the days of the Kingdom of Judah and thus is confident of its economic viability, for a sense of continuity has been established. The people of modern Arad do not consider themselves a lonely outpost in the wilderness, but the direct descendants of Solomonic Arad which guarded the approaches to Israel from the south."

# CHAPTER XII

## ISRAEL AIDS AFRICA, ASIA

I watched a tall, dark man from Africa surrounded by a cluster of curious sabra school children who bombarded him with questions about Tarzan of the Jungle.

I saw an Ethiopian touching the hand of a white girl for the first time as she guided him into a whirling hora.

I met a young Buddhist from Burma who came to Israel to study the moshavim and discovered in these agricultural cooperatives the translation of his own religious principles into the reality of day-to-day living.

And I sat in a classroom next to a Hindu from India who, in the company of students from Japan, Africa, the Philippines and other Eastern lands, absorbed Histadrut philosophies of labor economics, trade unionism, industrialization and social insurance.

At the Hadassah-Hebrew University Medical School, twenty students from Africa and Asia embarked on a six-year training course to enable them to teach medicine in their own countries.

Hundreds of men and women from Africa and Asia come to Israel each year to learn how to promote the development of their own new-born nations, and to raise

228

the living and health standards of their people.

At the same time, Israel sends to these emerging nations experts, instructors, survey missions and technical and professional teams. These Israelis go forth to export brains and know-how to places which have acquired importance on the map of the modern world; Congo, Ivory Coast, Togo, Mali, Senegal, Chad, Uganda, Ghana, Liberia, Nigeria, Sierra Leone, Kenya, Gambia, Dahomey, Nepal and Burma.

This is the "home-to-home" aspect of Israel's program of technical and economic cooperation with the developing nations in Africa and Asia and with scattered projects in South America.

By attracting a steady stream of students and government officials including prime ministers and cabinet members from abroad to train and observe in Israel, the Jewish State is making a lasting impression on the influentials of today and tomorrow in a vast part of the world that is steadily growing in importance. Israel's technical and economic aid to 87 Latin-American, Mediterranean, African and Asian nations is already paying off in increasing recognition and support from the United Nations where Israel is in desperate need of friends and understanding.

Israel's program of technical aid is earning dividends also in her trade relations with the new countries to whom she has given assistance. As early as 1960, more than $10,400,000 worth — or 12 per cent — of Israel's industrial exports went to Africa and Asia, and this was only the beginning. As the emerging nations, with the help of Israel-trained experts, bring their economies, agricultural methods and social systems into line with the needs and challenges of the twentieth century, their demands for Israeli products, machinery and services are expected to increase many times over.

Although Israel must compete with some of the

world's largest countries for orders, and even for the privilege of helping the young nations, which are being courted by the rivals in the "cold war" with free aid, advice and loans, the potential is unlimited.

Israel is not the savior of Africa, nor is the Afro-Asian market the one great hope for Israel's economy. The role of Israeli experts in the newly-established nations should not be overestimated. Yet it would be an equally great mistake to make light of Israel's part in the development and upbuilding of these infant republics.

To begin with, Israel is "in." In some countries in Asia and Africa, Israel is considered to have a stronger foothold than the United States and Britain, because there need be no fear that Israel has designs of imperialist expansion. As opposed to the emissaries from some other nations, the Israelis offer technical assistance and economic cooperation not as colonizers but as equals. Many emergent nations regard Israel as a kindred soul, another young, newly-established democracy which, beset by problems similar to their own, has evolved ways of solving these problems by cooperative institutions worthy of emulation and by the application of brain power to the maximum exploitation of her sparse natural resources.

Being regarded as "in," Israel is invited to organize joint enterprises with the governments and private interests of these new nations. Solel Bone, Histadrut's construction trust went into partnership with interests in Ghana, Nigeria, Sierra Leone, Burma, Nepal, Ethiopia, Iran, Turkey and Cyprus, and grossed $28,000,000 in overseas works in 1960 and approximately $42,000,000 in 1962. More than 350 Israeli experts are engaged in foreign projects which at present provide employment for a total of 30,000 natives in these countries.

Solel Bone construction projects include highways, housing, harbors, airports, government buildings, hotels, stadiums, farm settlements, schools and factories. To fulfill its far-flung obligations, Solel Bone is training tens of thousands of native laborers, foreman, superintendents, engineers, architects, carpenters and mechanics, setting up machine and carpentry shops, maintenance units, quarries, and importing heavy equipment, for transportation and production, so that the new nations may carry on the work on their own when the Israelis leave.

Zim, Israel's merchant fleet, went into partnership with the government of Ghana to form the Black Star Line, and remained as managing agent even after Ghana had taken over shipping operations outright.

Israeli doctors from the Hadassah-Hebrew University Medical School, Kupat Holim and government hospitals have established the Haile Selassie Hospital in Massawa, Ethiopia, and the eye clinic in Monrovia, Liberia; helped plan a 500-bed hospital and nursing school in Sierra Leone; and conducted medical surveys in Kenya and Tanganyika. Girls from Africa are coming to Israel to train as nurses.

Histadrut erected a building in Tel Aviv to house the Afro-Asian Institute for Labor Studies and Cooperation. Richard Zavidov, an instructor at the institute, gave us an insight into the human aspects of this project.

There is, of course, an enormous difference in education, culture, background and work experience between the students arriving from the Far East and those coming from tropical Africa.

Arrival in Tel Aviv may be as overwhelming an experience for the student from Tanganyika or Nigeria as the first flight to New York would be for a lifelong resident of Kibbutz Yagur.

"We have to be fathers and mothers to them," Zavidov said. Some of the students from Asia and Africa arrived in Israel's cold and rainy winter with tropical summer

clothes and had to be outfitted at once with new ward-
robes to withstand the chilly season.

The four-month course given by the Institute consists
of lectures, discussions, classwork, field studies, sightsee-
ing trip, (including four-day stays in various kibbutzim
and moshavim), and cultural programs of folklore, singing, dancing, exhibits, sports, and stage and screen performances.

Fiercely proud of their newly-gained independence,
the Africans want to imitate the white men in every
respect, even to playing tennis, which was the favorite
sport of the British colonists.

Occupied with the problem of integrating immigrants from the Oriental countries, the Israelis know
how to make their Asia and African guests feel at home
with them.

The colored students are invited into the homes of
Israelis on Friday nights to participate in the festive
Sabbath dinner. Social affairs are planned to welcome
them. They can be seen at concerts, movies, at the
theatres and the opera.

Instructors working with these visitors know how
deeply their colored students are hurt by such news of
racial discrimination from America as the refusal of
some Southern restaurant to serve a diplomat from an
African nation.

"The United States could give a hundred million dollars to an African state and one stupid Southern café
owner can spoil everything," said Zavidov, who was born
in Brooklyn but has been in Israel for all but nine of
his thirty-five years.

Israelis have quite a delicate task smoothing personal
relationships between their own people and some of
the African visitors, whose traditions and customs run
counter to Jewish and Western mores. For instance, Israeli girls and women who mingle with these guests at

receptions and folk dance festivals must be briefed in advance how to say a diplomatic "no" to blunt propositions from a student who already has four wives back in his own country.

When the enthusiastic observers from Asia and Africa are guided through Israel's kibbutzim and moshavim, they are cautioned not to attempt to transplant the uniquely Israeli set-up to their countries without modifications to adapt it to their own culture, tradition and general situation. Zavidov, who was raised at Kibbutz Urim, feels that the students from Asia and Africa do not seem to go for the completely non-individualist way of life that characterizes the kibbutz. "I don't blame them," he added. "The kibbutz is not going out of style, but it is not progressing. The human being is an individualist and wants to go it alone. The kibbutz way of life is not capable of solving all our problems."

The moshav or moshav shitufi, in which each farm family has its own home where it rears its children, and only the farm work and marketing are done on a collective basis, seems a better model for some of the new nations to follow. Burma has organized, on the pattern of the moshav, a large-scale model agricultural settlement built around a central area of clinics, schools, tractor stations, offices, shops and stores.

The Institute emphasizes that the change from primitive tribal custom to cooperative living for the common good is a long process. In Israel, the visitors from Asia and Africa learn that there are people who consider it an honor rather than a disgrace to be farmers and laborers. They are shown the evils of too rapid migration from the village to the city, and are taught the importance of giving assistance to the back-country population in raising their standard of living, attaining better health and devising cooperative methods for workshops and factories.

The Africans and Asians like much of what they see in the State of Israel. Contrary to those who visit the United States and feel that they can never hope to build in their own countries a manufacturing plant of General Electric or General Motors dimensions, the observers who come to Israel are made to realize that with a little concerted effort and outside assistance, it is entirely possible for their countries to attain Israeli-scale industries, collective farms, hospitals and social institutions in their lifetime.

Admittedly, the path of aid and cooperation with the Afro-Asian world is not always smooth for the Israelis. There are recipients of Israeli aid who do not exactly express their appreciation at the United Nations or in conferences with Arab leaders. Yet, at the grassroots level, the Israelis are freely told: "Don't pay attention to what Nkrumah may say in Belgrade. It means nothing. Don't mix one thing with another."

On the whole, it would seem that there is much good will for Israel in the countries of Africa and Asia.

Even the United States could learn a little from Israel. I feel that the American Government may profit if it were to ask Israeli experts to show our planners how to rebuild earthquake-shattered Alaska and make something of our underpopulated and underdeveloped forty-ninth State. For Israel, more than any other nation in the world, has succeeded in making the wilderness flourish.

One of Alaska's principal problems is how to get people to settle there and to do the actual work of rebuilding. Anchorage, the state's largest town, has only 46,000 inhabitants. The population of Seward, industrial and railway center, is a mere 1,700. Israeli know-how could be of great help in the American North, because Alaska is a vast, unpeopled and unexploited wilderness, and there is no better example of the development of a barren new frontier than the miracle that took place in Israel's Negev.

Israel could show Alaska how to set up development towns in the proper areas, channel investment funds into large-scale apartment projects and new industries, and furnish homes, schools and jobs to induce families to settle in that northern outpost. If little Israel could do this in the Negev, then, certainly, the mighty United States can populate Alaska and tap its undeveloped natural resources with the aid of new development towns on the Israeli pattern.

Alaska should not be neglected, not only because of its strategic location near Soviet Siberia but also because it could absorb thousands of unemployed, both white and Negro, who could be induced to leave the crowded metropolitan centers and start a new life in the North. Negroes who have already settled in Alaska agree that they have experienced neither bigotry nor discrimination there. Alaska has achieved its own miracle of integration of people of many ethnic, national, religious and racial backgrounds. Native Eskimos work, study, play and maintain friendly relationships with white and Negro Americans, and with immigrants from Canada, the Pacific Islands, China and Japan. Alaska, therefore, could attract many of the unemployed and disenchanted of all races and religions, not only from the crowded slums but also from the rural "poverty pockets" of the United States. According to recent statistics, 35 per cent of America's Negro youth in the population centers of the United States now roams about idle. To remedy this perilous situation, the United States would do well to develop Alaska to provide for unemployed of both races the same benefits which Israel has given to her Oriental immigrants in the Negev — schools, jobs and inexpensive housing. If Israel's example of mass immigration and intensive agricultural and industrial development were indeed to be adopted by the United States in Alaska, immigrant housing would have to be erected on a large-scale, thus giving rise to a booming housing and construction industry which in turn would spark an industrial boom.

What Israel has accomplished, Alaska can do also. While Israel depends on outside capital investments, foreign loans, German reparations, and Bond and UJA drives, Alaska, as one of the 50 States of the Union, could receive all the investment capital, loans and grants it needs from the Federal Government. Israeli law gives private investors every conceivable tax, loan, depreciation and hard-dollar export incentive. American business corporations should be offered similar economic incentives for investing in Alaska.

The development of the southern Negev desert area was urged by Ben-Gurion, who pointed out that "empty deserts cannot be defended against enemy attack."

In the same manner, an underpopulated Alaska, infinitely richer than Israel in natural resources, would be a tempting dish for neighboring Russia. The Soviets are still smarting with humiliation at the thought that a hundred years ago the Tsar's ministers could be duped into selling this land of unlimited potential to the United States for a mere $7,000,000.

Enterprising Israel, which has shared her technical skill and knowledge with 87 nations thus far, could do much for the free world's outpost in the great Northwest.

# CHAPTER XIII

# GREATEST LITTLE ARMY

The first question Americans ask of travelers returning from Israel is invariably about the danger of war, or the prospects of peace, with the Arabs. But in Israel, this is the least talked-about of all problems. Unless the visitor from abroad makes a specific inquiry, the only allusion he will probably hear to what he considers a burning issue, is a wishful sigh from some Israeli: "Ah, if only we could have two things — peace with the Arabs and a million Jews from Russia — we would be a great little country."

They may be surrounded by enemies who vow to drive the Jews into the Mediterranean Sea, but the Israelis are not tense or anxious in the least. They seem to worry no more about the possibility of Arab attack than Americans do about being prime targets for Soviet nuclear missiles. One might say that the Israelis and those who live among them for any length of time get used to "living dangerously." They go about their daily work, attend concerts, movies and plays, build up their country and absorb their immigrants as if they had not a foe in the world.

A half-billion dollars is being invested in Israel each year by foreign, domestic, private and public interests in cold-blooded bankers' confidence that this little country is here to stay. Jews are pouring into Haifa harbor and Lod airport from 80 countries without regard for the enemy who may be just across the street in Jerusalem or within shooting distance of isolated border kibbutzim and moshavim.

The single event mainly responsible for confidence and sense of security in the face of Nasser's threats of annihilation is the triumph of Israel's army in the Sinai campaign of 1956. Israel's five-day sweep through the Sinai desert to within ten miles of the Suez Canal proclaimed to all the world that the Jewish State would not go under.

Israel's Army, or *Tzahal* (abbreviation for "Defense Force of Israel"), as it is known, is unlike any other armed force in the world. It is not simply an army, but a school of citizenship for the never-ending waves of immigrant youth which surge into the country from every corner of the earth, bringing with them a welter of languages, customs and cultures which are poured into the melting pot that is Tzahal. Tzahal is army, navy and air corps all combined into one Israel Defense Force. There are no separate services.

Tzahal's French-made jet fighter-bombers, including the latest million-dollar Mirages and Mystères, constantly patrol the skies to guard the country against surprise attack from the air. It is only a few minutes by jet from Cairo to Tel Aviv or from Tel Aviv to Cairo. In Jerusalem, the enemy is just across the street; in Tiberias, he is on the other side of Lake Kinneret, and the kibbutzniks at Ein Gev have him looking down on them from the Surian hills right over them.

Tzahal is aided in its defense operation by *Nahal,* its youth volunteer auxiliary, whose members serve out part of their regular army term on border farm settlements to fill in for manpower shortages there. The long and dangerously zig-zagging border lines between Israel and Lebanon, Syria, Jordan and Egypt are guarded not by army posts but by kibbutzim, moshavim and other settlements, each one an independent, fortified outpost, trained and equipped to fight for survival without outside aid at least in the initial stages of enemy attack. These settlements are set up not where the soil is most fertile or in locations which lend themselves best to the amenities of civilization, but primarily with defense in mind.

Israel's state of perpetual readiness for total mobilization is not kept secret, because only a full appreciation of Israel's military might and determination can dissuade the Arabs from proceeding beyond threats, propaganda and economic boycott.

Egypt's Nasser faces the situation with surprising frankness and realism. In 1964 he warned the Arab world: "If I am not in a position to fight, I will say so, without shame. Should I lead you and my country to destruction?"

The secret of Israel's matchless record of victory over the Arabs is its military call-up system, designed to keep the entire nation under arms, but on reserve, as it were. Israel's standing army is one of the smallest in the world. It consists mainly of training forces of young men and unmarried women between the ages of eighteen and twenty going through their two-and-one-half year period of compulsory military service for boys and eighteen months for girls.

This ever-shifting body of soldier-citizens, built around a tiny nucleus of career officers, constitutes Israel's peacetime defense force. Most of these young men learn the art of war not in training camps but in the Negev, ever on the alert so that, if necessary, they may put their acquired military skills to immediate practical use.

If actual war comes, a citizen army can be summoned within one day and a night from streets, homes, shops, factories, farms, kibbutzim and moshavim. Every able-bodied man, and thousands of young women, can be mobilized and ready for action within 24 hours, as they were in the Suez campaign.

According to Brigadier-General Samuel L. A. Marshall, American military expert, author of *Sinai Victory*, and chief historian of the European Theater of Operations in World War II, this trained and ready reserve is approximately equal in strength to the total reserve of the United States, exclusive of the National Guard.

General Marshall, who has extolled Israel's army in several books and articles, wrote:

"There is great military power in Israel. There is no military ambition. The society is not militarized or even militant. Israel is the very opposite of these things. In the truest sense, Israel is an armed people, and there has been nothing quite like it since the time of ancient Rome."

The American officer, who made a six-week study of the Sinai campaign, attributes Israel's lightning conquest of the Sinai area — it was all done within one hundred hours — to "the consistency in all forces, the extraordinary boldness in planning at all levels, the sustained momentum of offensive power and an extreme vigor in ranks when under fire, which kept the attack moving according to plan."

"In Sinai," General Marshall stated, "the action of Israel's soldiers was distinguished by a uniform decisiveness — the ability to give an intrepid order almost instantly or to move on impulse against danger with no hesitation."

"Israel's army," Marshall wrote, "did it by extending the limits of military daring. Striking forces traveled farther over more formidable terrain in less time than any other combat body in history. Decision was won in three days. This alone is a feat at which to marvel. A fortified area about half the size of Nevada, and far more repellant than the harshest wastes in that state, was conquered by a small field army fighting as it drove forward almost at the rate of an unopposed motor caravan...The soldiers of Israel invariably looked their best in those hours when they were beset by the greatest combat difficulty and the enemy pressure became such that total disorganization should have ensued."

"What is their secret?" General Marshall, who claims that the Army of Israel, despite inferior and antiquated tanks, trucks and half-tracks, shows more sustained mobility than the Army of the United States, keeps asking. The secret, he discovered, is a fighting doctrine of calculated risk: "The shortest route to safety is the road to the enemy hill; when in doubt, strike out; when trapped by fire, move instead of digging in; always try for surprise; in attacking, risk, risk, risk, and yet avoid the useless waste of tanks and manpower."

The Sinai War, Marshall wrote, was won "in a whirl of such slender forces that it is almost a miracle that they were not beaten by space alone. They did it on sheer nerve more than with fire and deception."

General Moshe Dayan, Israel's former Chief of Staff and architect of the Sinai victory, said to General Marshall: "What gratifies me most is that we lost only one prisoner of war. He was a wounded pilot who was brought down behind enemy lines. He had no chance to escape. That kind of score is no accident. It means that all the men were doing their best. They all believe in the military worth of this army." General Marshall translated Dayan's statement in his own way: "The contagion of courage," he said, "is the source of all battlefield unity."

"The men of this small army responded as if what is all-important is to live life fully while one may," Marshall wrote. "Israel's army in Sinai is a case study in the generation of group power by consummate daring in the command."

By way of contrast, General Marshall's study revealed a shocking lack of responsibility in the Egyptian Command. Surrounded at Umm Shihan, the Egyptian commander told his garrison of 2,500 men that it was "every man for himself." The men thereupon set out on foot over a sea of sand for El-Arish, 52 miles in the direction of the Mediterranean Sea. Israeli pilots flying overhead saw masses of these stragglers, going mad from thirst in the blazing sun, crawling, tottering through the desert. Those who collapsed, were buried almost immediately by the shifting sands. Others were stalked and murdered by desert Bedouins, who were eager for their guns, clothes and trinkets. Only 700 of the original 2,500 lived to be taken prisoner by the Israelis.

Even now, Israel's General Staff still speaks with pride of Moshe Dayan. "Moshe did it for us," they will tell you. Dayan turned Israel's army, reservists and career soldiers alike, into duplicates of himself, and according to General Marshall, Dayan was a fighting man who "held to the conviction that, in battle, boldness usually pays off." Dayan's officers admired their commander-in-chief for his brilliant reasoning, his grasp of tactical detail as well as broad strategy, his ability to assess the enemy's strength accurately, and his absolute disdain for anyone on his staff who was not devoted to the welfare of the ordinary front-line soldier. His subordinates were impressed by his uncanny aptitude for singling out the crux of a problem, concentrating on that until he would arrive at a solution, and then implementing the methods of attaining that solution with a vigor bordering on ruthlessness. Dayan was able to do all this despite the fact that he was severely handicapped. He had lost one eye in World War II, and as a result, according to Marshall, was plagued with frequent blinding headaches.

The basic secret of Israel's triumph under Dayan lies in the Army's selection and training of men and officers. Every reasonably able-bodied Israeli male between the ages of 18 and 49 is either on active military duty or in the reserves. With its small population, Israel simply cannot afford to reject anyone not completely unfit for service. Its reject rate is only 7 per cent, as compared with 29 per cent in the Army of the United States. Israel's army accepts men with minor ailments including flat feet and visual defects; low intelligence and illiteracy do not make an Israeli exempt from military duty. Officers must come up through the ranks. "Pull," or "protektzia," as the Israelis call it, is practically unknown in the Army.

General Marshall found Israel's army training program twice and even three times as demanding as that to which American draftees are subjected. Most of the training takes place in the open field. Recruits sleep in the desert sand and live on iron rations, toughening up for the war they may have to fight tomorrow but which they hope will never come.

Captain Ben-Ami Cohen, a student at the Hebrew University, who participated in the Sinai campaign and was among the troops that reached the Suez Canal, said to me: "We all hate army life, but we know that this is the only way for us to survive."

"We did very well," he modestly says of the Sinai action. "We knew it was the only chance to get rid of the fedayeen who were murdering our people on the border. All of us were afraid, but no one tried to desert. Everyone did his duty. This is one of our advantages over our enemies. Everyone understand what is going on, why we are fighting, what our strategy is and what we are doing. Everything is explained to us. We are not treated as machines. The officer eats, sleeps and lives with his soldiers. He knows each of his men personally. He knows about their backgrounds and personal problems, and he can, and does, give them advice on where to turn for help, or for financial assistance for their families.

"Our boys are very brave in that they don't show their fear. I was with the captain of the Sinai parachutists for three months, and I was always afraid. In fact, we were all scared. I knew of only one man who was not, and he was called the 'madman.' But once you go into actual combat, you suddenly cease to be afraid. Fear is completely gone. Once the battle has started, you have no time to think about your own feelings. The Army takes boys and turns them into men and leaders of men. We have to be practical. You can't survive if you've nothing else but idealism. You don't want to kill human beings, but you have to do it, if you are to survive."

At the same time, Captain Cohen was quick to point out that service in Israel's Army was a valuable educational experience.

"Army service," he told me, "gives us a more intimate knowledge of our country. We learn to live on the soil under the worst possible conditions; it's cold in the desert at night, even in the summer. But even after living in the desert, we still love it.

"The Army is the best mortar for mixing the Orientals, the Sabras and the Ashkenazim. We're all young and have no prejudices. In the Army, you are taught to have an open mind and to develop your own philosophy of life. When you live, eat, sleep and fight side by side with men of backgrounds other than yours, you find out that they're all human beings just like you are yourself. You find out that while the Orientals may not all be educated, they're willing to learn, and the Army gives them that chance. I was surprised to see how helpful the Orientals are. They're not spoiled yet by the artificial ways of Western civilization. Once an Oriental's your friend he will do anything for you, even lay down his life.

"These two-and-a-half years in the Army," said Captain Cohen, "have taught me more than ten years of book learning."

The Army is of crucial significance in the integration of thousands of young immigrants.

"Tzahal is the melting pot in which our new Israeli society is created," an Army spokesman said to me. "We treat the immigrant boy as a soldier and as a potential citizen of tomorrow. Thousands of draftees go through our program of training. It is in the Army that many of them have their first contact with people from other parts of the world. In the towns and cities, they might have kept with their own countrymen in tight little *landsmannshaften*. But here, in the Army, they train and fight together with men and women from many nations."

I asked Colonel Gad Moses, Deputy Director of Information in the Army's Education Department, whether he had ever encountered instances of discrimination against immigrants from the Oriental nations in the service.

"In training and war alike, the Orientals are treated no differently from the Ashkenazim," replied Colonel Moses, who had fled to Palestine from his native Berlin when Hitler came to power in 1933. "The Orientals attain complete equality in our Army. They all wear the same uniform, eat the same food and do the same jobs. Our Army is the one place where they feel absolutely no discrimination. Here in particular they get the feeling of belonging to the nation and enjoying the same rights as the rest of us."

As a matter of fact, the Orientals are a privileged group in some respects. They need fewer points than the Ashkenazim for selection for officer training because the Army wants to encourage them to rise to command posts. Already, there are Yemenite captains, majors, colonels and air force pilots. Nor is Ben-Gurion's wish for a Yemenite Chief of Staff a dream for some far-distant future.

The Oriental soldiers proved to be gallant fighters in the Sinai campaign. Gad Wilman, who commanded a platoon composed of 25 newly-arrived immigrants from North Africa, Yemen, Iraq and Iran in the Sinai Campaign, recalled that, at one point, his platoon and three ancient U. S. Sherman tanks faced a deeply-entrenched Egyptian company equipped with superior armaments.

"A hail of machine-gun bullets came our way," Wilman declared. "I ran ahead and looked sideways. There were Simantov, who was forty and had five children at home, Hayim Yosef, Mahluf and all the others, running level with me." Defying mortar and machine-gun fire, the Oriental platoon moved forward bravely, never stopping even once, toward the Egyptian strongpoint, and stormed it. Said Mahluf, who hailed from Morocco. "Commander, I never thought I could be this brave."

The Army gives special attention to draftees of Oriental background who have had no secular education. To meet their needs, it has set up for them a program combining military training with compulsory classwork in Hebrew language, Bible, Israeli and world history, geography, mathematics and civics, to bring each recruit up to the minimum national standard of basic education and so speed up his adjustment to the environment, culture and language of modern Israel.

"To train productive, patriotic citizens in a democracy has become one of the principal tasks of Israel's military establishment," an Army official said. "No soldier leaves the service without having at least an elementary education. Once he has learned to read and write and knows what he is working and fighting for, the trainee is a better soldier during his term in the service and better citizenship material in civilian life."

In the Army, the recruits also learn the thousand and one technical skills which they will need not only as soldiers but as civilians later on.

"The Army turns out craftsmen and specialists in dozens of trades, many of which are useful in civilian life as well," Brigadier-General Shaul Ramati, author of a manual entitled *Israel's Defense Forces*, pointed out. "The increasing technological and scientific requirements of the Army have led to an expansion of pre-service schools for cadets and for ordnance and air force technicians. The Ordnance Corps stores equipment valued at millions of pounds, runs base workshops and adjusts all types of obsolete heavy fighting equipment to fit present-day requirements. Its technicians can take any gun, tank, technical instrument and machine — modern or of World War II vintage — that is used in the Army, strip it down to nuts and bolts, produce the spare parts needed to bring it up to date and reassemble it, ready for action. During the Sinai campaign of 1956 every case of technical breakdown was repaired by dawn the next day. The Ordnance Corps maintains schools where craftsmen and artisans are instructed in the various branches of modern ordnance. This is a valuable contribution to our national vocational training program."

Graduates of this technological training course are in

great demand in Israel's expanding civilian industries. The car, truck and bus repair shops in this country of crowded roads, where 10,000 new cars are purchased each year, are happy to hire men who have learned in the Army how to repair and rebuild damaged vehicles overnight. Radio station Kol Yisrael draws heavily on graduates of Army radio headquarters. El Al, Israel's national airline, relies on air force veterans to fill its ever-growing need for pilots, and for air and ground crews. Zim's fast-growing fleet has openings for men who have completed their tour of duty at sea.

The girls, who relieve the men for front-line fighting, also receive invaluable vocational training. They are taught to serve at military headquarters and army posts as mechanics, clerks, radio operators, parachute packers, telephone and teletype operators, instrument checkers, nurses, social workers and teachers. All these skills are in great demand in civilian industry, in offices, schools and hospitals. In Nahal, boys and girls learn farm chores and get a taste of kibbutz or moshav life. Some choose to remain on the soil and either join existing agricultural settlements or form new ones.

On the officer level, the Israel Defense Forces maintain an intensive educational program in a constant effort to upgrade the caliber of leadership and to raise the educational level of officers holding positions of command. More than a thousand Army officers are receiving a free high school education. Career officers are allowed a 50 per cent reduction in tuition fees at the Hebrew University and the Haifa Technion. Many are sent abroad to study at foreign military staff schools. Senior officers attend not only lectures on strategy but also courses in Jewish thought and culture.

Platoon and company commanders act as teachers to their units, delivering weekly lectures on the fundamental aims of the State, its foreign policy and domestic problems, and diplomatic developments in Israel and on the international scene. Any group of soldiers interested in a particular subject may request its commander to set up a study circle and to provide the required instructors.

The battle cry of the Officer Corps is not *"Kadimah (Forward)!"* but *"Aharai* (Follow me)!" The commanders do not merely push their men forward while they themselves remain behind in relative safety. They personally lead their men into battle. The cost of this concept of leadership runs high. Of 180 Israelis killed in the Sinai desert, a high proportion were in positions of command.

According to General Ramati, the only excuse accepted for failure by an Israeli officer to complete an assigned war mission is a casualty rate of more than 50 per cent in the group under his command. After every operation in the 1956 action an exhaustive analysis would be made to establish how each commander had performed during the battle. The man who would be rated the best, irrespective of his rank, would be assigned as leader of the next mission.

From the Officer Corps of Israel's Defense Forces comes the cream of the nation's young manhood, trained and tested for leadership and executive skill. When they leave the Army, these men quickly find managerial and executive positions in industry, commerce, education and government. Israel has retired her Chiefs of Staff from active service when they were in the prime of life, in their forties with many productive years still ahead. Yigael Yadin, who led Israel's Army in 1948, is now professor of archaeology at the Hebrew University; Yaakov Dori is president of the Haifa Technion; Mordecai Makleff is general manager of the Dead Sea Works; Haim Laskov is director of the Ports Authority, Moshe Dayan became Minister of Agriculture, and Zvi Tsur is director of the National Water Authority.

This policy of frequent rotation at top levels of command keeps the defense forces dynamic and receptive to new ideas.

"We can't afford to stagnate," said my army guide. "We have to be on the alert at all times. Our survival depends not so much on numbers as on quality. Our fighters are better than those of the enemy; so are our pilots and our technicians. And our educational program is designed to make our nation truly united."

The tour of duty for all soldiers, officers and enlisted men alike, includes an unforgettable encounter with the Negev. Captain Ben-Ami Cohen, for instance, was assigned to Mashabe Sade, south of Beersheba.

"I was convinced that nobody could live at Mashabe Sade," Captain Cohen said. "But suddenly we came upon a garden spot there in the middle of the wilderness — a kibbutz. That was my first meeting with the Negev. When you come to the Negev, you begin to understand what Ben-Gurion meant when he said that we could do great things there."

Many of Captain Cohen's friends have settled in the Negev after their Army training and taken technical jobs or managerial positions in the new industries that have arisen in the development towns.

"It is thrilling to build rather than just to accept things ready-made," Captain Cohen declared. "Human beings want to feel that they have created something new, and in the Negev you sense that you are truly doing a great deal for your nation.

"The Negev is a good opportunity for young men to get the best jobs, to start at the top," Captain Cohen added. "The Army is preparing a new generation for the industrialization of the Negev. All my Army friends have served there for at least six months. They got to know the Negev by getting its sand in their mouths and hair, and sleeping out in the desert in the cold nights wearing only an overcoat. But once you've been through that, you know you can live in the Negev. There's a fascination to this wild, wide-open country. It's like the frontier wilderness the Americans conquered in their Wild West."

*　*　*

Working for Tzahal and Israel deep within enemy territory is hashish, a drug which Nasser and millions of others in the Arab world smoke in cigarette form and which transports them into a haze of fantasy that stunts their progress, detaches their plans and policies from reality and is the cause of much of the military weakness and disunity that characterizes the Arab bloc.

According to Iraqi or Egyptian-born Israeli physicians, Nasser's radio harangues, which sometimes last as long as four hours, clearly show the effect of drug addiction on his mind. He wanders far afield in interminable, rambling orations and repeats himself over and over again as if he had forgotten what he had said earlier in his speech. He screams and rants in a manner unbecoming a chief of state and heaps vulgar insults not only on Israel but also on Arab leaders who dare disagree with him, and lately on America which feeds his nation.

Israeli doctors of Oriental origin who examined Egyptian and Arab prisoners of war captured in the Sinai campaign found that thousands of these captives had the hashish habit.

"As a physician," one of these doctors told me, "I would do all I can to eradicate this drug addiction. But as an Israeli who hears the Arab radio stations threaten us daily with extermination, I frankly admit that I am grateful for hashish. Hashish is the worst enemy of the Arabs because it weakens them and their leaders to an extent where they become irresolute and disunited and thus actually make us feel more secure."

This same doctor recalled that when he studied medicine at a European university, many of his Arab classmates were unable to finish the course and could not get their doctorates because they were slaves to hashish. In his native Baghdad, he told me, the boys and girls begin to smoke hashish when they are four-teen and fifteen years old.

If one really wishes to understand the attitude of the Arab world toward the Jews and Israel, one must talk with educated Israelis who originally lived in these countries, worked and studied side by side with their Moslem neighbors, absorbed their culture and differed specifically from them only with regard to religion.

Many prominent Israelis of Oriental origin say that if Eshkol's government made use of more Oriental talent in the Foreign Ministry, Israel might find it easier to reach an understanding with the Arab bloc.

Other Oriental thinkers are not quite so sanguine. They see the Arab-Israel rift as a deep one which is likely to take a generation or two to be bridged. They sum up the underlying causes of the present conflict as follows:

For over two thousand years, Jews have lived in close proximity, if not always in tranquility, with Arab and other Moslem majorities in North Africa, Yemen, Iraq and Persia. The Mohammedans, whose Koran was influ-enced by the Hebrew Bible and includes many stories and ethical ideas taken from it, regarded the Jewish mi-nority in their midst as the "people of the Book." Unlike the Christians, who blamed the Jews for the crucifixion of the founder of their religion, the Mohammedans had no religious reasons to hate the Jewish people. And among the masses of Moslems, who had no secular schooling, religion was the only thing that counted.

Then the English and French colonists brought their secular schools to the Arab countries and opened a new world of science, philosophy, history, languages and political knowledge to the Moslems who until then had studied nothing but the Koran. Thus has arisen in our time a new generation which, unable to reconcile the challenges of the secular world with the symbolism and teachings of Mohammedanism, was faced with a choice and opted in favor of the modern world. Therefore the present-day leadership class in Arab government, politics, education, industry and science is basically a non-religious group which, though it pays lip service to Islam and carries on its "holy war" against Israel in the name of Mohammed the Prophet, gives little thought to the ethical ideals that are part of the Koran. These Arab bigwigs certainly do not see why they should have any consideration for the Jews, and the policy which they plot for their countries is determined not by religious motives but by the influence of extremist elements who would murder in cold blood any Moslem leader who would attempt to make peace with Israel.

As Walter Eytan, former Director-General of the Foreign Ministry pointed out, the Arab states see no advantage in converting the armistice agreements they made with Israel in 1948 and 1949 into permanent peace treaties.

"It is a bitter truth," said Eytan, "that the Arab states have lost very little and gained a great deal from maintaining a state of war with Israel. The political advantages they derive from it are very great indeed." The fact is that Israel is the only point on which the Arab countries find they can agree. Israel is the common enemy that keeps the Arab bloc from falling apart and its members from turning against each other. It all adds up to the fact that Israel must continue to walk with care.

# CHAPTER XIV

# EVERY JEW IS A DOCTOR

"Every Jew is a doctor," the late Dr. Meir Vovsi used to say.

When asked to explain, Dr. Vovsi, who was a physician with the British Army in World War II and later served as medical director of Israel's Malben —JDC hospitals in Machne Israel and Pardes Katz, would reply:

"In England, it's the doctors who see the patient. If a patient comes to the British National Health Service and complains of a cough, the doctor asks him what kind of a cough it is. When the patient answers that he has a dry cough, the doctor prescribes codeine, three times a day, and that's the end of the interview.

"But in Israel, it's the patient who sees the doctor. He won't accept the quick quiz and prescription setup. He'll ask the doctor, 'Aren't you going to examine me?'. Besides, the Jewish patient never is satisfied with seeing just one doctor. Everybody in Israel runs to two or three."

Perhaps this is the reason why 2,500,000 Israelis can support more than 4,000 physicians — one doctor for every 625 persons — one of the highest doctor-patient ratios in the world. The combined Arab world, with 45,000,000 Arabs, has no more than 9,200 doctors, or one for every 7,200 persons in Lebanon and one per 40,000 in Saudi Arabia.

Israeli doctors complain that actually, the "support" they are getting is not overly generous. Two-thirds of the population is insured by the Kupat Holim (Sick Fund), leaving only a comparatively small number of wealthy business and professional people and their families to patronize specialists with private practices. Kupat Holim employs 2,100 physicians, 3,000 nurses, and 2,000 dentists, laboratory technicians and pharmacists.

The high percentage of doctors in Israel's present population has somewhat retarded the absorption of the greater-than-usual number of physicians now entering the country as immigrants. Despite the absorption of 700 new doctors in four years by Kupat Holim alone, 200 newly-arrived physicians were unemployed only recently. It is hoped that these will find work as industrial physicians, emergency doctors in the cities, heads of clinics in settlements and small towns, and that institutions such as Kupat Holim will find a way to engage them as badly needed additions to their staffs. Despite the high doctor-patient ratio, Kupat Holim members complain that they must lose half a day's work waiting their turn at overcrowded clinics and hospitals and that when they are finally called they are subjected to the British-style "quickie" examination at which they rebel. Critics of Kupat Holim contend that the Sick Fund could and should take in all the unemployed immigrant doctors to provide better and faster medical service for its one- and one-half million members.

A sore point with the medical profession in Israel is the inadequate remuneration received by physicians. Sixty per cent of the doctors live on salaries from Kupat Holim, Hadassah, Malben, the Ministry of Health or other public institutions, and they complain that Histadrut's low wage standards for physicians as compared to those for factory workers keeps doctors from attaining compensation even remotely in keeping with their long period of preparatory training, professional status and the comparative earning capacity of physicians in other advanced countries. Physicians' salaries average $250-500 a month, before taxes, which range between 20 and 33 per cent. Yet only few physicians go into private practice, for the number of patients in Israel able to afford private care is small.

Since 1912, Israel's doctors have been organized professionally in the Israel (formerly Palestine) Medical Association. Rather than seeking to eliminate "competition," the Association always insisted that every doctor, like any other Jew, has the right to come to the Land and to practice his profession here. In the half-century and more that has passed since the Association was first organized in Jaffa with nine charter members, it has never attempted to restrict the immigration of doctors or to subject them to restrictive examinations before permitting them to practice in Israel.

During the era of the British Mandate, when immigrant doctors could not obtain permits to practice, the Association did everything to enable the newcomers to find work even though they lacked licenses. During the first six years of the Hitler regime, two thousand doctors arrived in Palestine from the Central European countries. After the war, another large influx of physicians entered from Eastern Europe, and now Israel must absorb another immigration wave of medical men.

As an act of professional brotherhood, the Israel Medical Association raised a fund of IL 50,000 to assist immigrant doctors until they are absorbed. At present, it is planning to finance a home for retired physicians which will be open not only to Israelis but also to doctors from abroad who wish to spend their golden years in the Israel sun.

Physicians in the United States, interested in the welfare of their colleagues in Israel, have formed the American Physicians' Fellowship for the Israel Medical Association, with headquarters in Brookline, Massachusetts.

In 1962 the Israel Medical Association, in honor of the Golden Anniversary of its founding, held its fourth World Assembly at Tel Aviv's Mann Auditorium. At this gathering, Prof. Herman Zondek, as chairman, reported on the progress made by biochemistry in the search for the secret of life in cells. More specifically Prof. Zondek discussed the work of Prof. Isaac Berenblum at the Weizmann Institute on a two-stage cancer-producing mechanism.

Pointing out the "harmonious planning apparent in the organization of the living organism," Dr. Zondek delivered to the gathering a medical scientist's declaration of faith in God as the Creator of all things.

"Our cells and organs act in accordance with a harmonious preconceived plan, as if possessed by an inherent, unconscious reason," he told his audience. "But if we recognize an unconscious reason, we may safely accept the existence of a conscious reason.

"This conclusion leads us doctors and scientists to believe in the existence of some ultimate power which will forever remain incomprehensible to the human mind."

Since Israel's "Open Door" immigration policy does not exclude the sick, its medical services are engaged in a never ending battle to maintain and improve the nation's health. The Israeli Ministry of Health, operating more than 600 clinics at government hospitals, Kupat Holim, Hadassah, Malben and other public health agencies, must constantly cope with new viruses and endemic diseases imported by mass immigration, particularly by the heavy influx of newcomers from the Moslem countries.

Israel has a total of 102 hospitals with a total bed capacity of 12,250, and spends 10 per cent of its national budget on health. The disease-ridden Arab countries allocate less than 4 per cent of their budgets for this purpose.

Dr. Kalman Mann, director of Hadassah Medical Organization, pointed out that Israel is the healthiest nation in its part of the world. She has conquered tuberculosis, trachoma, malaria and other sub-tropical diseases. In the mass immigration wave of 1949-51, Israel was swamped with tuberculosis patients. Today, the incidence of TB in Israel is the third lowest in the world. With the tuberculosis death rate down to 4.7 per 1,000, many TB wards have been set aside for the care of general hospital cases and mental patients. Infant mortality in Israel is 0.3 per cent, as compared with 50 per cent in Yemen, 35 in Iraq, and 36 in Syria. And Israel's average life expectancy is 70.2 years for men and 72.2 years for women. In neighboring Egypt, it is 46 years, and in Iraq no more than 29.

To the outside world, Israel's progress in medical science is represented by the 400-bed, $30,000,000 Hadassah Medical Center — Hebrew University Medical School Hospital on the western frontier of the Jerusalem Hills which replaced the hospital on Mount Scopus, now in Jordan-held territory.

It was at the suggestion of Ben-Gurion that Hadassah built its new medical center on the mountain overlooking the Ein Karem section, six miles from the center of Jerusalem. In contrast to the isolation of the former Hadassah Hospital and Hebrew University buildings atop Mount Scopus, the new Hadassah Medical Center is being linked to the outskirts of Jerusalem at

Rehavia by a breathtaking chain of new housing projects, by intermediate villages such as Rassco, Katamon,
and the Biblical town of Ein Karem, which is hallowed
in Christian tradition as the birthplace of St. John the
Baptist.

"Hadassah gave impetus to the westward development of Jerusalem into the Tel Aviv corridor," said
Lucien Harris, director of information of the Hadassah
Medical Organization. "At the pace at which new housing and other developments are expanding in our direction, we expect that the open spaces between the Medical Center and the present outskirts of Jerusalem will
soon be built up. We have learned a lesson from the
loss of Mount Scopus. Had Mount Scopus, too, been
built up with Jewish settlements, we would never have
lost the University and our Hospital here."

In addition to consolidating, as it were, the western
approaches to Jerusalem from a security standpoint, its
location well outside the city allows the Medical Center
breathing space for future expansion.

A hospital employes' town, Kiryat Hadassah, is
planned around the 300-acre Medical Center. Until the
completion of this project, employees must commute to
the Hospital by bus from the city every day. On Sabbaths, Medical Center workers are transported by
special white buses marked "For Essential Medical
Staff Only." This is done to prevent the recurrence of
a distressing incident in which members of the extremist Neture Karta of Jerusalem's Mea Shearim district
stoned a bus carrying Hadassah doctors, nurses and other
employees to work on a Sabbath.

Recalling the incident, Harris pointed out that
Hadassah's sole interest is to make sure that its staff
gets to duty and relieves previous shifts on time. "We
are not in the transportation business," he said to me.
"We are part of the Jerusalem landscape. We under-

stand the feelings and sensibilities of religious people. We work closely with the Jerusalem Rabbinate. And now that the hospital is six miles away from the center of town, we sought to get the Rabbinate of the city to adopt an understanding attitude to the necessary transportation of hospital employes on the Sabbath."

An ironic twist in the "bus controversy" is that the old Orthodox settlement in Jerusalem has relied heavily on Hadassah's free medical services since the early beginnings of Hadassah's work in the Holy City.

The working population of Israel is covered by the Kupat Holim health insurance system to which members of the Israel Labor Federation contribute monthly. But the inhabitants of Mea Shearim and other ultra-Othodox sectors in the country, who are mainly teaching or studying at yeshivot and receive little or no income outside of funds donated by charity for the support of their institutions, have no such protection. Therefore they are dependent on Hadassah for free medical services.

What Hadassah means to the ailing poor of Jerusalem can best be observed in the spacious new lobby through which a thousand destitute sick men, women and children pass daily on their way to the outpatient department. There, on benches, sits a sample of the Ingathering — Yemenites, North Africans, Iraqis, Persians, Europeans, South Africans, Indians, Asians, Americans, Canadians, Arabs, people of every race and creed who come to Hadassah to be healed.

Hadassah's community health services include five branch hospitals in Jerusalem, and one each in Beersheba and Safed, and 27 clinics, a convalescent home, and a school hygiene center. And of course, there is the School of Nursing.

As the teaching hospital of the Hebrew University Medical School, Hadassah Medical Center accommo-

dates 450 medical students, plus classes in dentistry
and pharmacology. Each year the school awards degrees of Doctor of Medicine to 50 students, who largely
replace the aged physicians who retire or die in an
average year in Israel. Most of the graduates take positions with Kupat Holim. A few enter teaching, medical
research or public health.

"To save life and to restore the people physically
and emotionally — the dignity of the human being —this
is Hadassah's driving motivation," Dr. Mann stated. This
is an ambitious task, but Hadassah does it, and does it
well.

\* \* \*

Early in 1964, my wife "came home" to Mahne Israel
Rehabilitation Hospital. After a year in Denver, former Head Nurse Dora returned to visit her patients
and colleagues. It was a holiday for the cruelly handicapped human beings that fill the wards, beds and
workshops of the Malben Hospital and now welcomed
*Ahot* ("Sister") Dora with tears, hugs, embraces and
kisses.

As the word spread that their beloved head nurse
had come back, out came those who could leave their
beds, propelling themselves in their wheelchairs, hob-
bling on crutches, or weaving and bobbing in the stiff
gait of the semi-paralyzed. And the faces of the bedrid-
den grew bright with joy as they saw the sympathetic,
understanding woman who had cared for them with devotion and whom they adored in return.

These were the handicapped, the crippled and the
victims of progressive diseases of the nervous system,
who are helped to make the most of their lives and
abilities through the creative program of work and
rehabilitation sponsored by Malben, the service of the
American Jewish Joint Distribution Committee in Israel

for the care of handicapped immigrants. Here again was an Ingathering from all the ends of the earth, from Africa, Europe, Yemen, Iraq, South America and India, shouting greetings in Hebrew, Yiddish, German, Arabic, Russian, Polish and English as Dora came to each with a cheerful *shalom,* and inquired after their health, their family and their work.

Mahne Israel Rehabilitation, just across the road from Lod Airport, is just one of a network of hospitals, homes for the aged, clinics, day care centers, psychiatric services and institutions, sheltered workshops and other health facilities operated by Malben in Israel on an annual budget of $7,000,000 to serve a total of 84,000 sick, aged and handicapped immigrants. Mahne Israel has room for 160 patients. It receives the crippled, the distorted, the paraplegics, hemiplegics, amputees, and the victims of Parkinson's disease, arthritis, strokes, heart trouble, diabetes and sufferers from crippling diseases of the nervous system that defy attempts at cure.

We stopped to chat with Mussa Fared, the refugee from Nasser's Egypt who was still creating wonders of woodwork artistry from Jerusalem olive wood. Mussa weighs seventy pounds and is hardly more than a handsome head, perched atop a cruelly deformed body, with one leg crippled and crooked, childlike hands with several fingers missing. On his tiny, stunted hands he has leather protectors so that he can hold a chisel and tap it gently with the back of his other hand. In this manner he can operate a machine tool and the products of his skill — paper cutters, dishes, knives, forks, spoons, cigarette boxes — are sold in tourist gift shops. As he works, there is a sweet smile on his face. He is happy that he can do creative and productive work to earn part of his keep. He proudly showed us a picture of his girl friend, a victim of cerebral palsy.

Next we visited with Michaela, who spent her childhood in the Nazi death camps and was rescued by the American forces of liberation. Now in her middle thirties, she is afflicted with Parkinson's disease which has paralyzed both her legs and her left hand. Yet, with her one good hand, this courageous young woman propels her wheelchair, even manages to play the piano and to weave beautiful rugs on a loom. And she can talk, sing and laugh in twelve languages.

There was Moshe Shamogi, a painter and writer from Hungary, who wrote a book on the terrors of the Nazi extermination plants which he survived. Ten years ago Moshe showed the first symptoms of muscular dystrophy. Now in his early fifties, weakened and paralyzed, he gets around in a wheelchair and proudly showed us a picture of his son who is studying biology at Stanford University.

Yankele Blau, another survivor of Hitler's reign of terror, is crippled by multiple sclerosis. A skilled tailor, he is busy sewing. Yankele, too, happily brought out a picture of his son in the uniform of the Israeli Army.

And there was Sophie, a pretty young woman in her thirties, who came to Israel from Rumania, and who cannot walk. Sophie is a dressmaker and continues to make use of her skill in the hospital workshop.

These men and women are part of the wave of mass immigration which brought to Israel the sick and the healthy, the rich and the poor, the workers and the handicapped without discrimination. For such is the Law of the Return: Any Jew who needs a home may come to Israel for good.

The basic objective of the Malben program for the handicapped is to get the patients to help themselves to the greatest possible extent. If, for instance, a cerebral palsy victim is found to be 90 per cent disabled, his whole life is rebuilt around the 10 per cent of ability still left him. He is tested for the type of work he can do, then trained accordingly and encouraged to spend as much time at that work — one hour, two, three, four or more hours each day — as his strength will permit. With the help of a grant from the Government of the United States, Mahne Israel has set up a program of skill assessment and rehabilitation training for cerebral palsy patients who come to the hospital workshops for day work, and mostly return to their homes at night.

In cases where rehabilitation has advanced to a stage where a patient is capable of caring for himself with the aid of ingenious devices and household gadgets especially designed for the handicapped, he is encouraged to return to his family, if he has one, and to do contract work at home as an out-patient of Mahne Israel. Some even graduate into private industry, where employers have found them to be productive, faithful and steady workers. But "Rully" Goldman, American-trained rehabilitation counselor, told me that in Israel, like in the United States, much still remains to be done to educate employers to hire the handicapped

Dr. Yona Goldreich, the medical director of Mahne Israel, fled to Soviet Russia in 1939 from the German invaders of his native Poland. During World War II, he served as a doctor in the Red Army. He summed up Malben's goal in these words: "Our aim is to give these handicapped people a purpose to live. We do this by giving them the dignity of work, which in turn gives them a sense of personal dignity and worth." Only 10 per cent of the patients at Mahne Israel are not able to do any kind of creative work whatsoever, even for an hour a day.

Dr. Meir Shadel, Malben's director of rehabilitation and homes for the aged, revealed that Malben is planning a gradual transfer of responsibility for its institutions to local communities and to the Government of

Israel. With mass immigration continuing to pour new-comers into Malben hospitals, homes for the aged and mental institutions, it will be many years before this objective can be attained. In the meantime, Malben is forming "partnerships" with local and national government units for joint responsibility with a view to having these units eventually take over the administration and financial support of institutions set up by Malben.

"We are also changing our minds about the whole concept of hospital and institutional care," Dr. Shadel said. "We are coming to believe that outpatient care is better than the best hospital or old age home for those who can receive care, or care for themselves, at home."

In the case of the aged, much depends on occupational therapy. The senior citizens are encouraged to "do what you want to do, and do what you are able to do, for as long as you are able."

By allowing the aged to help out in hospital and institutional housekeeping services, Malben not only keeps the oldsters busy and in good spirits but also saves money in labor costs.

Malben services have adopted new concepts in the medical care of the aged. Dr. Shadel prescribes tranquilizers to calm aged patients when they become disturbed. "An old man cannot always control his emotions," Dr. Shadel told me. "When an old person gets in a tough spot, he regresses to childhood and cries. We handle the emotionally disturbed among the aged by giving them emotional support. We do not believe in treating them all as victims of 'senile dementia.'"

Dr. Shadel explained a revolutionary concept applied by Malben in the care of the chronically ill.

"When a paralytic patient shows a 10 per cent improvement, we consider it rehabilitation. When he becomes able to sit up in bed instead of remaining flat on his back, we consider him improved. There is continual functional reassessment. Pathology is not important to us. What is important is the patient's ability to function, his ability to do something. If he has only one hand, we see what can be done to help him make full use of that one hand.

"Tranquilizers are effective also with the chronically ill. By lessening tensions, we prevent breakdowns, and once tension is lowered, you see a different person. The personal approach, too, works wonders. Nobody wants to be a number. Once you call a patient by name, you have already won his or her confidence. The doctor cannot be only a doctor. He must treat the whole person, not just physically, but also psychologically and socially, because social and psychological factors are definitely involved in the history of each patient.

"All our patients have been uprooted. Many are survivors of death camps. To them, small things can be very important. One may want to change his room, or his roommate; another may insist on having his bed near the door. If you listen to the patient, understand his needs and show him that you have his personal interest at heart, you have already helped him.

"Another innovation in Malben's program is the regular physical checkup to spot signs of illness and prevent physical breakdown. People change as they grow older, and constant assessment and reassessment is necessary. We have 130 known aged cancer patients walking around because we either operated early or treated them in time with chemicals or hormones."

Surgeons, Dr. Shadel noted, do not like to operate on old people, but Malben has an amazing record of successful surgery with patients over eighty.

\* \* \*

Israel's Number One unsolved health problem is mental illness. Today, Malben, in partnership with the Ministry of Health, is responsible for the care of 50 per cent of all mental patients in the country. Israel has set up a National Mental Health Assessment Center designed to serve new immigrants and old settlers alike, assigning the mentally disturbed to private or government institutions, or to "sheltered halfway houses."

After making a survey of Israel's health facilities and rehabilitation centers, including Mahne Israel, Dr. Howard A. Rusk, medical editor of *The New York Times,* reported:

"No nation has faced a more difficult task than Israel in providing rehabilitation services for large numbers of severely handicapped persons. The problem has been compounded by the continuous flow of immigrants into the country, a newly developing economy and the necessity for devoting a substantial proportion of the gross national income to defense.

"As evidenced by its tremendous social and technological progress (in the short time of its existence), Israel is a nation in a hurry. However, the needs of the individual have not been overlooked. Throughout Israel — in every village, settlement and farm — one sees men and women at work with pride and dignity.

"They are eloquent testimony to Israel's success in solving her rehabilitation problems — and to her concern for the human person."

# CHAPTER XV

## POLICING THE INGATHERING

"The police has its finger on the pulse of daily life in Israel," Chief Superintendent of Police David Ben-Yishai said to me when we discussed the share of his 7,000-man (and woman) police force in Operation In-gathering.

In this land of pioneers from all over the world, the police is called most often not to catch a holdup man but to settle quarrels between neighbors.

"Here in Israel, we build houses with thin walls," Chief Ben-Yishai, who had arrived in Tel-Aviv in 1932 from Galicia as an illegal immigrant, explained in Yiddish. "Now let's see what happens when a family from Poland moves in next door to Iraqis. On Friday night, the Polish Jews may be listening to a radio recording of the voice of Cantor Yossele Rosenblatt. But the Jews from Iraq next door have their radio tuned in to their favorite Moslem music from some station in Jordan. There you have a problem we never had back in Galicia. Our grandfathers may have had violent arguments on the merits of Hassidism against those of the *Misnagdish* viewpoint, but certainly never on the subject of *Haz-*

*zanish* chants as against Arabic melodies. On a Shabbat, the Jew from Poland wants Yossele Rosenblatt.
Arabic music grates on his nerves like a knife on a dish.
So one word leads to another, and the next thing you
know, somebody's called in the police to settle the argument.

"Now this sort of squabble isn't one you can deal
with by invoking paragraph 400 of the Police Code.
Our police here has to operate differently from any
other police force in the world. We have to have an
understanding for the human elements involved. The
Israel policeman has to understand the Jews from Poland, Iraq, Morocco, Germany, Yemen and South Africa.
In other words, when we enter a house we have to be able
to smell immediately what's cooking, *gefilte fish* or *felafel*.

"If you want to be sentimental about this thing, you
could say that Ben-Gurion's Operation Ingathering is
an even greater miracle than the Exodus from Egypt.
Moses took 600,000 Hebrews out of Egypt. They all
spoke the same language, wore the same type of clothing and observed the same customs. Still, Moses wan-
dered around the wilderness with them for 40 years
until the older generation died out so he could bring
a united new people into the Promised Land. By contrast, Ben-Gurion brought in a million newcomers from
80 different countries, who had nothing in common, pro-
fessors from German universities and mountain people
from Morocco who are a thousand years apart as far as
culture is concerned. And he had a good deal less than
40 years to do it in. Our job is to unify the products
of those vastly differing civilizations. In order to do
this well, in addition to handling the problems common to police forces the world over, the members of
the police force of Israel must be human beings first
and foremost."

At National Police Training Academy at Shfaram in

the Carmel region, near Haifa, Israeli policemen are taught to keep order with kid gloves and with understanding.

"In Israel," Chief Inspector Avraham Schwenk, the Academy's commanding officer, told me, "we learn many ways to deal with people without force. The idea behind our program is to get our trainees to regard troublemakers not as criminals but as people with problems."

When Tom Blitz, who accidentally shot and killed a bystander in a holdup at a movie theatre in Northern Tel Aviv, escaped from prison and fled across the border to Syria, the Israeli press headlines screamed out the story as if he were a master criminal.

"But what's Blitz really like?" asked Chief Ben-Yishai. "He's intelligent, a good pianist, but a very unlucky boy. Unfortunate family background, an unhappy life. So he vowed to get even with the world. The holdup failed, he pulled the trigger and the bullet happened to hit an engineer. So Blitz was given a life term. When he escaped, the public got hysterical. But Blitz isn't dangerous. He's a sick man. He has asthma and bad eyes and frankly, I have *rachmones* (pity) on him. I'm really sorry for the chap, sitting in jail in Syria without the medical care he needs."

In one year, a total of 30 murders was reported in Israel, all "crimes of passion," committed in anger, rather than with premeditated intention to kill. That same year saw only three major robberies in the entire country.

Riding in a district patrol car in Tel Aviv for two and a half hours during the after-work traffic rush was a tame experience. The only two calls received were about a lost child and a motorcycle-pedestrian accident in Ramat Gan. My hosts, Sergeant Jacob Cohen, who came to Israel from Poland in 1933 and saw service with the Israel Army, and Sergeant Reuven Elat, a native-born Tel Avivian, a veteran of the British Navy and the Palestine Mandate Police, had plenty of time to point out the sights of the city, and the trouble-spots and hangouts on HaYarkon Street along the sea-shore. Petty theft and juvenile delinquency, Chief Ben-Yishai insisted, were not serious problems in Israel. "To put this into proper perspective for you," he explained, "I'll tell you a true story that's making the rounds here. A newcomer climbed up an orange tree and helped him-self to the fruit of the Holy Land without first asking whether he could. The man who owned the orange grove caught him and hollered up to the thief, 'The Tora says, Thou shalt not steal. So what did the *ganov* do? He kept right on eating oranges and said, "Isn't Eretz Yisrael a wonderful country? Here I sit in a tree, eat oranges and listen to Tora, all at the same time.' So much for our petty larceny."

"Teddy-boys?" the Chief continued, "Well, our boys are full of energy. So they whistle at girls. So what? But organized gangs of juvenile delinquents — those we don't have."

Although he felt that youth had not created prob-lems of major dimensions in Israel, Chief Ben-Yishai said that not enough was being done for the young people of Israel. And the police force was doing some-thing about that.

The Municipality of Tel Aviv operates a network of 26 youth centers, but there are not enough clubhouses for youngsters living in outlying towns. The police has supplied seventeen WIZO (Women's International Zionist Organization) youth clubs in development areas with special instructors to lead immigrant boys and girls in sports, arts and crafts, music, discussions and cultural activities. In addition, the police has an orches-tra composed of its own members which performs at youth clubs and also in settlements and hospitals.

Chief Ben-Yishai reported a drastic change in the attitude of the public toward the police. During the huge immigration wave which swamped Israel with hundreds of thousands of newcomers between 1951 and 1953, the Knesset had to adopt a law providing stiff penalties for attacks on police officers. But since 1955 the courts have heard less than ten cases of aggressive resistance to members of the police force.

"We succeeded in teaching our immigrants — mostly those from the Moslem countries who had no conception of democratic life — that the police are for them, not against them," Ben-Yishai said.

Probably the toughest and most heartbreaking assignment is the one which falls to the Jerusalem police when it has to break up violent demonstrations by members of the ultra-Orthodox Neture Karta. Chief Inspector Schwenk, who had practiced law in Germany before coming to Israel in 1937, said that Jerusalem's police force knew Mea Shearim, the quarter of religious extremists, inside out.

"We try never to use force against religious people, except in those few cases where there's no other way out," he explained.

In a recent incident when Neture Karta demonstrators stoned a bus carrying essential employees of the Hadassah Hospital to work on the Sabbath, the police had to exercise particular caution. It seems that the demonstrators deliberately sought to provoke the police into using force, so that they, the demonstrators, could be photographed by the press as victims of police brutality and the pictures taken on the scene could be published in their fund-raising literature in the United States.

The immigrants from the Oriental countries, on the other hand, pose no special problems to the police. "All we have to do is to understand the mentality of the laborer from Morocco, the teacher from Yemen, the businessman from Rumania, and so forth. If we can't do that, we just aren't policemen," said the commanding officer of Israel's Police Academy. "You have to approach each person according to his own mentality and background. The *Yekke* from Germany is used to accepting orders from authorities without asking questions. But the newcomer from Poland may give you a whole argument that maybe what you call white isn't quite so white or maybe what you call black is half black and half-white."

Composed of almost exactly one-half Oriental officers and one-half from Ashkenazi background, Israel's police faithfully reflects the approximate fifty-fifty composition of the country's general population. But national origins play no part in either promotions or assignments. The small permanent units in which policemen train and work represent an Ingathering in miniature from all over the world.

I was introduced to Inspector Arie Amikam, Chief of Shfaram's school for non-commissioned officers. As this Czech-born officer sees it, one of the worst headaches of Israel's police force is the traffic problem. The streets and highways are two-lane, totally inadequate for the present-day heavy traffic of cars, trucks, buses, taxicabs, motorcycles, scooters, bicycles, plus a motley assortment of more primitive conveyances. Traffic is handled by special details, including a policewomen's auxiliary whose members are so charming that violators usually accept tickets from them without argument.

The pay on the police force is low, starting at IL 220 (a little over $70) a month and increasing to an average of IL 260 (less than $90) according to rank, experience, and size of family. This modest compensation — a factory worker gets about IL 350 (about $116) — is expected to result in a preponderance of newcomers from the Oriental countries, whose general lack

of secondary and college education keeps them from
work with higher pay.

The pride of Shfaram is Jubal, winner of twelve
international awards, and one of 35 police dogs which
are trained at the Academy. Commands are given in
Hebrew, of course, and each dog has a vocabulary of
25 words by the time he's through training. Jubal, a
German shepherd, is world-famous for his fine sense
of smell with which he unerringly tracks down caches
of hashish, the chief narcotic of the Arab world. According to Sergeant Avraham Rubek, who has over
three decades of experience in training police blood-
hounds, the mere mention of Jubal's name is enough
to cause dope peddlers in Jaffa to quake with fear.

Another source of pride to the Academy is the training course for African policemen which has been set
up as part of Israel's program of technical assistance to
newly-independent nations.

There is no racial discrimination of any kind in the
selection of candidates for the non-commissioned officers' school, Inspector Amikam stressed. Selection is
made from candidates with more than six years' experience on the police force, on the basis of character, ability, attitude and potential for leadership.

Under Inspector Amikam's guidance, candidates absorb such subjects as criminal law, investigation, psychology and basic academic studies. In addition, they learn
the art of handling subordinates on the force as well
as the general public. For this skill, the Inspector said,
the candidate must have not only brains, but a *Yiddishe
herz*, a warm and understanding heart.

\* \* \*

I have been to prison to see the conscience of Israel
at work. It all began when I met Victoria Nissan, who

is director of psychological and social services for Israel's five prisons. Mrs. Nissan spoke of the tour which the State of Israel had arranged for a high official of one of the new African nations. Looking over the itinerary, the official commented that there was something missing — a tour of a prison. Surprised and mildly annoyed that the visitor should ask to look into the seamier side of life in the Land of the Bible, his hostess, Foreign Minister Golda Meir, inquired, "Why a prison of all places?"

"You planned a wonderful tour to show me the achievements of your country," the guest replied. "You want me to see what you have built, how you care for your immigrants, and I am to inspect your schools, universities, hospitals, housing projects and government institutions. All these things are marvelous to see. But when I visit a country, I also want to take a look at the prisons, for it is there, behind the bars, that I see the conscience of the country — the way in which it deals with those who break its laws."

And so I, too, asked to see an Israeli prison. Accompanied by Mrs. Nissan, who studied at schools of social work at Baghdad and Tulane universities, I visited Mahne Massiyahu near Lod Airport, an "open-type" institution with minimum security. The barbed wire fences and the simple wooden gate are guarded by a detail chosen from among the prisoners themselves. In theory, any prisoner who wants to make a bid for freedom can walk out any time.

This freedom to go — with its corollary of self-discipline — is one of the subtler steps toward rehabilitation, and rehabilitation of the law-breaker is the ultimate purpose of the prison in the State of Israel.

The rehabilitation process begins in the courtroom where the convicted defendant is given a sentence to fit the nature of his crime and the attendant circumstances. Character rebuilding starts with classification and prison assignment. The case of every individual sentenced to a term in prison is turned over to a social worker trained in correctional therapy who in turn presents it to a national Penology Committee which then summons the convict for an interview. At this interview, each convict learns where he will serve out his term, who his psychiatric social worker will be, and what vocational training he will receive in prison. Thus, instead of entering prison in despair, he is brought there with hope for a new life.

"I don't see a prisoner," said Mrs. Nissan. "All I see is a human being. What he did was bad. But he himself is not bad. He has a problem. I try to find out his strengths and his weaknesses. Then we try to utilize his strength and shore it up to help him create a new life for himself. As we assist him in learning a trade and furthering his education, his self-esteem rises, and his self-image is a very important thing. His self-realization is accomplished by the use of all the elements that have shaped his life. We encourage him to maintain contacts with his family, friends, employer and community. We prepare the way for his eventual return to society by making sure that when he has served his term, society will be ready to accept him and to help him rebuild his life."

When a prisoner has completed two-thirds of his term, he is entitled to have his case reviewed by a parole commission, which may commute the sentence by cancelling the last third if, in its judgment, the prisoner is ready to return to society.

The crux of the penal rehabilitation program, according to Mrs. Nissan, is "self-improvement to channel the drive for destructiveness into constructive living." This objective is accomplished by a five-fold program of reading, entertainment, education, vocational training, and a routine of daily work.

However, this rehabilitation program is of no avail if the prisoner is not ready to cooperate. Here psychotherapy comes in to unlock whatever psychological blocks may be holding him back. At weekly sessions, the psychiatric social worker helps the prisoner rid himself of the emotional burdens that have led him astray. As self-understanding gradually clears up inner conflict, the prisoner begins to take an interest in the program of study, training and work that has been planned for his benefit. A recent survey has revealed that most of those discharged from prison "go straight" and become law-abiding citizens. Not all of the inmates of Israel's five prisons (Israel's total prison population is about 1,000) undergo this intensive program of psychotherapy, education and vocational retraining. Some don't need it; others don't stay long enough to use it. Some stay in prison only for 21 days for such minor offenses as failure to pay debts. This apparent throwback to the eighteenth century "debtors' prison" shocks American observers, but leaves Israelis unaffected. Most Israelis look with horror on the excesses of installment buying in the United States; they insist that people should buy only what they can afford to pay for in cash.

There is an increase in the number of "white collar criminals," clerks, tellers, bookkeepers and other officials convicted of embezzling funds from their employers including the government, banks, institutions of various kinds and private business concerns. Many cases involve stories of wives who drive their hubands to desperation by nagging them to earn more money so that they may be able to afford a car, a better apartment and trips abroad.

Instead of cells and bars, the prison I saw has dormitory-style barracks, twelve upper and lower double bunks in each building. Instead of being confined to one cell block, prisoners have the run of the entire detention area. Characteristically, Massiyahu is called a Mahane, or camp, rather than a prison, and bulletin boards are headlined "Notices to Residents." And when the "residents" are discharged, they are not given papers attesting to their release from prison but a diploma of graduation from the "Ramle Trade School."

Warden Aharon Turjiman, who was a prisoner of war in Nazi POW camps for four years during World War II, shows his sympathy and understanding for his charges in his attitude of friendly informality and his sincere concern for the welfare and the feelings of each individual under his care. Warden Turjiman, who was born in Israel and served with the British Army until he was captured by the Nazis in Greece, proudly escorted us through the prison library, recreation hall, synagogue, dining hall, kitchen, infirmary, sports areas and workshops.

Mahne Massiyahu has a synagogue complete with Ark, Scrolls of the Law, a shofar and other ceremonial objects. Services are held every weekday morning and evening and, of course, on Sabbaths and holidays. At the time of my visit, worship was conducted by a Yemenite rabbi who was completing a 56 months term for defrauding a Yemenite shohet of IL 40,000. He had managed to part the shohet from his hard-earned savings by promising to make him be the Messiah. The would-be Messiah-maker, father of ten children who visited him regularly each week, stoutly protested his innocence. Although his family was practically destitute, the rabbi insisted that he would repay every *pruta* of the 40,000 pounds. On his release, he said, he would return to his synagogue in the ancient town of Ekron.

The prison's farm raises vegetables, and a crop of

gladiolas raised in Massiyahu's flower gardens has won first prize at an annual flower exhibit in Haifa.

Mrs. Nissan invited us to sit in on a rehabilitation conference involving an Iraqi who had stabbed his wife, though fortunately not fatally. It was the typical story of an immigrant from the Oriental countries who discovered to his dismay that his wife could earn more money in Israel as a cleaning woman than he himself who had come without a trade. The wife came to despise him and found another man more to her liking. Then, in a fit of anger, her husband stabbed her.

Now he was completing his term at Massiyahu but he had plenty of other troubles which required the combined help of a team of social worker, physician, welfare agency and vocational instructor. He was suffering from tuberculosis of the bones, and one of his legs was three inches shorter than the other. He had to be taught a trade that would enable him to work, seated, in a comfortable shop. In addition, he needed the assistance of the Rabbinical Courts since his wife had requested a divorce. He served the first six years at a maximum security institution, then he was transferred to Massiyahu where he was put to work as an instructor in the prison's tailor shop. He soon acquired a sense of personal usefulness and worth.

"There you have the difference between punishment and rehabilitation," said Victoria Nissan.

Meanwhile, what was happening to the tailor's three children? They were placed in an institution for orphans and abandoned children. The officials of the institution felt that the children should never see their father again. Mrs. Nissan, on the other hand, was equally insistent that they should be permitted to have contact with their father because she believed that they would otherwise suffer psychological damage, creating unhealthy fantasies about the man who nearly murdered their mother. She succeeded in making her point, and the director of the orphanage offered his own home as a meeting place. The father was brought there from prison camp, gave his children gifts and spent a happy day with them. From then on, father and children met regularly on "neutral territory."

The tailor's twelve-year old son had a deep-seated hatred for his father. A psychiatric social worker helped him overcome these hostile feelings by explaining to him that certain human beings will hurt others in rage just as a child will break a cherished toy when he is angry.

This is the way in which Israel's prisons help the prisoner reestablish healthy relationships with his family and with society.

"It is much easier just to lock a man in a cell for years," said Victoria Nissan. "But then he is certain to leave bitter and maladjusted and ready to commit more and greater crimes." As she spoke, she radiated warmth and compassion. This is the conscience of Israel.

# CHAPTER XVI

# THE UNDEFEATED YOUTH

"The youth of Israel are a constant subject of concern, speculation, exhortation, and prophecy. They have been accused of isolationism and indifference toward Diaspora Jewry, and they have been charged with disdain for the victims of the Nazi horrors who went to their deaths like sheep to slaughter.

"What I find lacking in the Israeli youth is the sense of mission without which, I believe, Israel is missing its chief credentials."

These are the words of Rabbi Israel Goldstein of Keren Hayesod-United Israel Appeal.

Is it true that Israeli youth lack a sense of mission? And if so, is it because the mission has been somewhat blurred in the rapid transformation that has overtaken this ever-changing country in the less than two decades which have passed since it gained Statehood after bloody conflict with the Arab invaders?

Perhaps the answer is indeed indicated in that quick change of history that has taken place between 1948 and the 1960's. In 1948, and in the preceding years of conflict with the British and the Arabs, the sense of mission

which Dr. Goldstein now finds lacking in Israel's young
was as crystal clear to the youth of Palestine as the faces
of Arab attackers or of British troops disarming Hagana
units and armories. It was to fight for freedom against
the British and the Arabs. When freedom was achieved,
the sense of mission lost its clarity and its urgency. But
there are new channels into which this sense of mission
may be directed with great gain for the new State. How
can the youth of Israel serve as pioneers in Israel's quest
for economic progress and spiritual growth? And how do
the young find their place in Israel?

I cast about for answers to these questions. I had a
lengthy interview with Ben-Ami Cohen, captain in the
Israeli army, veteran of the Suez campaign, and now a
student of economics at the Hebrew University. We
spoke of the challenge presented to youth by the vast,
unexploited Negev desert.

"It's not just a challenge for pioneering spirit," replied Cohen, whose "extracurricular activity" is to be
director of the Israel Student Travel Association. "It's a
good opportunity for young men to get to real jobs, not
just second-rate positions."

Another venture that attracts many young Israelis today is the Israeli "peace corps" of technical experts which
is being sent abroad to aid the emergent nations of
Asia and Africa.

"We want to know other people," Captain Cohen said.
"Being a new nation ourselves, we have a feeling for
them. We can give them good ideas and an example that
will help them. They need us in Asia and Africa, and we
have plenty of extra engineers and doctors to send to
them."

Cohen, who has chosen budget analysis as his specific
field of study, evaluates Israel's future in straightfor-
ward terms:

"We need economic independence," he asserted. "We

need peace to help develop the entire Middle East. We need to find a common language with other small nations so that we may all be heard at the United Nations. We need a common language to communicate with the others, people to people, so that Israel won't be isolated. That's why I took my job with the Israel Students Travel Association — to work with exchange students and to help them."

"They say we're rejecting the Diaspora," Cohen continued. "I feel that Israeli youth wants very much to find some common ground with the Jews of America. But that's not easy, especially when the wealthy American tourists come over and ask, 'Well, what have you done with our money?' It's true that we got help from the American Jews — mostly through the UJA — to transport, resettle and house our immigrants. But you have to remember that the citizens of Israel pay for all this too — with heavy taxes. And as far as the contribution from America is concerned, we want to say to our fellow-Jews there, 'You did give us great help. Therefore, we cordially invite you to come and see what we have done with your money. See the work that's being done here because you have helped. But please — try to live among our people while you're with us. Don't just tour the country and gripe about the hotels.' "

Cohen conceded that many visitors from the United States do come to Israel with open minds, open eyes and a great deal of good will. "You can really talk with those people," he said.

He urged American students to spend a year at the Hebrew University, Bar-Ilan or Tel Aviv University or the Haifa Technion. Three hundred American students are already enrolled at these institutions. Many of them decide to settle in Israel, marry Israelis, and build a new life for themselves in the Jewish State.

Cohen, who graduated from a religious secondary

school, has clear-cut opinions about the problem of religion in Israel. He was raised in an Orthodox kibbutz, keeps a kosher house and frequently attends synagogue, but he is frank in voicing the widespread desire of Israeli youth for an easing of the stringent rules of Rabbinic law.

"Actually, despite what the Chief Rabbinate says, the majority of the religious and the non-religious believe that each should live his own life and that neither side should seek to impose its view on the other," Cohen declared.

"When I come to your home on a Sabbath, I won't smoke, but I want an opportunity to live as I please, to listen to the radio on the Sabbath and to drive my car, too, if I wish. There are many good things in our national tradition and we can't afford to cast it aside. But the trouble is that Israel has no great religious leaders who would be willing and able to adjust our religion to the needs of the present day. The Chief Rabbinate is so afraid of the religious extremists that it will not even attempt to make changes or revision in the Law to meet the demands of modern living.

"The youth doesn't believe that the religious laws were intended to be so strict. I don't believe that whether or not electric power can be used on the Sabbath is the main point of Tora. Nor can it be the will of God that all work activity should be stopped on the Sabbath in a modern State. And I don't think that Moses wore a yarmulka.

"If the religious leaders will continue to isolate themselves from the people, the youth will not follow religion. It's our task to make our tradition a positive force and not just have it make life difficult.

"I think a national council of religious and non-religious leaders should be set up here to try to adjust our religion to practical life in twentieth-century Israel.

We're no longer living in the tenth century. But nothing's being done and the rabbis are afraid of their own shadows," said Ben-Ami Cohen.

\* \* \*

"Do you have the time, sir?" The young soldier in the next seat on the Haifa-Tel Aviv bus spoke with a cultured British inflection.

Allan Muller, nineteen years old, had left his car and the comfortable apartment he had shared with his mother in Rhodesia, and settled in Israel. He told me that he had been inspired by a speaker from the Hebrew University and by reading *Exodus*.

"Until I read *Exodus*," he recalled, "Israel had never really entered my consciousness."

I asked him how he liked Israel after seven months.

Intelligent, perceptive, and obviously careful not to speak in generalities, Allan explained that he was not yet ready to decide whether he would remain in Israel permanently. But he had already completed his basic training with the Israeli Army and was stationed with a group of twenty immigrants from South Africa at Kibbutz Gesher on the Jordan border.

"Would you consider remaining in the kibbutz?" I inquired.

"No, sir," Allan replied. "The first two months, the kibbutz appears to be an ideal place. The kibbutz people don't get money for their work, but they receive all their basic needs — food, shelter, clothing, medical care, education and personal necessities. They don't have to face the struggle for a livelihood. They have peace of mind. But for my part, after two months, I'd be climbing up the walls. I'd go mad. No, the kibbutz isn't for me. And not one of the 20 other boys from South Africa will stay in the kibbutz after our term in the Army is over."

"What about the sabras who were born and raised at Gesher?" I asked him. "Do they return to the kibbutz when they're through with the Army?"

"Less than half the sabras of Gesher come back to the kibbutz to live when they finish Army service," Allen answered. "Though that figure is a little higher in the older kibbutzim. Until they reach eighteen — draft age — the youngsters think kibbutz life is the best and the happiest possible. But then, after they've been through Army training, and after they've mixed with boys and girls from all walks of Israeli life and with immigrant youth, most of them lose the idealism of the kibbutznik and long for more of an element of challenge in their personal lives. Then, too, many marry people from the cities who don't want to share what they consider the boredom and isolation of life in a kibbutz. Even a boy from a kibbutz and a girl from a moshav often can't agree on which of the two forms of cooperative living they prefer, and unhappily choose the city by way of compromise."

Official sources admit that only 5 per cent of Israeli youth movement members who dedicate a summer or even a year to work on kibbutzim eventually elect to join a kibbutz on a permanent basis.

What has happened to the idealism of the pre-State generations who went out into the wilderness and built up the collective farm settlements which proved impregnable strongholds of defense during the War of Independence and helped Israel attain virtual self-sufficiency in food production?

Is it true what Arthur Koestler, the author of *Thieves in the Night*, a novel about kibbutz life, said about the "Espresso Generation" of Israeli youth?

There are as many answers to these and other questions about the "new generation" as there are people to ask.

One view would agree with Koestler's condemnation of the "Espresso Generation." The proponents of this opinion believe that Israel's youth is no different from the youth of America and Europe which has produced the "Teddy Boys" of London, the street gangs of New York, and the boy hoodlums of Paris, Rome and Berlin. In Tel Aviv, Jerusalem, Haifa, Natanya, Hadera and elsewhere, they say the young people's main concern seems to be: "What'll we do tonight?" Israel's new generation has been accused of aggressiveness, nihilism, and of using the cinema and the espresso café as escapes from responsibility. It has been charged with placing personal advancement above service to community and nation. It is said to prefer transistor radios, cars, scooters and motorcycles to study and spiritual values, and all in all, to be brilliant but selfish. Israel's young may regard themselves as "Zionists;" if called upon, they may even offer help to Diaspora Jewries, but they lack all sense of identification with the individual Jew of Brooklyn, London or Casablanca, the supporters of Koestler's view maintain, and predict a rise in delinquency, alcoholism, and sexual problems among the youth of Israel. And they are convinced that it will become increasingly difficult to persuade these young people to give up material comforts in order to settle the outlying areas of the country where they would be badly needed.

Those who hold these pessimistic views cite as evidence in their support the writings of some of Israel's outstanding young poets and novelists. They point to S. Izhar's 1,000-page epic, *The Days of Ziklag,* in which Izhar who is considered one of Israel's brilliant young writers, tells of Israeli boys who displayed heroic tenacity in holding off the Egyptians in the War of Independence but had no real knowledge of the cause for which they were fighting. And to prove the self-centeredness of Israel's youth, they quote the popular poet Yehuda Amihai, who cried out, "There is no bridge between you and me. Each one stands alone."

Ben-Gurion vehemently disagrees. He insists that there never has been in Israel a more heroic generation than the young men and women who fought and won the wars of 1948 and 1956 to establish and consolidate the State of Israel. His own generation, he says, fell far short of the standard set by the young people of today. He points out that many of the pioneers who came to Palestine with him half a century ago found the pioneering life too difficult and returned to Russia.

The former Premier speaks with pride of the collective farms on the borders, settled by youngsters who defended these kibbutzim and moshavim against the Arab invader even as they raised crops to provide food for their people.

"In every generation," Ben-Gurion said, "the older people think the young cannot measure up to the generation that went before them." Ben-Gurion, who was a guardsman in his youth and is now a member of Kibbutz Sde Boker, feels that there is no justification for the belief that if a person does not belong to a kibbutz he is nothing. He has set new standards to define the present-day "pioneer." A jet pilot in Israel's Air Force is a pioneer able to defend his country in a far more effective way than Ben-Gurion had done as a *shomer* in the old days. A cancer researcher at the Weizmann Institute in the 1960's is in a position to clear a far wider path than the kibbutznik of 1910 who drained the malaria-infested marshes of the Galilee. A schoolteacher in the frontier town of Dimona today is just as much a pioneer as her grandmother who taught at a school in Haifa forty years ago. A nurse caring for the most pitiful victims of cerebral palsy, spinal meningitis and other dreaded progressive, chronic cripplers at Mahne Israel Hospital is a pioneer. So is the youth center worker who is toiling in the slums of Jaffa to weld together an Ingathering of young immigrants from eighty different countries.

There are others who take a less extreme view. They see Israel's youth neither as thrill-seeking delinquents nor as shining heroes. Hillel Barzel, deputy director of Tel Aviv's Municipal Department of Education, Culture and Youth, cautions against speaking of Israeli youth as one monolithic "type."

Barzel, a fifth-generation sabra and descendant of a long line of Hassidic rabbis, points out that if we are to understand Israel's youth, we must remember that we are not dealing with one homogenous entity. The young sabra has little in common with his immigrant contemporary. The children of low-income families from North Africa, Iraq and Yemen who live in the slums, naturally will be different from the Ashkenazi boys and girls whose parents are well-to-do and who have airy, modern apartments in one of the newer apartment houses. The young of the kibbutzim are worlds apart from their metropolitan contemporaries in Tel Aviv, Haifa and Jerusalem. And, of course, the yeshiva students of the Neture Karta of Mea Shearim, with their black frock coats, earlocks and broad-brimmed velour hats, who throw rocks at those who drive on the Sabbath, are worlds and centuries removed from the young *haverim* and *haverot* of Kibbutz Gesher who have no synagogue and think nothing of eating pork.

It would be a mistake, of course, Barzel said, to deny that the young people of Israel are influenced by the trend to self-centeredness, "careerism," escapism and "cinema culture" that can be noted in youth all over the world.

The reason for much of the instability seen among present-day youth in many nations is that, in today's specialized, atomic-age society, the young are accorded adult status at a much later age than earlier generations. According to Jewish law, Barzel pointed out, a boy of thirteen is a man. In Biblical times, he was considered ready for marriage. Today, a bar-mitzva boy is still a child. What with the academic and technical training required in today's world, the entry of the adolescent into self-sufficient adulthood is frequently delayed until he is well in his twenties. As a result, the modern adolescent is not sure where he belongs. He is physically ready for adulthood, but his parents at home, and his teachers, treat him as a child. He wants to feel like an adult, and he wants to have a sense of belonging to a group in which he is regarded as a full-fledged person in his own right. These needs of his are met by the teen-age gang.

"We live in the atomic age," Barzel said. "The youth only reflects our adult society. The young people say, 'Tomorrow the world may be destroyed in a nuclear war. So let's enjoy life today.' This probably is the basic cause of the nihilism, escapism and selfishness which we find among many of the young today."

Turning to the specific problems of Israeli youth, Barzel frankly conceded that the pioneering spirit that pervaded the young prior to Statehood in 1948 is no longer the spirit of all the youth of the 1960's.

"One aim of Zionism was to build a normal society with a normal youth in our Jewish Homeland," he sighed. "Now we do have what you might call a normal youth. But we're not satisfied."

I attended a symposium at Tel Aviv's ZOA House, where the sabra youth in particular was examined from head to foot and literally psychoanalyzed.

Emerging as the winner — if a discussion can be said to have a winner — was one of the spokesmen in behalf of the young people who had been born and raised in Israel. He was Avraham Shavit, whose family produces

80 per cent of the ovens used by Israeli housewives. Avraham served as a captain in Israel's air force in the War of Independence. Tall, strapping, intelligent and brilliantly articulate, Avraham, born and raised in Tel Aviv, was able to convert every criticism of the sabra into a point in his favor. Shavit was a living demonstration of the theory that, actually, there is nothing wrong with Israeli youth that education, economic opportunity and a bit of *mazel* couldn't cure.

Despite all the epithets such as "brash, crude, lewd, shrewd, conceited, free, immodest, noisy, boisterous, humorless, unmannerly, disrespectful, aggressive, provincial, chauvinistic, irreligious, boastful and unsportsmanlike," that are so readily hurled at the sabra youth of today, the panelists were generally agreed that Israeli youth is not only the product of the time and of the revolutionary conditions that gave birth to the Jewish State but is, in fact, the best type for this burgeoning young democracy.

Avraham Shavit denied many of the accusations leveled against his native-born generation. He spoke of differing values in different lands. Eating with chopsticks may be perfectly good manners in a Chinese restaurant, he said, but it is considered crude in a French restaurant, and certainly inappropriate in an Ashkenazi home in Jerusalem. But who can say what constitutes "bad manners" for a Yemenite family in Dimona which is merely following a ritual taught for many generations when it scoops its food with its hands from a common pot?

Shavit admitted that young Israelis hate to lose at sports, but could one honestly blame them, he asked, if they unconsciously carried over into the athletic field what they had been taught for years in the Hagana and in the Army, that there is no alternative to victory but death? Can fighters, who hear each day that the enemy must be defeated on the field of battle if the Jews are not to be driven into the Mediterranean, turn into gracious losers on the playfield at a moment's notice?

The pride — which irks some as boastfulness — with which Israeli youth speaks of its victories in 1948 and 1956 derives not only from self-confidence gained on the field of battle but also from the "superman" image of the young Israelis which has been projected in the best-seller book and the film *Exodus*. According to Shavit, this exaggerated image of superhuman virtues is downright embarrassing to many a sabra.

If the sabra of today is not religious, Shavit said, it may be due to the fact that his parents mocked God. He criticized the older generation for supplanting the Deity with the ideal of Statehood. When Statehood finally was attained in the War for Independence, he charged, "no other God was brought into our life."

Yitzhak Danziger, a member of the faculty of the Haifa Technion, questioned the propriety of lumping together all Israeli-born youth under the term of sabra. Danziger, who was born in Berlin and came to Palestine in 1923 at the age of seven, agreed with Hillel Barzel that while a yeshiva student of Jerusalem's Mea Shearim quarter, a young kibbutznik, and an engineer at the Dead Sea Potash Works may all be sabras, there is very little that they have in common.

Like Barzel, Danziger drew a sharp contrast between the sabra of the 1960's and his counterpart of the years preceding Statehood. Prior to 1948, he said, the sabra was either an idealist by nature, or was impelled by circumstances to be idealistic. Immersed in the country's life-and-death struggle for Statehood, he could not take time to plan his personal future, because he might get a notice at any time to report at six the next morning for a Hagana assignment which carried no guarantee of a safe return.

The sabra of today still gives two weeks to a month each year to Army reserve training, but the rest of the time he is free to plan for his education and his career, and to acquire an apartment, a car, and some of the luxuries of living. But today's sabra also requires new challenges, said Danziger, whose activities include sculpture and town planning. Such a challenge, he pointed out, is provided even now by the development of new industrial towns in the Negev which offer great opportunities for constructive work as well as self-advancement.

Elisha Almogar, sociologist and director of the ZOA House, noted that many of the sabras' less appealing character traits may have been engendered by the contradictory philosophies and values propounded in the turbulent times in which they live. At present, said Austrian-born Almogar, Israel is a land without traditions. The religious traditions of Judaism are accepted only by a minority of the people. Most of the men and women of Israel have thrown off old traditions but failed to develop new ones to take their place. The boisterous behavior of the young on the bus and in the street may be a cover-up for the confusion that this situation holds for them.

The young sabra who has been in battle faces additional problems. At the front, the soldier of eighteen was given the same responsibilities as the more mature man who fought at his side. But when he returns to civilian life, he is just another ex-soldier and in many cases a misfit.

Many of the older generation look askance at the sabra youth's seeming disregard for the social amenities, particularly for the etiquette of chivalry. But, as Almogar reminded the audience, many sabra boys and girls fought side by side in the Palmah, sharing responsibilities and dangers. Girls carried their own rifles and were assigned to tasks no less perilous than those given the boys. In a society where girl soldiers were accustomed to lug their

own rifles and ammunition, the tradition of boys carrying
the girls' books and packages must be learned all over
again.

As for learning in general, Moshe Posner, a British-
born teacher of English, reported that there is a tendency
among sabras never to want to say "I don't know," and
to hold forth at length on any topic from science to
religion whether they know anything about it or not.
Yet, he emphasized, sabras by and large are eager to
learn, "provided that the subject matter is of interest to
them."

*　　*　　*

The young people of Israel, sabra and foreign-born
alike, give considerable thought to the future and do not
hesitate to admit that they regard the problems they
encounter as formidable.

According to Yehuda Erel, director of Tel Aviv's Department of Recreation, the greatest concern of the
young men and women in the cities who contemplate
marriage and "settling down" is how to find an apartment they can afford.

"And after they get that apartment," Erel added,
"they face up to the task of building a family and attaining a high standard of living, which means a two-room
flat, a trip to Europe in a few years, and a little second-
hand car, one of those jobs we call 'Israeli push-me's' because they stall so often."

You cannot rent a flat in Israel's cities without a few
thousand dollars of "key money." For those who purchase their apartments, prices, compared with average
earnings, are astronomical. A working-class flat, with two
rooms utilized interchangeably as bedroom or living
room and a kitchen and bathroom, costs from $7,500 to
$10,000. Depending on the number of rooms, the age of
the house, various "extras" and the neighborhood in

which the apartment is located, an apartment may cost as much as $20,000.

While an immigrant family which decides to settle in outlying development areas gets a new apartment for no more than a token payment of $5 a month, Tel Avivians must raise a cash down payment of one-half to two-thirds of the total cost of the flat, a feat impossible for newlyweds without parental assistance, which frequently entails great sacrifice.

As soon as a child is born, parents save every penny, first for his high school tuition, which is $500 a year, and then for their contribution to the down payment for his apartment when he marries. In-laws must figure on about $1,000 for basic furniture, including $500 for an electric refrigerator which is a vital necessity in this subtropical country with its long, hot summers and the resultant peril of food spoilage.

With wages averaging from $40 to $45 a week, how do the young families manage? One answer is that 27 per cent of the wives work to help make ends meet and to save up for that dream trip to Europe and the "push-me" car. Despite hypothetical arguments over the question whether a housewife and mother should hold down an outside job, the working woman gets full approval and encouragement from the new State. Beba Idelson, member of the Knesset and a lifelong campaigner for women's equality, insists that the married woman's personality is developed and her horizons are broadened by the contacts she makes in her work outside the home. Scornful of the tea-drinking, gossiping and sidewalk-café sessions in which many a non-working wife indulges to kill time, Mrs. Idelson has called upon working housewives to avail themselves of labor-saving household appliances, and has urged Israel's industry and commerce to break down their work requirements into part-time jobs to enable mothers to accept employment for at least half a day, until one p.m., when the children's school day is over.

As the children are born, the two-room flat may be sold, often at a profit as property values join the inflationary climb. The proceeds are applied to the purchase of a three-room apartment, but the new home may still saddle the family with a debt of $5000. By the time the parents reach their forties, they are faced with the $500 annual high school tuition fee.

Yet, despite the tight squeeze between low salaries, high taxes and rising prices, the young men and women of Israel are optimistic. Fewer of them are leaving the country now; they enjoy the feeling that they can now have all the amenities of modern living even in Israel — modern apartments, cars, refrigerators and vacations — if they can afford it. They may not be able to afford all these things, but they insist that it is better to know that they are available in Israel if you have the money than to learn that they cannot be had there even if you would be in a position to pay for them. This knowledge impels the new generation to strive for a higher education, and economic advancement. Old-timers and kibbutzniks lambaste this attitude as "materialistic conformity," but such is the way of life of Israel's younger generation in the cities.

With all their optimism, the young Israelis are not oblivious of the continued Arab threat to the independence of their country. While one astute observer of the Tel Aviv scene reassured me that "the war threat does not disturb our optimism," he also made it plain that Israel's new generation was not living in a fool's paradise. The young men and women are ready at all times to go into battle to defend their country, their way of life, and their people. But they do not allow the ever-present danger of war to disturb their everyday lives and the happiness of their families.

"The sabra," Hillel Barzel noted, "still has in him some of the sadness of the Jewish soul. He's not a new type of human being. Go a little below the surface and you'll find many of the old traits that are regarded as typically Jewish. He's no coward. He's a good fighter, if need be, but contrary to the exaggerated image of the sabra that's been spread, he's not the Spartan of the Middle East. He doesn't regard military life as the ideal way of living. When his term of service ends, he's glad to return home."

\* \* \*

Returning to the less "materialistic" aspects of the problems of Israel's youth, Barzel spoke of the lengths to which some boys and girls of Oriental immigrant families go in order to conform to what they feel are sabra standards.

Observing that sabra girls appear to be rather free in their bestowal of kisses and other demonstrations of affection on the opposite sex, the dark-skinned Oriental maidens tend to believe that the Israeli girl dispenses love freely. They miss the sophisticated sabra nuance between the content of a serious love affair and the institution of marriage. If a sabra girl falls in love and is convinced that her boy friend is not exploiting her but truly returns her affection, she will let down the barriers without insisting on marriage first. More likely than not, she regards marriage as the natural result of an intimate relationship. But, contrary to what the Oriental girl may think, the average sabra does not believe in promiscuity and "free love."

While parents would be shocked to learn that their own daughter is a partner in this sabra version of companionate marriage, and parents and youth movement advisors continue to teach the young the traditional objections to pre-marital relationships, Barzel says:

"Israel is no different from the other Western countries where the so-called sex revolution has brought greater frankness, freedom and openness to this subject to individual relationships as well as to literature, movies and the stage. The sophisticated sabra looks primarily for love with a faithful partner and according to the modern view she does not need to wait until marriage for fulfillment. Of course, there are cases in which this freedom is misused, but we have a very low incidence of illegitimacy."

Barzel asserted that the municipality of Tel Aviv is a pace-setter for the rest of Israel in its awareness of youth's problems. The city has allocated a total annual budget of $600,000 to Barzel's department which supervises 36 youth clubs, 80 playing fields, 26 athletic areas, 26 youth centers and 70 summer camps, and is manned by 260 professional group workers.

"Our youth is good," said Deputy Mayor Moshe Goldstein, who, as director of the department, is Barzel's immediate superior. "They're energetic and must be kept busy. I don't believe in all that 'Espresso Generation' talk. Basically, our young people love work, they're simple and uncomplicated human beings and they'll do the right thing if you just have the right approach to them."

As for the charge that the young people of the cities are not answering Ben-Gurion's call to settle in the development areas of the Negev, Tel Aviv's Deputy Mayor said that many boys and girls from Tel Aviv's youth movements are now in outlying settlements in the Negev and Galilee.

"Tel Aviv has young people from 80 countries, speaking 40 languages," the Deputy Mayor, a former newspaperman and youth leader who came to Palestine in 1933 from his native Vilna, remarked. He noted that

there are pronounced differences between the young
people who have come to Israel from the Oriental countries and their parents, and defends today's young people
against those who would downgrade them in comparison
with the earlier generation.

Goldstein's department has taken constructive steps to
solve the "Friday night problem" for many young Tel
Avivians who are not particularly religious and are at
a loss for things to do on Friday nights when movie
theaters, commercial amusement places and public transportation do not operate. The Department of Education,
Culture and Youth has organized about a thousand Tel
Aviv boys and girls into small groups meeting at the
homes of various members on Friday night for discussions followed by singing and dancing to music provided
by the members themselves.

The political parties sponsor their own youth movements, imparting their respective ideologies to boys and
girls from the age of twelve onward. While these party
movements serve many positive purposes, such as in-
stilling the pioneering spirit into the young, critics note
a number of negative by-products, primarily that Israeli
adolescents tend to cling to the ideology of their particular party group even into their university days when
they might be expected to subject the pat formulas of
earlier years to critical evaluation and revision. The
Israeli penchant for splinter parties tends to perpetuate
itself from one generation to another. Frequently, political youth movements serve to divide, rather than to
unite, the young people of Israel.

\* \* \*

I went to the movies on HaYarkon Street to see "The
Young Savages." The reaction of the youthful audience
which had flocked to the show suggested a measure of

identification with the Puerto Rican and Italian teen-age gangs who met in savage warfare in the streets of Manhattan on the other side of the world.

It occurred to me that Israel has its potential "young savages" in the teen-age sons and daughters of the immigrants from the Moslem countries, boys and girls who, because of the cultural and educational gap of many centuries between themselves and their Ashkenazi and sabra counterparts, feel inferior and hence are super-sensitive to any slight that may smack of discrimination.

Having rejected the religious values of their "old-fashioned" parents, these dark-skinned youths from Morocco, Tunisia, Algeria, Egypt, Iraq, Iran and Yemen feel a lack of purpose in their lives. While many of their Ashkenazi and sabra contemporaries look forward to better employment opportunities because they have completed secondary school and, in many instances, university, these young people fear that they will have to spend the rest of their lives at menial tasks. It is not that higher education is deliberately denied the Orientals; indeed, the Israeli government extends scholarships and tuition allowances to encourage them to avail themselves of learning beyond the compulsory elementary level. The trouble lies in the home. With acute poverty, and fathers and mothers having little understanding or appreciation for the value of secondary education in secular subjects, the youngsters from the Oriental countries are forced to go to work as soon as possible to help support their families of eight, nine, ten or twelve brothers and sisters.

In the face of such frustration so similar to that suffered by many a Puerto Rican boy and girl in New York, I wondered, as the drama unfolded on the screen, why there were no "young savages" in the Jewish State.

"We're in the nation of the Bible," Hillel Barzel reminded me when I posed the question to him. "The

Bible still exerts a tremendous influence on the lives of our people. The Oriental Jewish family may live in a slum, but it has reverence for the ethical code of the Tora, and the parents have instilled in their children the conviction that rape and murder are monstrous crimes."

While the younger generation in Israel is clearly under the influence of trends which social and technological change and the resulting increase in the complexity of life have brought on throughout the world, Barzel stressed that there is one basic difference between the youth of Israel and that of Europe and America — "Jewish consciousness."

"In all schools, religious and non-religious alike," Barzel explained, "the children are taught that we Jews are an 'am segula, a chosen people, and that we must behave ourselves. The tragedy that destroyed our brethren in Europe has taught us that we must be better than the others if we want to survive. Therefore the teacher, the Army instructor, the employer all insist on high standards. In Israel, adherence to high standards is not a matter of being 'good.' It's a question of survival."

Jewish consciousness" is taught in all schools as a special subject in the form of Bible study, with emphasis on the significance of its moral teachings in Jewish history and ethics.

Thus, while the sabra may lack courtesy and good manners, serious delinquency has never been a problem in Israel. Percentage-wise, the local police files have as many youth dossiers as the Swiss police. But qualitatively, there is no basis for comparison. To-date, there have been no arrests for murder, rape or grand larceny among Israeli youth. If adolescents get into trouble with the law, it is chiefly for petty theft. Alcoholism is practically non-existent among young Israelis. Israel as a whole keeps only 6 per cent of its wine, whiskey and beer production for domestic consumption; the other 94 per cent are exported, and young Israelis "make life," as the Hebrew has it, with *gazoz,* a carbonated soft drink.

Barzel agreed with Danziger of the ZOA House symposium that the industrialization of the Negev provides a much-needed challenge to the youth of Israel. He mentioned an Army friend who studied engineering and went down to the Negev. Today, at 32, he is in charge of production in a factory there.

"This is *the* opportunity for our young people," Barzel exclaimed. "In what other country could he have gotten a job like that at 32? Where else could he have gone up the ladder so fast? Only in a pioneering country — or more specifically only in the Negev. In Tel Aviv, an engineer with his background would have to wait till he is 50 before they'd put him in charge of production at a plant that size."

He was caught up in the general enthusiasm which was then sweeping the country for the 70 young pioneers who volunteered to go down to the Negev and to establish an industrial cooperative, a desert city at Mitzpe Ramon, midway between Beersheba and Elat.

"It was all strictly spontaneous," Barzel said. "This project wasn't initiated by some bureaucrats. The young people did it all themselves."

Project Mitzpe Ramon is especially close to the heart of Ben-Gurion who is putting his personal prestige to work to see that it doesn't fail for lack of loans and other assistance.

The idea for this industrial cooperative was born in a sidewalk café on Ben Yehuda Street in Tel Aviv, where five of the original organizers started to enlist the aid of their friends for the venture. They went to Sde Boker to confer with Ben-Gurion at his kibbutz retreat. The "Old Man" was enthusiastic. He personally selected that particular spot near the Dead Sea, and he told the youngsters to be happy there and to "have many children."

"That depends on the girls," one of the young men replied.

"No," retorted Ben-Gurion, "it depends on you, *haverim*."

Said Dani Samroni, formerly of Tel Aviv, "I came here to the desert to begin a new life. After I was through with the Army, I got a job as a clerk in Tel Aviv. But I got fed up with city life. The café talk was boring. Apartments were out of reach — $10,000 to $15,000 for just a small apartment, with a down payment of 75 percent, and wages were low, only $40 a week before the stiff taxes. How could I ever have gotten married in the city with those obstacles to overcome? Here, housing's provided for pioneers for very little money, and I expect to earn more than I ever made in the city."

The pioneers of Mitzpe Ramon overcame their sense of isolation in the desert by organizing a multitude of activities including social circles, town meetings, semi-weekly movie programs, lectures by guest speakers, dramatics, arts and crafts, music, classes in Biblical and Israeli lore, English, painting, and a program of training in industrial skills.

The young men and women of Mitzpe Ramon plan to develop their new town with the aid of government loans. They intend to start small plants for the manufacture of mechanical parts, electrical and electronic products and ceramic goods.

Situated 2,500 feet above sea level, Mitzpe Ramon, which overlooks the Dead Sea valley, has a cool and dry climate. The pioneers hope to make it into a health and vacation resort in due time.

If Project Mitzpe Ramon succeeds, the young generation of Israel will have good cause to look upon it as its own milestone of adventure and pioneering in Israel's growth. A far cry from "The Young Savages" indeed.

# CHAPTER XVII

## SWITZERLAND OF ASIA MINOR

"Israel is planning to build a Switzerland in the Middle East!" This was not the pipe dream of a Cabinet minister or some government official who never had to meet a payroll, but a matter-of-fact statement by Israel Dikenstein, managing director and major owner of Albar, Ltd., Israel's largest aluminum factory, a glittering $3,000,000 example of the country's half-billion-dollar a year program of industrialization.

Albar sprawls over eight acres at Kfar Saba, in the fertile coastal farm country north of Tel Aviv. Dikenstein told me that the factory, which grossed $2,500,000 in one year, already was too small and would have to double its capacity to meet export demands. The most recent addition to Albar's list of exports is aluminum foil, which goes to Turkey for cigarette packages and milk bottle tops.

"I never dreamt that we would be able to compete abroad, but we are doing it," said Dikenstein. Now in his late fifties, he came to Palestine with his parents in 1923. He first went into manufacturing in 1940 with a starting capital of 1800 Palestine pounds, the proceeds from the sale of a plot of land he owned at Natanya. He acquired the capital for later industrial growth by turning out war materiel for the British Middle East Army during World War II.

Financed by a combination of Israeli and foreign investments, Albar Aluminum is an example of what Israel's industries have accomplished with an annual influx of $170,000,000 in private capital from abroad in addition to government investments and loans, Histadrut and domestic private investments, stock market and Israel Bonds, German reparations payments, United States Government grants and World Bank loans.

Albar, which employs 220 workers, of whom 80 per cent are immigrants from North Africa, Yemen, Iraq and Iran, is one of the more than 400 new enterprises approved annually by the Investment Center of Israel's Ministry of Commerce and Industry. Plants like Albar serve to industrialize the country, provide employment for mass immigration, meet the growing local consumer demand, help reduce the spending of foreign currency for imports, earn hard currency by exports, and so speed Israel toward economic independence.

Albar alone saves Israel $1,000,000 a year in foreign currency by eliminating the need for imports of aluminum foil and semi-finished materials. This saving was enough to pay for one full year's machinery imports.

Dikenstein, who built up world-wide business contacts on purchasing missions for the Israeli Army during the War of 1948, smiled broadly as he pointed to boxes stamped "ISTANBUL." He recalled that in 1955, a Swiss aluminum manufacturer had laughed at the idea that Israel would ever be able to make inroads into the monopoly of Alcoa and Aluminium of Canada.

"Today, the world aluminum industry knows of our existence," Dikenstein said. "They feel our competition," and this despite the fact that Albar must import raw aluminum ingots from Canada and France.

I asked Dikenstein how Israel manages to attract $170,-
000,000 in foreign private investments. The tall, suave
manufacturer attributed the influx of capital to government encouragement, tax benefits, confidence abroad in
Israel's economic future, trade agreements with 26 countries and close economic ties with the developing nations
of Asia and Africa. A Government-sponsored Israel Export Institute assists Israeli manufacturers seeking world
markets. Exhibits of Israeli products are arranged at
international fairs, and commercial attaches stationed
all over the world promote Israeli exports.

"Israel now compares favorably with advanced West
European countries as a profitable and secure place for
foreign investment," Dr. Z. Dinstein, director of the Investment Authority of Israel's Government, explained.
"Israel has a modern banking system with branches
throughout the world, modern postal and dial telephone
services, international telex, new highway and railroad
facilities, shipping and airline services to all parts of the
world, a nationwide electric grid system, compulsory
elementary education, vocational training schools, productivity drives, and a skilled and efficient labor force
which is constantly augmented by large-scale immigration. This, combined with relatively low average wages,
and the availability of engineers, scientists and other
professional personnel, is one of the country's greatest
inducements for incoming industries."

Albar does its share in the absorption and integration
of immigrant. At Albar's presses and machines, the
sabras are working side by side with newcomers from
Europe, South and North Africa, Iraq and Yemen. According to Israel Dikenstein, 50 different languages are
spoken at the mill, but every one of the workers knows
Hebrew.

I had been told that while Ashkenazim tended to
regard the factory as a temporary place of employment

where they intended to stay only until they saved up enough money to go into business for themselves, the Orientals looked upon factory work as a lifetime vocation and strove diligently to improve their skills in order to advance to better-paid tasks.

Dikenstein did not agree. "As far as I'm concerned, I don't see any difference between Ashkenazi workers and the Orientals," he said. "Our boys are all ambitious. They devour every book on the trade, and they advance to highly technical jobs. Incidentally, quite a few of our men are graduates from ORT schools in Tel Aviv and from ORT's technical school right here in Kfar Saba."

Dikenstein saved $7,000,000 in the building of his mill by acquiring junked presses and other used machinery in France, and rebuilding them with new key parts and smooth rollers in Albar's own machine shop.

"It takes courage and resourcefulness to start with old, rebuilt machines," he said with a smile. "But new bearings and rollers are really all that's needed to do the trick."

Above Dikenstein's desk hangs a huge portrait of Theodor Herzl, who said to the Jewish people: "If you will it, it is no dream."

Albar, Ltd., is just one example of the manner in which the industries of Israel are helping translate Herzl's vision into reality.

\* \* \*

Business is booming in Israel. "Any more modest word," wrote a *New York Herald Tribune* correspondent early in 1964, "would be inadequate" to describe the present situation in the Jewish State.

The evidences of prosperity in Israel are impressive when you recall that only ten to fifteen years ago this immigration-bloated infant nation was beset with stringent food rationing, a devastating trade deficit, and heavy unemployment with a quarter-million newcomers languishing in tents and ma'abarot.

Today, Israel has a food surplus to export. Its expanding industries are handicapped only by the shortage of skilled hands which persists despite mass immigration. Out of a total labor force of 830,000, only 3,500 are unemployed.

Early in 1964, the Economic Planning Authority of Israel's Treasury, in conjunction with the Bank of Israel, issued the following optimistic forecast for Israeli business and industry: The export volume during 1964 would increase to $700,000,000. In 1963, exports had been $500,000,000. The rise in imports would be slight, from $1,031,000 to $1,160,000. The trade gap would widen from $420,000,000 to $460,000,000, but this figure included the import of a great capital investment in the form of nineteen new ships worth a total of $68,000,000 by ZIM.

Capital inflow, including investments, German restitution payments, and loans, would rise above the 1963 total of $500,000,000. This increase would cover the trade deficit and swell Israel's foreign currency reserves by $55,000,000 to a total of $650,000,000, making possible the repayment of debts totalling $50,000,000 including the redemption of $24,000,000 in Israel Bonds.

Investments from Israeli sources would rise 12 per cent above the 1963 level to a total of 2,000,000,000 Israeli pounds.

Production would rise 9.5 per cent above the 1963 gross national product of $2,600,000,000.

In 1963, savings in Israel rose to IL 450,000,000, mainly due to German restitution payments totalling $140,000,000 made to victims of Nazi persecution. The Tel Aviv Stock Exchange, with a daily turnover of IL 3,000,000 from 150,000 small investors in addition to large-scale investors such as banks, trusts and mutual funds, became an important channel siphoning off savings for capital investment in corporations. However, much of the investment went for other than productive enterprises, going instead to land boom speculation and to a surfeit of new bond issues floated by banks and land companies. Within one year, land prices soared from 50 to 70 per cent in an unhealthy development of speculation which forced land values up to IL 150,000 per dunam, or $37,500 per quarter-acre. German reparation payments to the State of Israel ended in 1963, with a total of $820,000,000 paid to the State since 1952.

Dekel, the Israel Discount Bank's new mutual fund, established in 1963, ended its first year of operation with a 35 per cent rise.

Taxes in 1963 raised a total of IL 1,900,000,000, an increase of 18 per cent, due to the economic boom.

Israel's development budget for 1963 totalled IL 1,300,000,000; of this amount, 52 per cent came from foreign sources including Israel Bonds and German reparations, as compared to 56 per cent in 1962. The development budget was broken down into IL 144,000,000 for agriculture and irrigation; IL 290,000,000 for housing, including 10,000 apartments for immigrants; IL 30,-000,000 for mining; IL 42,000,000 for new power stations; IL 22,500,000 for industrial expansion; IL 65,000,000 for communications, and IL 60,000,000 for ports, highways and the Beersheba-Dimona railroad.

The two heavy clouds on Israel's economic horizon have been defense expenditures — the largest item on the national budget — and the ever-present threat of inflation.

Preparedness for Arab attack entailed great financial sacrifices on the part of the Israeli taxpayers, and averting inflation necessitated holding the line on the price-wage spiral under heavy pressure.

According to Pinhas Sapir, Minister of Finance, Commerce and Industry, the Eshkol Government's efforts to maintain stability in wages, taxes, production costs and prices "have been crowned with success." The alternative Sapir said, would have been "economic anarchy."

In 1963, foreign investments in Israeli industry dropped to $17,000,000 from $24,000,000 in 1962, but approved domestic investments in industrial enterprises increased from IL 48,000,000 to IL 71,000,000, which more than offset the loss of foreign capital. Dr. Dinstein attributed the decrease in foreign investments to a change in Israeli policy which put the accent on selection of investment projects, with priority given to those planned in development areas or to commitments to export a minimum of 50 per cent of Israel's production output. Approval for investment propositions in financial institutions, real estate, or services, was either refused or given on a limited scale only. Untold foreign investment propositions have been turned down because they do not meet the Israeli economists' requirement that they earn dollars through exports; or because the investor is unwilling to pay the prevailing Histadrut union wage scales and social benefits. A proposal by I. G. Farben to pour $250,000,000 into Israel's petro-chemical industry was turned down because the nation which so recently tried Eichmann for the death of six million Jews is not yet emotionally ready to open it doors to large-scale German industry. Dinstein revealed that since the enactment of Israel's "Law to Encourage Private Investment" in 1959, his office has approved investment projects totalling the equivalent of a half-billion dollars in foreign currency plus a half-billion Israeli pounds.

The influx of a half-billion dollars in foreign investments in addition to the Israeli capital has scotched ideological slogans predicting "Socialism in our time." The

1959 law has definitely swung the course of Israel into a combination economy based on private capital working together with cooperatives, Histadrut trusts, Kibbutzim and State-owned communications and railroads.

Amnon Ben-Zeev, spokesman of Israel's Finance Ministry, pointed out that mass immigration has served to create a growing domestic market. This, of course, is only a partial explanation for the country's economic boom of the early 1960's. As other factors, Ben Zeev cited the heavy investment by Israeli and foreign stock exchange funds in the industrialization of Israel; the upbuilding of the economy made possible by German reparations payments and Israel Bonds; the rapid development of Israel's agriculture from food deficit to surplus-export farm production; and the large-scale international loans and grants, mainly from the United States, the World Bank and the Import-Export Bank for such major projects as the Dead Sea Potash Works, Ashdod Harbor, roads, irrigation and communications. In 1964, loans and farm surplus shipments to Israel from the United States totalled $40,000,000.

"Without the tremendous burden of our security budget," Ben- Zeev told me, "we might have achieved economic self-sufficiency by now. If the United States would supply us with as many arms as Russia gives to Egypt, we would be in fine shape. But unlike Egypt, we have to pay for the arms we want. Our $600,000,000 foreign currency reserve, therefore, is not actually ours. We have long-term debts to pay."

Ben-Zeev also informed me that as of January 1, 1964, Israel's Ministry of Housing has taken over the financial responsibility for immigrant housing. Out of a total of 30,000 housing units to be built annually, 15,000 are for newcomers — because Jewish Agency funds, obtained through the United Jewish Appeal, must largely go to cover the cost of transportation, initial resettlement and training of immigrants and special training and care for newcomers who are old, ill or handicapped.

*　*　*

Remaining stubbornly outside Eshkol's coalition cabinet is Herut, the Revisionist (lit. "Freedom") group, Israel's second largest political party, led by Menahem Beigin.

Beigin feels that a better balanced relationship between the strength of the government on the one hand and the opposition on the other is a good thing for the individual citizen because the opposition serves the important purpose of ensuring his rights.

While Beigin is regarded by many of his countrymen as a demagogue who arouses mass hysteria at public gatherings, he is soft-spoken, sensible, logical and conservative in private conversation. With his emphasis on private enterprise, individual freedom, and his demand that the position of the Histadrut in Israel's politics be reduced to that of an ordinary trade union, he has considerable appeal to American business men who look askance at the brand of mixed socialism and capitalism espoused by Ben-Gurion and Eshkol.

Histadrut, an overall labor organization, stands unique in the free world as a combination of trade unions which also acts as owner of many of the greatest industrial enterprises in the country. Thus, Histadrut represents the employees and actually serves as their employer at the same time. According to Beigin, this is an anomalous arrangement which may have served its purpose in the days before the establishment of the State but which is out of step with Israel's present needs of large-scale investments for the industrial development of the Negev and the absorption of mass immigration.

"We cannot live in the past," Beigin told me. "We need a sound, self-sustaining economy. To attain this goal, Herut believes that Histadrut should become simply a trade union. It should not own industrial enterprises and compete with private industry. Of course the change can't all be made in one day. But it can and must be made — carefully, one enterprise at a time — for the benefit of Israel and also for the good of her workers."

Beigin pointed out that in the never-ending struggle of the worker for higher wages, Histadrut in its present form often is in a position where it clashes with its own member workers. Employees in a privately-owned factory are free to go on strike in order to force a wage increase. But the men and women working in Histadrut factories are confronted by their own Histadrut-controlled union which forbids strikes against its own plants. This unhealthy alliance, the Herut leader said, makes for low wages all around. Beigin gets a salary of approximately $62 a week as a member of the Knesset. The average wage earner, with a weekly income between $30 and $40 before stiff taxes, can't make ends meet. What has kept 100,000 Israeli families above water is the restitution money paid out by the government of West Germany to victims of Nazi persecution. A total of approximately $500,000,000 has been turned over to survivors of the Hitler regime in Israel thus far, in addition to $800,000,000 reparations paid to the Israel government.

Beigin said that these reparations and other forms of foreign aid are keeping Israel afloat artificially by covering her $300,000,000 trade deficit.

"We have a controlled economy," Beigin charged.

"This is an obstacle to foreign investment." Herut is strongly in favor of the abolition of the law requiring import and export permits.

*HaAretz,* a newspaper which is independent but reflects the economic thought of Herut and Liberal elements, criticized Histadrut's announcement that it would earmark $250,000,000 from its union pension and sick funds for investment in the Negev.

"What moral right does the Histadrut have to use or to borrow these monies for the purpose of imposing its will upon whole regions of Israel?" *HaAretz* demanded. "How does the Secretary-General of the Histadrut know that the newcomers who will be settled in these areas really desire this type of colonization?"

At the dedication of the Histadrut building in Dimona, which I attended, Histadrut speakers pounded away at the theme that it was their organization which was building the Negev, and integrating the immigrants, providing them with work, education and social services. Actually, the Negev today is being built up mainly by private capital with the aid of Government development loans including Israel Bonds.

It is true that Histadrut provides the development towns with many social services, including health insurance. But this, too, has become a political issue. Yosef Sapir, leader of the Liberal party, contends that most of the social services, including comprehensive health insurance, which are now supplied by Histadrut, should be taken over by the Government.

Premier Eshkol has ready answers for his critics. In reply to Beigin's objections to Government investment in industry, Eshkol stresses that the Government extends loans to all approved enterprises, and at the same time underscores the need for more private capital. Every encouragement is given to private investors, including tax benefits, fast depreciation write-off, land leases, and the right to ownership entirely independent of Histadrut. Eshkol wants to see all four in Israel together, side by side — more private enterprise, more Histadrut factories, more government loans to new industries and more immigration to provide the manpower for new industry.

As to the future course of Israel's economy, Eshkol declared that the more foreign investment is poured into the country, the more it will turn to the right. But "to the right" is the way of Menahem Beigin.

Levi Eshkol is an old socialist, but as long as he attains his dream for Israel of a population of four million, economic self-sufficiency and of the wealth of a "Switzerland of the Middle East" by 1970, he couldn't care less which way Israel will go — right, left or center.

Meanwhile, foreign investors are proving their growing confidence in the future of Israel.

Baron Rothschild of Paris announced that he would head a combine of thirteen banks in France, Great Britain, West Germany, Italy, Belgium, Switzerland and Israel, to be known as the Israel-European Company (ISROP), which would support the creation of new enterprises in Israel and purchase securities on the Tel Aviv Stock Exchange.

Sam Federmann, co-owner of the 400-room, $3,000,-000 Dan Hotel of Tel Aviv, part owner of the King David, Accadia and Dan-Carmel Hotels, and partner in the Federmann-Miami investment group which expanded its holdings from $1,000,000 in 1953 to an estimated book value of $30,000,000, said:

"Capital looks for a safe place to invest. When Jewish people want to put their money to work, they seriously consider Israel, because, next to Europe, they find Israel the most secure place in which to invest, with returns of from 5 to 30 per cent."

Federmann feels there is no cause to fear that Israel might nationalize all private industry some day. "The

Israeli government would never think of nationalizing private industry because that would only hurt the country and its economy," he explained.

Federmann's group has extensive investments in the Heletz oil field, in the Isasbest cement, asbestos and pipe factory, in orange groves and in low-cost housing.

"I'm satisfied that my investments are secure here. But more than that, I also gain a tremendous satisfaction from the knowledge that my money helps to create new industries, new jobs and to rebuild our own State of Israel. It is wonderful to be able to say: 'This is my own; I helped bring this about',", Federmann, a one-time German refugee declared.

"This is my message to Jews abroad," he concluded. "When you invest here, you help people and you help create jobs for new-comers. And beyond that, you strengthen your own position wherever you may live in the Diaspora."

According to Federmann, non-Jewish investors, whose original motivation was strictly business, soon became even more enthusiastic about their projects in Israel than many Zionists.

Looking ahead to that hoped-for day when Israel will be able to live in peace with her Arab neighbors, Federmann predicted that eventually Israel would become the supply center not only for the entire Middle East, but also for Asia and Africa. "What with our Jewish know-how," he asserted, "Israel certainly should become a model of progress and development for this part of the world."

\* \* \*

When the United States Operations Mission (USOM) in Israel wound up eleven years of invaluable technical assistance to the new Jewish State in 1962, it was able to record in its final report that the Government of the United States, as of that date, had given to Israel a total of $800,000,000 in financial aid.

Nor did the termination of USOM's activities mean the end of American grants, loans and surplus food shipments to Israel. It simply indicated that Israel was now ready for more sophisticated types of assistance in the form of long-term economic development loans from the World Bank and the Export-Import Bank.

The World Bank has extended to Israel a loan of $50,000,000 for the expansion of the Dead Sea Potash Works, a loan of $27,500,000 for the building of Ashdod Harbor, and one of $20,000,000 for highway construction. Another loan of $35,000,000 from the U.S. Development Loan Fund was approved for the purchase, in the United States, of computers, steel, non-ferrous metals, trucks, construction equipment, chemicals, pharmaceuticals, plastics and other industrial materials. This loan is for 20 years, at 0.75 per cent interest, with no repayment of principal required for the first five years.

Washington has been sending Israel surplus grain which, by the terms of the agreement, is converted each year into $40,000,000 to $50,000,000 in counterpart funds by sale to Israeli bakeries. The proceeds go to Israel's development budget for the construction of factories, roads, communications and new farms.

Dispelling fears that the end of technical assistance may presage the termination of all economic aid from the United States, Premier Levi Eshkol said that "American economic aid will continue to be given to Israel, though the emphasis will now be more on long-term loans than on outright grants."

The story of the U.S. technical assistance program in Israel deserves to be inscribed in every public and religious school textbook as a present-day realization of Isaiah's vision of brotherhood: "They helped everyone his neighbor, and everyone said to his brother: 'Be of good courage'."

During its eleven years of operation in Israel, USOM spent $14,700,000 to bring 640 Israeli specialists to the United States and other countries for training and study, and to send 340 American experts to work in partnership with the Israelis on a total of 182 mutual assistance projects.

These project covered virtually every aspect of Israeli life. Philip Gillon in the *Jerusalem Post* interpreted the meaning of this assistance in everyday terms:

"We envisage a kaleidoscope of such images — a tap in the desert; farmers putting down hoes and mounting tractors; men testing hot tarmac for a new road; day-old chicks being flown thousands of miles to start life in a new country; drillers piercing the bottom of the Dead Sea; milk flowing down the stainless steel sides of a cooling tank; men sitting in an office analyzing program and costs to the last penny; endless committee meetings; scientists helping in the absorption of immigrants by their discoveries; an immigrant from a fifteenth-century world working a twentieth-century lathe in a training-center at Beersheba; an expert walking along an assembly-line and pointing out an error; managers going back to school; two men wading through sludge to solve a sanitation problem; the last of the 'iron horses' puffing to a well earned rest, yielding place to Diesel locomotives gliding smoothly over the rails; American experts landing at Lydda Airport and Israelis landing at Idlewild..."

Bruce McDaniel, the modern-day saint who served as USOM's first director, gave his own moving vision of this American-Israeli hands-across-the-sea program:

"This living story of international collaboration began in 1951, and was born of the humble idea that nations, by exchanging skills and sharing humanitarian responsibilities, could build a better world," he wrote. "It is written in green fields and burgeoning factories, in reservoirs of sweet water, in schools and hospitals, in the faces of children, in the hearts of lonely men at sea in fishing boats, and in the memories of women tending flocks in the Negev. . . .

"On some distant day at Etzion Geber, looking beyond the fleet of nuclear-powered merchant ships in the bustling harbor of Elat toward the solar-energy plant on the hill pumping desalinated sea water for irrigation to Arab and Israel farms alike, a nostalgic grandfather will explain to his grandson the meaning of this golden thread in the tapestry, will tell him the legend of the time, long ago, when the Americans came to newly-born Israel bringing wheat and skills and understanding.

"To the amazement of some of its friends, and, one suspects, of quite a few Israelis, and despite land blockade and constant harassment by its enemies . . . the Republic of Israel has surmounted economic, social and political dilemmas which could have confounded seasoned nations. . . . There came into action in Israel that rare and magic catalyst which, from time to time, unites and endows men with the unconquerable spirit which moves mountains. American revolutionists and pioneers had it. In part, perhaps, in Israel, it came from centuries of longing and hope, in part from dogged determination, the stubborn refusal to concede defeat. There were, too, the bonds forged by constant threat of attack, the sharing of hunger and faith, the common compassion for the flood of incoming immigrants, and the determination to prove that Israel could produce what historical slander for centuries had declared to be impossible: fishermen, fighters, miners, cowboys, brain surgeons and nuclear physicists."

Israel counter-balances her meager natural endowments with brain power. The arrival of some of the world's finest scientists, physicians, engineers and teachers fleeing from persecution fitted in perfectly with the American program of technical assistance. In every field, Israel has been able to place skilled and trained specialists alongside U.S. experts to pick up American know-how and to adapt it to conditions in Israel.

The goal of USOM was to "work itself out of a job" and it has achieved this end. Within the past decade, Israel has emerged from the category of "underdeveloped nation" to the point where she herself is now exporting technical know-how to underdeveloped countries in Asia and Africa and cooperating with newly-independent republics in the building of new economic enterprises.

During the decade of U.S. technical and financial assistance, Israel's agricultural production has increased five-fold. When USOM first began operations in Israel, food rationing and austerity were the bywords of the day. When USOM completed its mission, Israel achieved a food surplus, exporting citrus fruit, poultry, eggs, vegetables and other farm products. Her industrial output has raced ahead of the phenomenal growth of her population, and Israeli factories, having met domestic needs, rely on exports for further profits.

Point Four, an outgrowth of the postwar programs devised by President Harry S. Truman and the late Secretary of State George C. Marshall to rehabilitate the countries ravaged by World War II, was a life-saver for Israel.

When USOM first came to Israel, the new Jewish State, which only a few years before had won a miraculous victory over a half-dozen invading Arab armies, was on the verge of collapse from an inundation of 640,000 immigrants who had poured into the new-born republic during the first three years of its existence.

With the pitiful shortage of food and hundreds of thousands of immigrants forced to live in miserable tent camps, it was a miracle that Israel did not explode in unrest and riots.

Abba Eban, then Israel's ambasador to the United States, was charged with the task of conveying Israel's desperate economic plight to President Truman and Secretary of State Dean Acheson in 1950. Eban laid the facts on the line for Washington leaders, and met personally with many Congressmen and Senators, including a young man from Massachusetts named John F. Kennedy, to convince them that Israel was in urgent need of help if she were to survive.

Congress then passed the Douglas-Taft Israel Aid Bill, authorizing Truman to make an outright gift of $73,000,-000 to the Ben-Gurion government for immigrant absorption.

That gift, along with income from the Israel Bond Drive, begun in 1950, from the United Jewish Appeal, and from German reparations, saved the day for Israel.

Eban, Israel's Deputy Premier, points out that America's program of aid to Israel has remained constant through the changes in administration from Truman to Eisenhower to Kennedy and Johnson, and that Israel's use of U.S. aid has been a model of efficiency and maximum utilization. Because of Israel's pilot plant role, the U.S. foreign aid program as a whole has been easier to sell to a recalcitrant Congress, and today Africa and Asia are the chief recipients of this assistance from America.

Eban has eloquently reminded his friends in Washington that they have no cause to regret their foresight in establishing the program of aid to underdeveloped countries by helping Israel in her hour of need in 1950.

"The ultimate prize," says Deputy Premier Eban, "may be nothing less than a family of nations united in a growing equality of dignity and creative growth."

As for the future — does Israel still need help from

abroad? The answer: Technical aid, no. Economic help? Bruce McDaniel, the pioneer of USOM, gave the answer.

"Despite remarkable progress," he stated, "Israel's leaders know that much is yet to be done; [Israel is faced with the task of] reducing the number of people still not productively employed; securing new sources of capital; ... adjusting balance of payments in line with manageable essential absorptive capacity; accelerating hard currency earnings from added higher values in exports, from international services and in the proven profitable area of tourism; developing the port of Elat and the industrial potential of the Negev; expanding trade with African and Asian markets in correlation with the growth of Israel's merchant fleet and significant developments in the European Common Market; harboring reserves to meet unexpected immigration loads and the rising costs of modern defense ... reducing the plethora of political groups ... augmenting research and secondary education facilities ... capturing solar energy ... desalinating sea water for irrigation ... technical assistance to other nations (and) trade with Central and South America .. Mr. McDaniel knows that Israel is not content to rely upon help from the outside without putting her own resources to work.

"Since its creation, the leaders of Israel, wisely, have realized that Israel's most precious resources abide neither in its land nor in its water, valuable as they are, but in the fertile mind of the people; that the worth of a nation is no longer dependent primarily on its location, its land area or the size of its population. Research and new skills, hard work and promising horizons in human relations, coupled with access to almost unlimited sources of energy, today can endow the hapless 'little nations' of yesterday with the productive potential of giants."

# CHAPTER XVIII

# ESHKOL'S VISION

What manner of man is Levi Eshkol, David Ben-Gurion's successor at the helm of the State of Israel?

His choice came as something of a surprise to many circles abroad who expected the Premiership to go to General Moshe Dayan, the hero of Sinai, or to Abba Eban, the silver-tongued spokesman of Israel at the United Nations.

The fact is that Levi Eshkol, Israel's powerful Minister of Finance, was a most logical candidate for the job. The alter ego of his chief, Ben-Gurion, Eshkol had his strong hands on the controls of Israel's economic life. He had virtual *carte blanche* from Ben-Gurion to pile an ever-increasing load of income taxes and customs duties upon an already overburdened population, to manage the money market and to devaluate the Israeli pound. As Minister of Finance, Eshkol held life-and-death licensing power over import and export trade. As Chairman of immigration in the Jewish Agency, he directed the world-wide program of immigration and resettlement which brought to Israel, within the span of one decade, the greatest influx of human beings in its history.

323

Who is Levi Eshkol? What, specifically, have been his accomplishments that brought him the Premiership? What does he believe? And how does he measure up to his famous predecessor?

The answers to some of these questions will have to await the verdict of history. But enough is known now about Eshkol from his stewardship of Israel's economy and his first eighteen months as Prime Minister to say that he has risen to the awesome responsibilities and challenge of his high office.

The big, burly, youthful-looking ex-kibbutznik who emigrated to Palestine from Russia in 1914 when he was a youth of nineteen, is first and last a man of the people, a son of the soil and an old-style *Yiddel* who delights in peppering his Hebrew and English with Yiddish wise-cracks. He is a man of monumental strength and healthy "horse sense," with implicit faith in his people and in its democratic traditions.

On the speaker's platform, the Premier does not create a favorable first impression, for his delivery is halting and cumbersome.

In private conversation, he is kind and fatherly, exuding warmth, humor and affection. The enthusiasm with which he speaks of Israel's future is infectious.

When he holds forth on Israel's past progress, her mass immigration and enormous program of industrialization and housing, his fervor is that of an evangelist of the Billy Graham school.

His mind is sharp and precise. He quotes statistics from memory and rarely has to refer to a subordinate to recall details. Eshkol knows all the answers because he thought up the questions.

A founder of Kibbutz Degania Beth by the Sea of Galilee, Eshkol has been in the land for half a century. Originally an idealist who sought the realization of his dreams in the communal life of the kibbutz, he eventually realized that while idealism had launched the Zionist experiment in the 1910's, a more practical, pragmatic approach, mixing cooperative economy with free enterprise, was vital to keep the economy of Israel in step with mass immigration in the 1960's.

When in 1959 Eshkol brought to Ben-Gurion for approval the "Law to Encourage Private Investment," Israel took a sharp turn from the original orthodox socialism of the Mapai party to a mixed economy with components of capitalism, Histadrut cooperatives, labor-union-owned industry, government loans to private industry for factories in the Negev, and various combinations of all these.

The right wing, as represented by Israel's Herut party, feels that Ben-Gurion and Eshkol have not gone far enough from the left. But Levi Eshkol quite frankly told me:

"When I first came here in 1914, we never said or even believed that it would be possible to have Israel built as a socialist state in our generation. I doubt that people know how to build a state on a foundation of democratic socialism. From the very first day that I came here, we went both ways, socialist and capitalist, at the same time.

"We have always had a mixture of private enterprise and public ownership. We had Kibbutz Degania side by side with Petah Tikva's privately-owned orange groves, and in Tel Aviv we have had Histadrut-operated factories together with plants run by private enterprise.

"Even the left-wing parties, Mapam and Ahdut Ha-'Avoda, know that, in order to build our nation, we need billions in private capital investments. The economic structure of the Jewish people in the Diaspora is based on money, education, technical skills and culture. We need these things to build a strong Israel and to absorb a maximum number of Jews.

"At the same time we would like public money to support the public ownership sector and thus strengthen the hands of the working people. We are building a nation on the foundation of social justice. We are building a new social order in which people may decide for themselves where and how they want to live — in a kibbutz, in a moshav, or in a city or town. It is up to the individual to make the choice. I see no conflict in Israel between the socialist ideal and private enterprise. What counts is initiative, daring and skill — know-how, that is what we need."

Eshkol pointed out the benefits to be gained by Israel from healthy competition between private enterprise and public interests, each spurring the other to invest, to build and to develop the open spaces. Private interests in Israel, he said, do not live in fear of nationalization or socialism.

"The government of Israel has no inclination to be a partner in business enterprises except where national security is at stake, or when an industry must be put on its feet. Once such an industrial enterprise is on its way, the government puts its share on the Tel Aviv Stock Exchange for the public to buy. The government has too many other uses for its development funds in the Negev to hold on to an enterprise after it is able to stand on its own feet," Eshkol said.

The Premier, a former Histadrut official, told me he would want Histadrut to increase its investments of its own funds, for there is no limit to initiative and investment. At the same time he is opposed to Histadrut's former policy of seeking to enter into partnerships with private industry. The 1959 private investment law encourages complete private ownership. At present, 70 per cent of Israel's industry is privately owned.

"The more Jews will come to Israel, the greater will the proportion of private ownership become," he declared, and predicted that Israel should have a population of 4,000,000 by 1980. Immigration, he said, is vital to the future of the country, since it provides the labor force required for the industrialization created by large-scale investment.

"With Jewish skill and devotion, we are on the right path," said the Prime Minister.

That Israel's new Premier is a master politician was demonstrated when Ben-Gurion gave up trying to organize a new coalition government and left the onerous task to Eshkol, who completed it after three months of negotiation. In my 1962 interview with Eshkol, long before his break with Ben-Gurion over the revival of the Lavon affair late in 1964, Levi Eshkol extolled his former chief's wisdom and breadth of vision, and his refusal to compromise when he felt a cause would be best served by having the related issues fought out in public.

Eshkol described his predecessor as a lonely man who has few intimate friends, and prefers reading, writing and contemplation at home to entertaining and socializing. The former Premier sleeps only five hours a night, works late and keeps in close touch with everything that goes on in Israel. Weeks after the broadcast of an address by Eshkol to the Knesset, Ben-Gurion would call to remind him of a small detail in that speech. While Ben-Gurion was still Prime Minister, he did not interfere with Eshkol's manifold economic activities and concerned himself primarily with issues of defense, education and immigrant integration.

Recalling the events that led up to Statehood and the War of Independence, Eshkol declared: "Without Ben-Gurion, we wouldn't have a State today." Ben-Gurion had stubbornly and uncompromisingly put through the plan to establish the State in the face of much internal opposition, and, of course, the avowed enmity of the Arabs and the non-cooperation of the British mandatory authorities. And when the Arabs invaded the new State, Ben-Gurion proved himself a master military strategist and diplomat, insisting on the liberation of besieged Jerusalem despite opposition from influential military quarters.

As regards international issues, Eshkol thinks along Ben-Gurion's lines. He favors peace talks with the Arabs but refuses to bow to their demands with regard to territory and refugees. He is enthusiastic about Israel's program of aid to African and Asian nations.

Eshkol gets along better with American Zionists and philanthropists than did Ben-Gurion who likes to poke fun at them, defining them as "individuals who give so that another Jew can go to Israel" instead of coming to the land themselves. Eshkol, a frequent visitor to the United States, has seen the Jews of America in their own communities and knows American officialdom both in Washington and at the United Nations. It was Eshkol who managed to secure more than $50,000,000 in World Bank loans for the construction of Ashdod Harbor and for the expansion of the Dead Sea Works.

In March 1964, Premier Eshkol set forth his policies to the General Council of the Zionist movement which was then meeting in Jerusalem.

"It is our responsibility to be prepared," he said, "so that if (war) should come, Israel will be prepared to thwart the machinations of the enemy and to carry the battle from our own territory to terrain beyond. It is clear to us here that the deterrent strength of the Israeli defense forces and of the people of Israel are the surest guarantees for peace."

Luckily, Eshkol emphasized, Israel does not stand alone. "In addition to our relationships in Europe and America, we have stretched out, over the heads of the enemy states around us, a hand of friendship to the farthest nations of Asia and Africa. We have shown our readiness to come to the assistance of young nations in need of our help and have found reciprocal friendship. . . .

"Beyond all this, we must primarily bear in mind our loyal and unchanging covenant with the Jewish people in the Diaspora. Throughout the long years of our history before the emergence of the State and during the brief period of the State's existence thus far, this covenant has found expression in help, both material and spiritual, and in manpower. It is upon the Jewish people that our first claim must be made.

"Much has been done to make this covenant with the Jewish people a tangible one, and our share has been by no means small. In the work of *kibbutz galuyot* (the Ingathering), we are about to deplete the large reservoir of poverty in many Jewish communities. We have brought them to Israel and now it remains for us to absorb them, to educate them, and to integrate them. This mighty enterprise will demand our resources for another generation or so. But the time has come to think about the next stage of the Ingathering. Now that we have almost reached the peak of our efforts in the absorption of immigrants from the countries of stress from which the Jews may be driven out, we must devote our attention to other sources of aliya.

"For Israel to continue to fulfill its mission, there must be an incessant expansion in its population. Now this is not merely a question of (having) three, four or even five million Jews in the State. Our task does not end there. This is not the end of the Zionist mission. We have responsibilities toward the remainder of the Jewish people, and the Jewish people has responsibilities toward us, as regards our strength and the composition and size of our population.

"There are about three million Jews in Soviet Russia. We all share the anxiety over the fate of this community, as well as the hope that it will be allowed eventually to make its contribution to the future of the Jewish people in its homeland. We must not forget this community for even one moment. We believe that their deliverance will eventually come to pass, and that the peoples of the Union of Soviet Socialist Republics and their leaders will come to realize the utter necessity and the great positive value of this act of liberation. But our demands alone will not be sufficient to bring this liberation to pass.

"We must, therefore, turn our attention to the Jewish communities in the lands of freedom, communities which do not form part of the stress area in the present generation. Objectively seen, these communities are capable of helping supply our immigrant needs both in quantity and in quality. They are in a position to provide the State with an aliya capable of absorbing others, and bringing with it material and spiritual assets conducive not only to its own full absorption but also contributing to the absorption of other newcomers.

"(But) apart from fulfilling our own historic mission by our very existence and growth, have we succeeded in providing the State with ideal and spiritual content? Surely, apart from serving the immediate needs of relieving the distress of the Jewish people, we have all wanted this State to be the repository of our spiritual values. We must become once again a nation that creates values. We must measure up to the demands and expectations of the Jewish diaspora and perhaps also to those of the nations of the world, so that these values may spread light to the nations and to the Jews in dispersion. We are preparing the instruments. We are constructing the lyre of David, but whence will come the gentle wind that will cause it to play of its own accord? In our own generation we are witnessing the miracle of the dry bones drawing near to one another. We have succeeded in constructing the frame; perhaps we have also succeeded in providing it with the sinews, the flesh and the skin, but will our strength alone be sufficient to infuse a spirit of life into it so that these dry bones may live?

"Let us now turn from the State of Israel to the Jewish people. To us falls the responsibility of securing the future of the Jewish people. Zionists may not draw a distinction between these two complementary components — the State and the people. We are enjoined to wage war against assimilation, against the dangers threatening the Jewish people from within, even where it is not threatened by danger from without. This struggle, too, is actually a struggle for the future of the State. Just as the struggle for the existence of the State and the fulfillment of its mission was a *sine qua non* for the assurance of Jewish continuity, so the duties of the Jewish people toward itself and the State are closely linked. . . . We must find new ways and means to mobilize the Jewish people, in quality and in quantity, around ourselves and around the State . . . Let the abilities that the Jewish people have acquired in the Diaspora find their way to us! It is no longer a question of 'stress' aliya, but of voluntary immigration — an aliya opening the road to pioneering efforts of wide vistas and compelling deeds.

" . . . I do not hesitate to say that we must find a way to the heart of the present-day youth and establish a pioneering movement in keeping with the needs and the living standards of the 1960's and the 1970's — a movement that can make an all-out effort for new conquests in the spheres of both matter and spirit.

"Nor is this distant and utopian. After all, we are now calling them to an Israel which is not what it was scores of years ago. Today, in our independent State, we have succeeded in creating reasonably good conditions of life, and in schools, institutions of higher learning, and research institutes capable of attracting research workers and scientists. We have set up specialized branches of agriculture, economy and industry, and great development projects in the fields of chemistry, electronics and others, and we are making new strides forward every day.

"Is it no longer possible to attract youth by the very challenge of an idea rather than by the allurements of profit and comforts alone?

"In the United States a 'Peace Corps' was established by the late President Kennedy, and I hear that quite a number of Jews have joined its ranks. Should we not derive a lesson from this? We see here young people who enjoy every comfort in a land of affluence and who nevertheless answered the call to go forth to developing countries far away, not for gain or glory but for the sake of an ideal. This is a human challenge. Cannot we, too, issue such a human, such a Jewish challenge? Do we, too, not speak in the name of the vital needs of our people, in the name of the new social values which are the source of our strength and pride?

"Let a Jewish reserve come (here to Israel) to develop our society, our economy and science, and to expand our cooperation with the developing countries.

"We are all doubtlessly aware of the vital importance of water for the existence of our country. Moses brought forth water from the rock by Divine command. We cannot emulate him. If we have succeeded in bringing forth water from the rocks, we have done so with the aid of twentieth-century science. We are now coming to the end of our potential of discovering underground water, but we are on the brink of a new era when vast quantities of water will be harnessed from the sea, under economically feasible conditions, for the expansion of agriculture and industry. Perhaps Jewish scientists will come and assist us in carrying through this feat. This may even provide an answer to the problems of other

nations. Perhaps we may envisage the State of Israel
as the scientific center for the study of water desalina-
tion for our entire region. Perhaps, due to the stress of
our own development needs, Israel may become the pilot
plant and nations near and far may draw on our experience.

"I know full well that we shall not reap the crop of
aliya without first ploughing deep, without sowing and
hoeing in good season, without constant and prolonged
Zionist education . . . We must work long and hard for
the education of the young generation, for the opening
of their hearts.

"In order that, together, we may carry this great
burden, we need a new set of interlinked instrumen-
talities. We are in need of interacting mutual influences; a call must go forth from Israel, the Zionist State,
to the Zionist movement and the Jewish people everywhere.

"No matter what the terms or the language in which
the call will be framed, the demand remains the same.
There can be no deviation from the principle that
Zionism calls for deeds, for action!

" . . . Israel is still awaiting the time when scores,
hundreds of thousands of Zionist families will set an
example for others by coming to settle in this country.
That will be a great day for Israel and a great encouragement both to the Zionist movement and the younger
generation."

# EPILOGUE

Levi Eshkol's evaluation of the miracle that is Israel, his hopes and dreams for its future, are shared, I am sure, by nearly every Jew whose heart has been stirred by Israel's creation and growth, and by her friends of other faiths in the new ecumenical movement embracing the world.

Having addressed many Jewish and non-sectarian audiences on the manifold phases of Israel's unrivalled drama over the years, and written and edited the day-by-day unfolding of the history of Zion Reborn, I have been witness to the vast reservoir of goodwill accumulated by the valiant men and women of the Holy Land in war and peace.

It has become a cliche to say that the rise of Israel has given the Diaspora Jew a "new look," a more favorable image of which he is proud, and which he values as a vital factor in the steady postwar decline of anti-Semitism, and the recent development of interfaith dialogue.

To our children, Israel is part of the global landscape, as if it had always been there. A teenage youth or college student, who either was born after 1948, or had been too

young to have read the war news then, is a world apart
from the older generation that suffered directly or indirectly during the Hitler nightmare and then exulted at
Israel's phoenix-like rise from the ashes. For those youngsters fortunate enough to spend a summer in Israel there
is hope that they will help build bridges between the new
generations in America and the Holy Land. The great
challenge facing both communities is to learn about each
other, to gain mutual understanding through knowledge
and contacts, and to forge links to unite brethren across
farflung lands and seas.

The American-Israel bridge must be a two-way thor-
oughfare.

The bromide, "I give to Israel," ought to be discarded.
As I explained, the Israeli citizen pays out in taxes for
immigration two dollars for every dollar contributed by
his American cousin, so that nothing remains from Federation fund-raising for the established employed Israelis,
who need no charity, or for their government.

To dramatize this point, I made the provocative statement to a B'nai B'rith Institute on Judaism that Israel has
done more for American Jewry than American Jewry has
done for Israel. Not a single member of my audience
challenged this declaration and I proceeded to document
this upside-down accounting of U. S.—Israel relationships.

How can American Jews set a price upon the feeling
of pride and self-assurance derived from the new image of
the Jew created by the Israeli army, by the halutz farmer,
by the Hebrew nation-builder? How much of the decline
of anti-Semitism in America can be ascribed to this proud
"new look" carried so buoyantly by the Jew in the United
States?

In 1948, when the Israel War of Independence aroused
American Jewry to unprecedented heights of Jewish consciousness and deepest concern for the survival and victory
of their brethren in embattled Israel, United Jewish

Appeal—Federation campaigns all over the United States established new records in fund-raising.

As the war in Israel opened flood-gates of generosity, the local welfare federations and their constituent beneficiary agencies such as homes for the aged, hospitals, centers, and defense services rode on the coattails of the Israel Appeal to launch building and expansion projects in numerous communities. I heard Golda Meir complain on one of her U. S. fund-raising missions that Israel is building a network of hospitals, community centers, homes for the aged, and other institutions for the American Jewish community. She was referring to the widespread practice of Federation fund-raising using the appeal and publicity of Israel, allocating around fifty per cent of the total funds thus gained to the United Jewish Appeal, but keeping half the monies at home for local causes.

In the process of raising record-breaking sums for the combined appeals, something happened to thousands of American Jews caught up in the machinery of campaigning. Businessmen and professionals discovered a new purpose in their lives. Identifying themselves with the drama of Israel and later with "saving lives," volunteers by the thousand across the United States attended meetings, solicited their friends and associates, became more deeply involved in allocation sessions and board deliberations, assumed chairmanships and Federation offices. Their pictures were published in the newspapers and campaign publications. They attained a proportion of prominence previously undreamed of within communities. Benefitting from the experience of addressing meetings, many who had never had training in public speaking learned how to become articulate and forceful before a crowd. Working together for a common cause they formed new friendships. Other organizations and institutions enlisted campaigners who proved themselves in the "big leagues" of fund-raising. In the case of these men and women it might not be out of line to say that the whole drama of our times revolving around the creation and rise of Israel has done more for them than they have done for Israel.

As for the hundreds of thousands of contributors to these campaigns, Israel raised their sights and "taught them how to give."

The women, banded together in Hadassah, Pioneer Women, Mizrachi Women, and other Zionist organizations, found a cause to touch their hearts. They raised funds at donor luncheons, fashion shows, theatre parties and banquets for hospitals, childrens' institutions, welfare work and vocational training in Israel. The women benefitted, even to a higher degree than the men, in the campaign school for leaders, speakers, organizers and publicity writers. The ladies outstripped their husbands in the intensity and year-round devotion to their organizational tasks. For the wife and mother who has raised her children and suddenly finds herself in middle age without a vital task, organizational work can be a veritable lifesaver. In an even more profound sense than for the male campaigner, organizational work gives the woman a sense of purpose and meaning in life.

Israel has done a great deal for American Jewry in many other ways. The critical shortage of Hebrew teachers in American Jewish religious schools is being alleviated by the importation of educators from Israel, as well as b⁻ part-time utilization of Israeli students at Americar versities.

American Jewish culture, indeed American cu' self, has been enriched by a steady stream of Isr singers and dancers entertaining audiences in this ⸏y. The Israel Philharmonic Orchestra, one of the ⸏rld's greatest symphony ensembles, won the acclaim of music critics and concert lovers on two American tours. Inbal, Israel's Yemenite Dance Theatre, enthralled American audiences with portrayals of Biblical themes and scenes.

The Gadna Youth Orchestra increased respect in American musical circles for Isaeli talent. The Habimah Theatre left the Tel Aviv stage to perform before U. S. audiences in the east. The parade of Israeli government officials, generals and other dignitaries across the speaking platforms of Jewish fund-raising meetings, forums, non-sectarian civic club luncheons and university gatherings constitutes a year-round procession telling the story of Israel's miraculous growth and shedding new light on its vexing problems, quite aside from presenting in person what Buber called the "new Jew."

There is hardly a Jewish home without an Israeli seder plate or menorah. The synagogue gift shops in every community display and sell an ever-growing variety of Israeli-produced religious objects of art. Israeli paintings and sculpture are being displayed in American art exhibits and find a ready market.

Hebrew literature, published in Israel in unequalled volume on a per capita comparison with other countries, must be translated into English to be appreciated by the non-Hebrew reading American Jews.

The word of the "Law from Jerusalem" has still not been accepted as final by American Jewry, even in its orthodox branch, because of the barriers which block a unified approach to consideration of the rulings of the Chief Rabbinate in the Holy City. On the other hand, American Reform Judaism and the Conservative movement hope to provide religious alternatives for Israelis who at present are faced with an "either/or" choice of either entering the Orthodox life in their country, or being outside the synagogue altogether.

Except for concern over Israel's security in the face of Arab threats and border incidents, religion raises more questions among American Jewish audiences than any other problems. There is little understanding of the true place of the religious issue in the daily lives of the Israelis.

The vast majority of Americans have the impression that Israel is torn by religious conflict. Those who live in Israel or have spent considerable time in Israeli homes will tell you that in their daily lives Israelis hardly feel the effect of the so-called *Kulturkampf*. Ordinary Israelis are made conscious of it only by persistent discussion in the Hebrew newspapers and occasional flareups that dominate the headlines and the radio news bulletins.

While seeking to compromise with the national religious parties which participate in the coalition cabinet, the Israel government has consistently attempted to postpone the inevitable showdown between the religious and the non-religious element. Surrounded by Arab enemies and quadrupling its population in sixteen years with mass immigration, Israel knows that it must not risk fragmentation by allowing its religious problem to come to a head now. Actually, there is no urgent necessity to settle the *Kulturkampf*. The Orthodox communities live in peace and tranquility, worshiping as they please in their religious enclaves in Mea Shearim, Bene Berak, and in their synagogues all over the Holy Land. The eighty-five per cent of Israelis who do not vote for the national religious parties go about their own way of life, seldom hampered by Rabbinical law except perhaps in certain problems connected with marriage and divorce. Each is free to pursue his or her own way of life. Many who never attend synagogue keep kosher homes, prepare the traditional Sabbath evening dinner, light candles, recite *kiddush*, sing *zemirot*, and observe all the Jewish holidays which, in Israel, are celebrated as national festivals. Children in non-religious public schools study the Bible, Jewish history, and thereby acquire a Jewish education superior to that of their American cousins. To inquiries from tourists why Israelis are not more religious, my wife Dora offered this reply when she resided in Tel Aviv: "To be religious, we don't have to go to synagogue as you American Jews do.

We speak Hebrew. We live in the Land of the Bible. We study the Bible in school. All around us are the Biblical place names in our hills and towns and countryside. We breathe the air of our prophets. We observe the Sabbath as a national day of rest. And yet each one enjoys the Sabbath in his own way. The Jewish holidays are our national festivals. We live in the Jewish State. The atmosphere is Jewish. This is our land, the Land of Israel. We lead a full Jewish life here. And we think we live a more Jewish life than even the most religious Jew in America or any place else in the Diaspora."

For the tourist, a visit to Israel is a revitalizing dose of Jewish pride in what Jews can accomplish in building and defending a pioneer land. The Jewish State, its history, its achivements and its rise as a light to the nations and a real source of help to the emergent nations in Africa and Asia, lift the American Jew to new heights of inspiration.

In the words of Abba Eban, the orator statesman of Israel, the Miracle of Israel is that it "re-established the youthful vigor of an ancient culture; opened the gates of hope and freedom to hundreds of thousands in distant lands; brought consolation to a people at the moment of its unfathomable grief; gave the community of nations a new dimension, a new link with its oldest spiritual roots." No one can sum up the miracle of Israel better than Eban: "A land endowed with deeper grace and broader fertility than it had known since the days of the ancient Hebrew kingdoms; a culture charged with the combined virtues of age and youth; inspired both by a sense of innovation and by pride of descent from a lineage of three thousand years; a citadel of democracy, in a region where political freedom has few other bulwarks; a lively center of social idealism and technological progress; an arena in which the pent-up energies of immigrants and Pioneers still have wide fields to conquer; a focus of pride for all throughout the world who cherish the Jewish faith and tradition as the central impulse of their daily lives; a testimony to the power of the human will to overcome the calculations of material chance; a new banner planted in the family of nations which would lack completeness without its presence — these are amongst the consequences of Israel's rebirth."

This is the miracle of Israel, this and Israel's attainment of full employment, surplus food production, adequate housing, an expanding economy and a deterrent military force in the face of mass immigration and threats of annihilation by its Arab neighbors.

This is the miracle of Israel.

## DATE DUE

| JA 11 66 | | | |
|---|---|---|---|
| MY 24'66 | | | |
| AP 23'68 | | | |
| MY 22'68 | | | |
| MAR 10 78 | | | |
| DEC 1 78 | | | |
| DEC 16 74 | | | |
| | | | |
| | | | |
| | | | |
| | | | |
| | | | |
| | | | |
| | | | |
| | | | |
| | | | |
| | | | |
| GAYLORD | | | PRINTED IN U.S.A. |